A COMPARATIVE STUDY OF PROFESSIONAL ACCOUNTANTS' JUDGEMENTS

STUDIES IN MANAGERIAL AND FINANCIAL ACCOUNTING

Series Editor: Marc J. Epstein

Volume 1:	Setting the Standard for the New Auditors Report: An Analysis of Attempts to Influence the Auditing Standards Board
Volume 2:	The Shareholders Use of Corporate Annual Reports
Volume 3:	Applications of Fuzzy Logic and the Theory of Evidence to Accounting
Volume 4:	The Usefulness of Corporate Annual Reports to Shareholders in Australia, New Zealand, and the United States: An International Comparison
Volume 5:	A Power Control Exchange Framework of Accounting Applications to Management Control Systems
Volume 6:	Throughout Modeling: Financial Information Used by Decision Makers
Volume 7:	Applications of Fuzzy Sets and the Theory of Evidence to Accounting II
Volume 8:	Corporate Governance, Accountability, and Pressures to Perform: An International Study
Volume 9:	The January Effect and Other Seasonal Anomalies: A Common Theoretical Framework
Volume 10:	Organizational Change and Development in Managerial Control Systems: Process Innovation for Internal Auditing and Management Accounting
Volume 11:	U.S. Individual Federal Income Taxation: Historical, Contemporary and Prospective Policy Issues
Volume 12:	Performance Measurement and Management Control: A Compendium of Research
Volume 13:	Information Asymmetry: A Unifying Concept for Financial and Managerial Accounting Theories
Volume 14:	Performance Measurement and Management Control: Superior Organization Performance

STUDIES IN MANAGERIAL AND FINANCIAL ACCOUNTING VOLUME 15

A COMPARATIVE STUDY OF PROFESSIONAL ACCOUNTANTS' JUDGEMENTS

BY

CHRIS PATEL

Department of Accounting and Finance, Macquarie University, Sydney, Australia

Emerald

United Kingdom – North America – Japan
India – Malaysia – China

Emerald Group Publishing Limited
Howard House, Wagon Lane, Bingley BD16 1WA, UK

British Library Cataloguing in Publication Data
A catalogue record for this book is available from the British Library

ISBN: 978-0-7623-1062-3
ISSN: 1479-3512 (Series)

CONTENTS

ACKNOWLEDGEMENT

This research monograph is based on my dissertation completed at Macquarie University. Parts of this study have been published as follows: "Some Theoretical and Methodological Suggestions for Cross-Cultural Accounting Studies", *International Journal of Accounting, Auditing and Performance Evaluation*, 2004, Vol. 1, No. 1, pp. 61–84; "Some Cross-Cultural Evidence on Whistle-Blowing As An Internal Control Mechanism", *Journal of International Accounting Research*, 2003, Vol. 2, pp. 69–96; and "Cultural Influences on judgements of Professional Accountants in Auditor-Client Conflict Resolution", *Journal of International Financial Management and Accounting*, 2002, Vol. 13, No. 1, pp. 1–31.

ABSTRACT

This research monograph is an empirical examination of cultural influences on professional judgements of Australian, Indian and Chinese Malaysian accountants in relation to auditor–client conflict resolution, and whistle-blowing as an internal control mechanism. The importance of cultural values in influencing accountants' professional judgements has been examined by a number of researchers; however, no research has systematically examined this influence on judgements related to auditor–client conflict resolution or whistle-blowing. Importantly, this study informs and guides both the theoretical specification and treatment of culture and its operationalisation and methodology. In the theory development and hypothesis formulation, the study draws on Hofstede's five-dimensional cultural taxonomy, specifically on the dimensions of Power Distance, Individualism (Versus Collectivism) and Long-term (Versus Short-term) Orientation. However, rather than relying solely on these works, the study also provides insight into the specific cultural values of Australians, Indians and Chinese Malaysians by (i) drawing on historical, psychological and sociological literatures, including features of Hinduism and Confucianism with respect to Indian and Chinese Malaysian cultures and (ii) conducting interviews with university academics to provide a more holistic understanding of cultural values in the three countries. Data were gathered through a survey questionnaire administered to a sample of senior professional accountants from big-five accounting firms in Australia, India and Malaysia. The questionnaire incorporated Values Survey Module to measure culture, and used scenarios to elicit responses about judgements of professional accountants. The study uses the Multidimensional Ethics Measure to capture judgements of professional accountants. This measure allows the study to go beyond a simplistic understanding of "what" respondents believe and provides insight into "why" they believe it. The study also measures and provides insight into social desirability response bias (SDRB) among professional accountants from the three countries studied. The results provide support for the following hypotheses: Australian professional accountants are less likely to resolve audit conflicts by acceding to clients than Indian and Chinese Malaysian professional accountants, and are also less accepting of resolving audit conflicts in this way;

Australian professional accountants are more likely to engage in whistle-blowing as an internal control mechanism than Chinese Malaysian and Indian professional accountants, and are also more accepting of doing so. The results also show the usefulness of the Multidimensional Ethics Measure to examine complex comparative judgements of professional accountants. The findings of the study have implications for the management of multinational enterprises, the international convergence and harmonisation of accounting and auditing standards and for cross-cultural accounting research and accounting education.

CHAPTER 1
INTRODUCTION

The objective of this study is to examine the influence of cultural values on judgements of Australian, Indian and Chinese Malaysian professional accountants in "big-five" multinational accounting firms with respect to two important issues in accounting, namely, auditor–client conflict resolution and whistle-blowing as an internal control mechanism.[1] The study draws out the various features of cultural differences between Indians and Chinese Malaysians in one cluster, and Australians in another cluster, to formulate and test the following hypotheses:

H1a: Australian professional accountants are *less likely* to resolve audit conflicts by acceding to clients than Indian and Chinese Malaysian professional accountants.

H1b: Australian professional accountants are *less accepting* of resolving audit conflicts by acceding to clients than Indian and Chinese Malaysian professional accountants.

H2a: Australian professional accountants are *more likely* to engage in whistle-blowing as an internal control mechanism than Chinese Malaysian and Indian professional accountants.

H2b: Australian professional accountants are *more accepting* of engaging in whistle-blowing as an internal control mechanism than Chinese Malaysian and Indian professional accountants.

The chapter is organised as follows. The first section provides the motivation and the contributions of the study. The motivation is discussed in terms of the importance of professional judgement in accounting and the potential role of culture in affecting that judgement. This is followed by a discussion of the two issues selected for examination, namely, auditor–client conflict resolution, and whistle-blowing as an internal control mechanism. The second section justifies the selection of Australian, Indian and Chinese Malaysian professional accountants for examining cross-cultural differences in their judgements with respect to the two issues. The third section provides a discussion of how culture is operationalised in the study. This section describes the Hofstede's (1980) and Hofstede and Bond's (1988) five-dimensional model of culture which is drawn on, together with the historical, psychological and sociological literatures, to underpin the theoretical development and empirical operationalisation of culture in the study. This is followed by a summary of the research method. The chapter concludes with a description of how the study is organised and also provides a brief summary of the seven chapters that comprise this research monograph.

MOTIVATION AND CONTRIBUTIONS OF THE STUDY

An enhanced awareness of the importance of studying accounting and accounting information in different countries has resulted from a multiplicity of factors that are largely driven by forces of globalisation. In addition to the current focus on international convergence and harmonisation of accounting and auditing standards, other factors propelling globalisation include the recent substantial increase in international financial markets, aggressiveness of multinational corporate strategies, increasing demand for business services, international economic and political interdependence, new technologies and the activities of international regulatory organisations (Radebaugh & Gray, 2002; Choi & Meek, 2005; Doupnik & Perera, 2005). Accounting has inevitably interacted with these complex global changes. Consequently, the relevance and reliability of accounting information, systems and procedures used in various countries are of increasing concern to professional accountants, investors, creditors, governments, multinational enterprises, accounting researchers, students and other interested parties.

It has been recognised for some time that accounting is a socio-technical activity in which the values and judgements of professional accountants and users of financial information are important (Jaggi, 1979; Patel, 2004). Accounting and information system managers are increasingly realising that the crucial issues in designing and administering accounting and information systems are no longer simply a matter of getting the technical aspects correct. Rather, equally crucial issues are those associated with professional judgement in accounting and the various factors that may influence professional judgement.

As early as 1937, Mapp in discussing the importance of professional judgement in accounting noted that, "Factual information and accuracy in its procurement are essential, but its value is submerged unless with it is synchronized the development and training of the judgement" (p. 258). More recently, the International Accounting Standards Board (IASB) has used the term "substance over form" to describe the importance of professional judgements in accounting (IASB, 2005, Framework, para. 35). That is, the idea that greater attention should be placed on the economic "substance" of the business transactions, rather than the legal "form". With respect to auditing, professional judgement pervades virtually all aspects of contemporary financial statement audits. Moreover, audit manuals of most multinational accounting firms reinforce that the single most important element in applying the firm's audit approach is the exercise of informed judgement at the various stages of the audit. Also, recognising the importance of professional judgements in auditing, the International Auditing and Assurance Board (IAASB) is currently working on a number of projects to examine various issues related to professional judgements.

As a socio-technical activity involving professional judgement, one of the important issues for study is that of culture. This is because of the importance of culture in its ability to influence individual and collective values and judgements in different countries (Cohen, Pant, & Sharp, 1995, 1996b; Patel, 2004). There is growing support for the belief that differences in cultural values, rather than differences in material and structural conditions, are the ultimate determinants of human organisations and behaviour, and thus of growth (Frank, Hofstede, & Bond, 1991; Hofstede & Hofstede, 2005). For example, the founder of the European Community, Jean Monnet declared: "If I were again facing the challenge to integrate Europe, I would probably start with culture. Culture is the context in which things happen; out of context, even legal matters lack significance (Trompenaars, 1993, p. 8).

The importance of cultural values in influencing accountants' professional judgements has been examined by a number of researchers in this area (Gul & Tsui, 1993; Yamamura, Frakes, Sanders, & Ahn, 1996; Tsui, 1996; Patel & Psaros, 2000; Doupnik & Richer, 2004); however, no research has systematically and holistically examined that influence with respect to these judgements. Similarly, while the various national and international standard setters have recognised the importance of various contextual factors including culture, which may influence professional judgements, these standard setters do not explain or examine cultural values. This study, therefore, seeks to extend the research in this area by examining two important aspects of professional judgements in an audit context, namely, auditor–client conflict resolution, and whistle-blowing as an internal control mechanism, and focusing specifically on the influence of culture on these judgements. The next section presents the motivations for examining these two aspects of professional judgement.

ASPECTS OF PROFESSIONAL JUDGEMENTS EXAMINED

Auditor–Client Conflict Resolution

Research into various areas of auditing, including examination of professional judgements, has made significant progress particularly over the last two decades. However, Hopwood (1996, pp. 217–218) concluded that "Auditing remains a relatively poorly understood phenomenon. Despite a series of major research initiatives, many key features of the audit process and context remain little investigated .... Too much of the practice and functioning of auditing remains a black box". While a number of researchers continue to provide some insight into this "black-box", it is suggested that multidisciplinary and more holistic theoretical and methodological approaches are required.

Researchers have generally studied auditors' judgement as either a technical or a cognitive phenomenon, wherein cues representing characteristics of the client (for example, relative size of the transaction) are examined in terms of their influence on auditors' judgements. While such studies are useful, researchers have been encouraged to enlarge the context in which audit judgements are examined. Audits take place in larger and more complex contexts than those portrayed in most cognitive research in auditing studies. Specifically, how forces of globalisation and culture influence accounting and auditing have been identified as important areas of study (Carpenter, Dirsmith, & Gupta, 1994; Roberts, Weetman, & Gordon, 2005).

This study enlarges the "context" of auditing research. In particular, the influence of culture on audit judgements has emerged as an important issue for further research because of the current focus on globalisation and on international convergence of accounting and auditing standards. Specifically, the influence of culture on how professional accountants from Australia, India and Malaysia resolve auditor–client conflict is selected for examination because of the importance of the issue to management of international enterprises in general, and the big-four accounting firms in particular. If multinational firms are to function effectively in a complex and interdependent world, then research needs to be undertaken to determine how to reduce the frequency of conflict as well as how to manage this conflict in a constructive manner.

Related to auditor–client conflict resolution is the concept of auditor independence and objectivity. Independence is the cornerstone of auditing because it adds credibility to the financial information of an entity by the expression of an independent opinion (International Federation of Accountants (IFAC), Code of Ethics for Professional Accountants, 2005a, b, Section 290). Auditing standards and ethical pronouncements of the professional bodies in the countries selected in this study recognise two aspects of external auditors' independence. These are independence "in fact" and "in appearance". Credibility of auditors depends not only on facts but also on perceptions of independence (Mautz & Sharaf, 1961; Shockley, 1981; The future of the Accounting Profession, 2003). While the facts can be assessed by determining the significance of certain financial, business or family relationships that may affect client services, perceptions of independence are said to be a matter of one's mental attitude, and therefore potentially influenced by one's cultural background.

Auditor–client conflicts are generally centred around issues such as the need to make adjustments to the financial statements, the propriety of the client's accounting policies and the adequacy of disclosure in financial statements (Fried & Schiff, 1981; Knapp, 1985; Lindsay, 1992; Bazley, Hancock, Berry, & Jarvis, 2003; Bloom & Schirm, 2005). Indeed, the demise of Arthur Anderson in 2002, Ernst and Young's violations of audit independence rules and the court action that forbade them from accepting new public company audits for six months (Securities and Exchange Commission of the USA (2004), Initial Decision Release 249, 16 April), and other large audit failures suggest that clients often appear to be successful in coercing their auditors not to question their accounting practices. A comprehensive report prepared by the United States General Accounting Office suggested that "too frequently, relationships between the auditor and the management being audited have become too accommodating" (Wyatt, 1997, p. 128). Arthur Levitt, the longest serving chairperson (from 1993 to 2001) of the Securities and Exchange Commission of the USA and who has contributed significantly to strengthening the rules related to independence of auditors, concluded that "Too many corporate managers, auditors, and analysts are participants in a game of nods and winks. In the zeal to satisfy consensus earnings estimates and project a smooth earnings path, wishful thinking may be winning the day over faithful representation.... Managing may be giving way to manipulation; integrity may be losing out to illusion" (Securities and Exchange Commission of the USA, 28 September 1998, p. 1). The Asian financial crisis of 1997–1998, the recent corporate scandals such as Enron, WorldCom and the scandals surrounding the demise of Arthur Anderson, all provide ample evidence to support Arthur Levitt's conclusions. Furthermore, the 103rd American Assembly in their report entitled "The Future of the Accounting Profession" (2003, p. 4) conclude that, "As the bubble economy encouraged corporate management to adopt increasingly creative accounting practices to deliver the kind of predictable and robust earnings and revenue growth demanded by investors, governance fell by the wayside. All too often, those whose mandate was to act as a gatekeeper were tempted by misguided compensation policies to forfeit their autonomy and independence".

The plethora of recent criticisms facing the accounting profession internationally makes a comparative study of auditor–client conflict resolution particularly relevant. While scandals surrounding Enron, WorldCom, Xerox and Merck and the subsequent enactment of the Sarbanes–Oxley Act of 2002 have received significant global attention, it is important to recognise that these accounting and auditing scandals are not new. For example, recall the US National Savings and Loan Industry crisis where bail-outs were estimated at $1.4 trillion (Lehman, 1992, p. 1), in which three of the big-six accounting firms were implicated for failing to uncover dubious financial practices (Lehman, 1992, pp. 1, 5). Another example is the collapse of the Bank of Credit and Commerce International (BCCI) which has been described as "the mother of all scandals" (Truell & Gurwin, 1992, p. xviii), and which could not have been perpetuated without the active cooperation of one of the big-six accounting firms (Truell & Gurwin, 1992, pp. 420, 423). Examples in Australia include the accounting scandals surrounding the collapse of Bond Corporation, Quintex Ltd. and Rothwells Ltd. (Clarke, Dean, & Oliver, 1997) and high-profile collapse of HIH which had approximately $5 billion liabilities gap (Bazley et al., 2003). Likewise, earnings management has been identified as a major problem in India (Mahimalia, 1997, pp. 36–40; Indian Financial Markets, 2005, http://www.rediff.com/money/2005/apr/12guest1.htm, pp. 3–5). In Malaysia, nepotism is suspected and earnings management implicated in the loss of billions by the government-controlled Bank Bumiputra, and during 1996 when $2.75 billion in bad debts was written off by the government-controlled Perwaja Steel (Time, January 13 1997, p. 29).

In addition, there are claims that auditors' failure in ethical resolution of conflicts has led to runaway litigation that has the power to destroy the accounting profession (The Future of the Accounting Profession: Auditor Concentration, 2005). On many occasions, "...professionals in largest and most respected accounting firms have yielded to management pressure, permitting management to file incomplete or misleading financial statements" (The Future of the Accounting Profession, 2003, p. 4). As such, there is an urgent need to restore investor confidence at both global and national levels. Indeed, issues related to international auditing and corporate governance are receiving increasing attention (Doupnik & Perera, 2005).

Furthermore, preliminary evidence suggests that professional accountants and accounting students are "not developing ethical reasoning capacities commensurate with individuals having similar social, economic, or educational background" (Ponemon, 1993, p. 5). For example, students from liberal arts courses and practising physicians in the USA scored higher on tests that measure ethical reasoning than accounting students and professional accountants (Ponemon & Glazer, 1990). As both the subject and consequences of unethical business behaviour increase in importance, so does the need to study its antecedents, dynamics and consequences.

Ethical resolution of conflicts in accounting has been identified as an important area of research (Ponemon, 1990; Ponemon & Gabhart, 1993; American Accounting Association (AAA), 1983; Jeffrey, 1993; Cohen, Pant, & Sharp, 1993a; IFAC, 2005b). Despite the importance of the topic in evaluating the relevance and reliability of accounting information, systems and procedures used in various countries, very little empirical evidence exists about the influence of culture on accountants' judgements in relation to resolution of auditor–client conflicts. Because of the current focus on international convergence and harmonisation of auditing standards, there is an urgent need to examine the question of how professional accountants from various countries differ in resolving auditor–client conflicts. This study aims to provide insight into the influence of culture on judgements of Australian, Indian and Chinese Malaysian professional accountants with respect to resolution of auditor–client conflicts.

Whistle-Blowing as an Internal Control Mechanism

Internal control systems determine whether acceptable policies and procedures are followed, established standards are met, resources are used efficiently and economically and the organisation's objectives are being achieved. However, increasing organisational complexities, especially in multinational enterprises, the growth of corporate mergers, acquisitions and restructurings and the ever-increasing corporate management accountability have weakened the effectiveness of traditional internal control systems (Choi & Mueller, 1992; Roberts et al., 2005). Additionally, International Standards on Auditing (ISA 400), "Risk Assessments and Internal Control" has identified the following inherent limitations of internal control systems:

> most internal controls tend to be directed at routine transactions rather than non-routine transactions; the possibility of circumvention of internal controls through the collusion of a member of management or an employee with parties outside or inside the entity; the possibility that a person responsible for exercising an internal control could abuse that responsibility, for example, a member of management overriding an internal control; the possibility that procedures may become inadequate due to changes in conditions, and compliance with procedures may deteriorate.

Despite the inherent limitations of internal control systems, a number of studies in Australia, the US, UK and Singapore have shown that a significant number of financial report users believe that the detection of irregularities is a primary audit objective and the auditor has a responsibility for detecting all irregularities (for Australia, see Monroe & Woodliff, 1994, for US, see Epstein & Geiger, 1994; Wyatt, 1997, for UK, see Humphrey, Moizer, & Turley, 1993, for Singapore, see Low, 1989).

To address some of the inherent limitations of internal control systems and to assist auditors and managers in detecting irregularities, it is increasingly being recognised that whistle-blowing as an internal control mechanism is useful (Miceli, Near, & Schwenk, 1991; Werhane, Bowie, & Radin, 2003). Whistle-blowing as an internal control mechanism is defined as "the disclosure by organization members (former or current) of illegal, immoral, or illegitimate practices under the control of their employees, to persons or organizations that may be able to effect action" (Miceli & Near, 1992, p. 15).

The topic of whistle-blowing as an internal control mechanism is important because it contributes to improvements in both internal control systems and in evaluations of the control environment by management and external auditors (Hooks, Kaplan, & Schultz, 1994; Johnson, 2002). Moreover, whistle-blowing can improve long-term organisational effectiveness because whistle blowers may suggest solutions to organisational problems (Brief & Motowidlo, 1986; Power, 1999; Werhane et al., 2003). More importantly, organisational members, investors, creditors and society in general can benefit from the cessation of organisational wrongdoings revealed by whistle blowers (Miceli et al., 1991; Power, 1999; Jha, 2005).

Indeed, recognizing its importance, the Chartered Institute of Public Finance and Accountancy in the UK has called for effective whistle-blowing procedures to be established in order to restore public confidence in accounting standards (Mitchell, 1995, p. 79). In the US, the Committee of Sponsoring Organizations (COSO) of the Treadway Commission (1992), has emphasised the role of communication in internal control. In particular, COSO advocated the importance of whistle-blowing but warned about maintaining balance because entities may become bogged down with unfounded assertions. In Australia, a study by the Australian Society of Certified Practising Accountants and the Institute of Chartered Accountants in Australia (Middleton Report, 1994) also emphasised the importance of whistle-blowing as an issue for the profession. Further importance of this topic is shown in Knapp's (1993) collection of well-known audit cases and the importance placed on whistle-blowers' assistance in detecting fraud.

More recently, throughout the industrialised world, 2002 will be remembered by the people as the year when corporations failed them. Incredible stories of corporate greed and wrongdoings created headlines. The importance of whistle-blowing as an internal control mechanism is most clearly illustrated by Time (30 December 2002) selecting three whistleblowers as persons of the year for 2002. Enron's vice-president Sherron Watkins has emerged as a hero for warning that Enron might, " ...implode in a wave of accounting scandals" (p. 53). Cynthia Cooper of WorldCom has also become famous for informing its board that the company had covered up $3.8 billion in losses by means of accounting fraud. FBI agent Coleen Rowley blew the whistle on her agency for mishandling a probe of a 11th September terrorist suspect. Time said Coleen Rowley, Cynthia Cooper and Sherron Watkins were selected "for believing – really believing – that the truth is one thing that must not be moved off the books, and for stepping in to make sure that it wasn't" (p. 10). Another story that made headlines is that of Barron Stone, a CPA who blew the whistle on his employer, Duke Energy Corporation that kept the price of electricity artificially high in the Carolinas with questionable accounting. Moreover, Eliot Spitzer's aggressive pursuit of Merrill Lynch and, subsequently, a dozen other Wall Street firms could have benefited from potential whistle blowers. These incidents in the US have triggered increasing attention on the topic of whistle-blowing as an internal control mechanism in other industrialised countries such as Australia, UK, Canada and France.

In India, the topic of whistle-blowing was clearly highlighted when Satendra Kumar Dubey was murdered on 27 November 2003 for whistle-blowing on corruption in the National Highways Authority of India (NHAI). Satendra had written to the Prime Minister's Office about corruption in NHAI and had specifically requested that his name be kept secret. However, his request for anonymity was ignored, and his letter was sent to his superiors at the NHAI. In March 2004, this case received international attention when the London-based Index on Censorship posthumously honoured him with the "Whistle-blower of the Year Award" (Jha, 2005, pp. 11–12). This and other similar cases reveal that in an economic climate where corporations and governments cannot be trusted to be ethical, whistle-blowing may be one, if not the only way of revealing wrongdoings.

Despite its importance, very little attention in accounting research has been paid to whistle-blowing, possibly because of the pejorative tone of the term (Hooks et al., 1994). Yet, both internal and external auditors would be very well served by the use of whistle-blowing if such reporting was based on reliable information concerning illegal acts, ethics violations, or fraud in the organisation (Ponemon, 1994).

Research on the organisational and individual characteristics of whistle blowers spans a number of disciplines, including psychology (Brabeck, 1984;

Near & Miceli, 1986), organisational theory (Dozier & Miceli, 1985; Miceli & Near, 1984; Tourish & Hargie, 2005), business ethics (Glazer, 1983; Greenberger, Miceli, & Cohen, 1987; Near & Miceli, 1985; Bowie, 2002; Jha, 2005) and accounting (Miceli et al., 1991; Arnold & Ponemon, 1991; Schultz, Johnson, Morris, & Dyrnes, 1993; Hooks et al., 1994; Power, 1999).

Studies in whistle-blowing have shown that moral judgement development or ethical reasoning may influence whistle-blowing behaviour and auditor judgements (Ponemon, 1990; Ponemon & Gabhart, 1990; Arnold & Ponemon, 1991; Lampe & Finn, 1992; Ponemon, 1992). Ethical reasoning, in turn is influenced by the relationship between self and society's values and expectations (Kohlberg, 1984, pp. 624–639). That is, it is influenced by cultural values.

This study contributes to cross-cultural research by examining differences in judgements of Australian, Indian and Chinese Malaysian professional accountants with respect to their acceptance and likelihood of engaging in whistle blowing as an internal control mechanism.

The next section of the chapter discusses the reasons for selecting Australia, India and Malaysia for examination and then goes on to discuss how the conception of culture was operationalised in the study.

SELECTION OF COUNTRIES

Australia, India and Malaysia have been selected for examination because they are classified as members of the British Commonwealth model of accounting development (Mueller, 1968; Mueller, Gernon, & Meek, 1991; Nobes & Parker, 2004). Through the influence of colonialism, these three countries inherited corporate legislation and accounting practices from the UK. The concept of a "true and fair" view of the financial affairs of an entity and the exercise of professional judgements are important aspects of accounting in these countries (Radebaugh & Gray, 2002; Nobes & Parker, 2004). Additionally, in each country, the objective of accounting is generally based on the concept of "decision usefulness" which is principally oriented towards the decision needs of investors.

The similarities in accounting development among Australia, India and Malaysia provide content equivalence in the accounting constructs being examined. This is a crucial consideration in cross-cultural studies. The failure to establish content equivalence in such studies may confound the findings because the differences found in subjects' judgements between and across countries may be the result of differences in the rules and concepts at issue (such as when and how to recognise revenue), rather than differences in their cultures. This study provides some confidence about content equivalence by selecting Australia, India and Malaysia as countries for study because they belong to the British Commonwealth model of accounting development. This issue is discussed in detail in Chapters 2 and 4.

Another reason for selecting Australians, Indians and Chinese Malaysians as subjects in the study relates to their identified importance to international business and globalisation. To facilitate international trade, Chang (1995, p. 955) identified five major "global tribes". These include: the British and the English-speaking progeny, Asian Indians, Chinese, Jews and Japanese. This study has selected professional accountants from three of the five major 'global tribes' for examination.

OPERATIONALISATION OF CULTURE

The concept of "culture" has been defined in a number of ways and remains one of the most elusive terms in the social sciences (Gillin, 1944; Jahoda, 1984). For example, Child (1981, p. 323) states that "the 164 definitions of culture cited by Kroeber and Kluckhohn (1952) together encompass a whole range of components: knowledge, values, preferences, habits and customs, traditional practices and behavior, implements and artefacts". Triandis (1994, p. 22) further argues that there are many definitions of culture and that "they are all valid". However, both Child (1981, p. 323) and Triandis (1994, p. 22) suggest that the adoption of one or more of the many definitions of culture in a particular study is largely dependent on what a particular investigator wishes to study.

The broad dimensions of social meanings, norms, values, beliefs and customs associated with culture require researchers to analyse thoroughly the specific components of culture relevant to their studies (Child, 1981, p. 330). In other words, the contemporary approaches in the structural functionalist perspective on culture tend to "unpackage" culture into its component parts (Bhagat & McQuaid, 1983, p. 685; Child, 1981, pp. 330–331). For psychologists, this "unpackaging" takes the form of identifying constructs that relate to behaviour, such as values, motivations, beliefs, expectancies for reinforcement and personality traits (Whiting, 1976; Smith & Bond, 1993, p. 221).

Most of the discussion of culture in this study is based on the structural functionalist perspective that conceptualises "cultural reality" in terms of norms and values in a given society. In contrast, the symbolic interaction theories consider that culture does not determine individual or collective action, rather it is created and re-created by people. In this context, "people are seen as active participants who, through their interpreting, reinterpreting and challenging of values engage in a constant interaction with culture, rather than being passive and obedient followers" (Lachowicz, 1997, p. 1). The non-values-based conceptualisation of culture adopted by the symbolic interaction theories provides useful insights, however, this approach does not "unpackage" culture. Thus, each of the two approaches to conceptualisation of culture has its strengths and weaknesses.

This study adopts the values-based structural functionalist perspective on culture. However, the study addresses some of the limitations of this perspective by adopting three complementary approaches to provide a richer and more holistic insight into cultural differences between Indians and Chinese Malaysians in one cluster and Australians in another cluster. These complementary approaches include: (i) drawing on the five-dimensional cultural model of Hofstede (1980) and Hofstede and Bond (1988); (ii) providing additional insight into Indian, Chinese Malaysian and Australian cultures by drawing on historical, psychological and sociological literatures, including features of Confucianism and Hinduism with respect to Chinese Malaysian and Indian cultures, respectively; and (iii) conducting in-depth interviews with university academics to further elicit the cultural values of these societies as they may influence the two accounting judgement issues examined in the study. The cross-cultural differences between the two clusters are then drawn on to formulate and test the hypotheses of the study.

Since the study draws on the cultural dimensions of Hofstede (1980) and Hofstede and Bond (1988) as one of the three approaches to operationalise culture, the next section provides a brief discussion of these dimensions.

Hofstede's Dimensions of National Culture

Geert Hofstede's (1980) taxonomy is perhaps one of the most useful in operationalising the values-based conception of culture (Child, 1981; Bhagat & McQuaid, 1983; Triandis, 1994). Additionally, the reliability, validity and applicability of Hofstede's research has been documented in a number of studies including Smith, Dugan, and Trompenaars (1996); Ronen and Shenkar (1985), Hofstede and Bond (1984, 1988), Rieger and Wong-Rieger (1988) and Laurent (1983). Furthermore, the cultural dimensions in Hofstede's cultural taxonomy have been extensively applied in various accounting contexts (Harrison, 1990, 1992, 1993; Ueno & Wu, 1993; Schultz et al., 1993; Lau, Low, & Eggleton, 1995; O'Connor, 1995; Cohen, Pant, &

Sharp, 1993a, 1995, 1996a; Jaggi & Low, 2000; Hope, 2003; Patel, 2004; Doupnik & Richer, 2004; Yamamura, Stedham, & Satoh, 2004).

Hofstede (1980, p. 25) defined culture as, "the collective programming of the mind which distinguishes the members of one category of people from another". The category of people can be a nation, region or ethnic group, women versus men (gender culture), a social class and can also include a family. The programming of the mind manifests itself in the values and beliefs of a society. Values are "a broad tendency to prefer certain states of affairs over others" (Hofstede, 1980, p. 19). Values also direct feelings of good and evil, and also affect behaviour and perceptions of how things are (Hofstede, 1991, p. 347). Culture affects not only our daily practices; the way we live, are brought up, manage, are managed; but also the theories we develop to explain our practices. No part of our lives is exempt from culture's influences (Hofstede, 1991, p. 170).

While culture is a composite concept, a "dimension" of culture is something that can be measured relative to other cultures. A framework which identified specific dimensions of culture was developed by Hofstede (1980). Based on a survey involving subsidiaries of International Business Machines (IBM) in 64 countries, and 117,000 questionnaires in 20 languages, Hofstede (1980) analysed differences in work-related values across countries. IBM constituted an effective organisation for identifying differences in national value systems because its employees represented almost perfectly matched samples. The samples were similar in most respects except nationality.

Statistical and other analysis of the IBM survey data revealed four distinct dimensions that reflected the cultural orientation of a country. These were Individualism Versus Collectivism, Large Versus Small Power Distance, Strong Versus Weak Uncertainty Avoidance and Masculinity Versus Femininity. In a later study, Hofstede and Bond (1988) developed a fifth dimension, Long-term Versus Short-term Orientation (also referred to as Confucian Dynamism). The five dimensions are as follows:

- *Individualism Versus Collectivism*: Individualism stands for a preference for a loosely knit social framework in society wherein individuals are supposed to take care of themselves and their immediate families only. Its opposite, collectivism, stands for a preference for a tightly knit social framework in which individuals can expect their relatives, clan or other in-groups to look after them in exchange for unquestioning loyalty (Hofstede, 1984a, p. 83).
- *Large Versus Small Power Distance*: Power Distance is the extent to which the members of a society accept that power in institutions and organisations is distributed unequally. People in large Power Distance societies

accept a hierarchical order in which everybody has a place, which needs no further justification. People in small Power Distance societies strive for power equalisation and demand justification for power inequalities (Hofstede, 1984a, p. 84).

- *Strong Versus Weak Uncertainty Avoidance*: Uncertainty Avoidance is the degree to which the members of a society feel uncomfortable with uncertainty and ambiguity. Strong Uncertainty Avoidance societies maintain rigid codes of belief and behaviour and are intolerant towards deviant persons and ideas. Weak Uncertainty Avoidance societies maintain a more relaxed atmosphere in which practice counts more than principles and deviance is more easily tolerated (Hofstede, 1984a, p. 84).
- *Masculinity Versus Femininity*: Masculinity stands for a preference in society for achievement, heroism, assertiveness and material success. Its opposite, Femininity, stands for a preference for relationships, modesty, caring for the weak and the quality of life (Hofstede, 1984a, p. 84).
- *Long-term Versus Short-term Orientation*:[2] The following "Long-term Orientation Values" are applicable to Chinese-based countries (such as China, Hong Kong and Singapore), including Chinese settled in other countries (such as Malaysia) and India:
  - Adaptation of traditions to a modern context.
  - Respect for social and status obligations within limits.
  - Thrift, being sparing with resources.
  - Large savings, funds available for investment.
  - Perseverance towards slow results.
  - Willingness to subordinate oneself for a purpose.
  - Concern with "face" (the importance of face is the consequence of living in a society that is very conscious of social contexts).
  - Concern with respecting the demands of virtue (Hofstede, 1994b, p. 173).

  The opposite, "Short-term Orientation Values", are applicable to countries such as Australia, the USA and Great Britain, and include the following characteristics:
  - Respect for traditions.
  - Respect for social and status obligations regardless of cost.
  - Social pressures to keep up with the Joneses even if it means overspending.
  - Small savings, little money for investment.
  - Quick results expected.
  - Concern with self-respect.
  - Concern with possessing the Truth (Hofstede, 1994b, p. 173).

THE FIVE-DIMENSIONAL MODEL OF CULTURE

In this model, each country is identified and ranked by a score on each of the five dimensions. By locating the position of different cultures on a five-quadrant model, Hofstede (1980) and Hofstede and Bond (1988) enable cross-cultural comparisons to be made on an a priori basis. This is attributable to the fact that each of the dimensions is relative, indicating that in order to derive meaning from each of the five indices, they must be compared with the other countries' indices. Such operationalisation of culture is "essential if the discipline is ever to build a theoretical structure for explaining cross-cultural differences in behaviour" (The Chinese Culture Connection, 1987, p. 144). The relative location within the model makes it possible to derive hypotheses concerning the relative influence of the cultural dimensions on organisational dynamics.

The five dimensions of culture may be expected to be related to accounting because as Hofstede (1991, p. 157) suggests, "The less an activity is determined by technical necessity, the more it is ruled by values, and thus influenced by cultural differences. Accounting is a field in which the technical imperatives are weak: historically based conventions are more important to it than laws of nature. So, it is logical for accounting systems and the ways they are used to vary along national cultural lines".

A framework based on the work by Hofstede (1980) and Gray (1988) is applied in this study to examine the influence of cultural values on professional judgements. In this framework, societal values (comprising Individualism, Power Distance, Uncertainty Avoidance, Masculinity and Short/Long-term Orientation) are affected by ecological influences such as geographic, economic, historical, technological and urbanisation. These ecological influences in turn are modified by external factors such as international trade and investment, conquest and the forces of nature.[3] Societal values have institutional consequences in the form of the legal system, political system, nature of capital markets, patterns of corporate ownership, education and religion. These institutional consequences reinforce both ecological influences and societal values (Hofstede, 1980). The value systems of accountants (accounting values) in turn are derived from societal values (Gray, 1988).[4] The exercise of professional judgements among accountants from various cultures is influenced by their societal values. It is on this latter relationship that this study is premised. As noted earlier, the exercise of professional judgement is an important aspect of accounting to study, both in its own right and in cultural contexts.

While it is useful to classify culture into distinct dimensions, a more holistic approach is needed to provide an insight into the specific nature of the cultural dimensions applicable to Indians, Chinese Malaysians and Australians. Recall that this study supplements the five-dimensional model of culture in each of the three countries by incorporating relevant evidence from other disciplines, particularly the sociological, psychological and historical literatures. This evidence, as well as the five-dimensional model, is drawn on in developing the theory and formulating the hypotheses on auditor–client conflict resolution, and whistle-blowing as an internal control mechanism.

RESEARCH METHOD

Data to test the hypotheses are collected using a survey questionnaire administered to a sample of senior professional accountants from the big-five accounting firms in India, Malaysia and Australia. The study uses "scenarios" to capture judgements of professional accountants from each of the three countries. Scenarios are defined as "short descriptions of a person or a social situation which contain precise references to what are thought to be the most important factors in the decision-making or judgement-making processes of respondents" (Alexander & Becker, 1978, p. 94). Scenarios allow studies to frame the research questions to incorporate complex issues reflecting decision making in the real world (Cavanagh & Fritzsche, 1985). This allows empirical researchers using scenarios to elicit from respondents their beliefs, preferences, intentions, reasoning, judgement or intended behaviour regarding ethical issues (Weber, 1992, p. 137).

This study uses the "multidimensional ethics measure" designed by Reidenbach and Robin (1988, 1990) and tested for validity and reliability in an accounting context by Flory, Phillips, Reidenbach, and Robin (1992) and Cohen, Pant, and Sharp (1993b, 1996a) to capture judgements of professional accountants based on the scenarios. The multidimensional ethics measure consists of eight bipolar scales and is based on the theoretical importance of the Moral Equity, Relativism and Contractualism ethical philosophies (details are provided in Chapter 4). The use of a multidimensional ethics measure allows a researcher to go beyond a simplistic understanding of "what" respondents believe and begins the process of understanding "why" they believe it (Reidenbach & Robin, 1988, 1990).

Furthermore, the study also uses the univariate single-item measure. The use of both the single-item and multidimensional measures enables the study to provide empirical evidence on the proposition that the explanatory power of the multidimensional ethics measure is greater than that of the univariate (ethical/unethical) meàsure.

Since the multidimensional ethics measure comprises eight items as dependent variables, Multivariate Analysis of Variance (MANOVA) is used to determine if culture (the independent variable, operationalised as country) influences respondents' judgements on the eight dependent variables. An alpha level of 0.05 is chosen as the level of significance in this study.

The study also measures and provides insight into SDRB among professional accountants from Australia, India and Malaysia. SDRB refers to the desire, at either a conscious or an unconscious level, to give a particular picture of oneself by the way one responds to questionnaire items (Watkins & Cheung, 1995, p. 490). SDRB is also described as maintaining a "holier than thou" ethical perception (Tyson, 1990, p. 715), and is a pervasive problem in behavioural ethics research (Rossi, Wright, & Anderson, 1983; Tyson, 1992). SDRB leads individuals to perceive peers as less ethical than themselves. A study of SDRB is important because this bias encourages the development of an unethical organisational culture. Individual organisational members are likely to resort to unethical behaviour because they may believe that the strategy is necessary to compete with colleagues who are perceived as unethical. SDRB is also likely to influence the reliability and validity of any findings where accountants' attitudes or judgements are solicited. For example, studies such as Harrison (1992, 1993), Pratt, Mohr weis, and Beaulieu (1993), Schultz et al. (1993), O'Connor (1995), Kachelemeier and Shehata (1997), Chow, Kato, and Shields (1994, 1999), Patel and Psaros (2000) and Doupnik and Richer (2004) while contributing to cross-cultural accounting research, failed to discuss the potential confounding effects of SDRB bias in their findings.

To measure culture, respondents completed Hofstede's (1994a) Values Survey Module that measured scores of the cultural dimensions of Individualism, Power Distance and Long-term Orientation for each of the three countries under examination. The Values Survey Module (1994) is a modified version of the survey module of Hofstede (1980). Furthermore, as explained earlier, the study also relies on in-depth interviews conducted with university accounting academics with an interest in culture in each of the three countries to further understand the cultural values that may influence auditor–client conflict resolution and whistle-blowing as an internal control mechanism.

CHAPTER OUTLINE AND ORGANISATION

The study is organised as follows. Chapter 2 is the literature review and provides an evaluation of the theoretical and methodological strengths and weaknesses of selected cross-cultural studies of professional accountant and auditor values, perceptions and judgements. Additionally, it provides recommendations for improving cross-cultural research in auditing and financial accounting with particular reference to studies on professional accounting and auditor values, perceptions and judgements. This chapter concludes by describing how this study addressed some of the theoretical and methodological limitations identified in the review of the relevant literatures.

Chapter 3 is the theory development and hypotheses formulation. The first section of this chapter provides reasons for selecting the cultural dimensions of Power Distance, Individualism and Long-term Orientation, and for excluding the Uncertainty Avoidance and Masculinity dimensions in the theory development and hypotheses formulation. This section also discusses the location of Australia, India and Malaysia on each of Hofstede's cultural dimensions of Power Distance, Individualism and Long-term Orientation, and classifies Indians and Chinese Malaysians in one cluster (comprising large Power Distance, low Individualism and Long-term Orientation), and Australians in another cluster (comprising small Power Distance, high Individualism and Short-term Orientation). This section then goes on to summarise important features of cultural differences between the two clusters based largely on Hofstede's cultural dimensions. The second section of this chapter provides insight into the specific nature of cultural dimensions that are applicable to Chinese Malaysians and Indians by drawing on the relevant features of Confucianism and Hinduism, respectively. Additionally, relevant historical and sociological literatures are summarised to provide insight into those aspects of Australian culture that are particularly applicable to the issues examined in the current study. The final section draws out various relevant features of cultural differences between Indians and Chinese Malaysians in one cluster and Australians in another cluster, to formulate hypotheses on auditor–client conflict resolution, and whistleblowing as an internal control mechanism.

Chapter 4 outlines the research method and explains the strategies employed to enhance the reliability and validity of the results of the study. Chapter 5 provides the results of the research with respect to calculations of the cultural indices of Individualism, Power Distance and Long-term Orientation of the three countries based on professional accountants' responses to Hofstede's (1994a) Value Survey Module. Additionally, this chapter provides a discussion of the results of the interviews with university academics with an interest in culture in each of the three countries.

Chapter 6 is the results of the hypotheses tests and includes the following: (i) a summary of the various methods used for the distribution and collection of survey questionnaires and the response rates for each of the three countries; (ii) a tabulation of the descriptive statistics for the dependent variables measured using the survey questionnaire and also the reliabilities of the multidimensional ethics measure; (iii) a discussion of the results of the hypotheses tests including an explanation of SDRB; and (iv) empirical evidence to show the usefulness of the multidimensional ethics measure over the univariate measure.

Chapter 7 summarises the conclusions and contributions of the study. This chapter also acknowledges the limitations of the study and provides suggestions for further research.

In interpreting the results of the study, it is important to note that the study has adopted the ethical philosophy of "relativism", which suggests that values are a function of culture, and as a result, there are no universal ethical rules (Reidenbach & Robin, 1990, p. 651). Although the study deals with ethical issues associated with auditor–client conflict resolution and whistle-blowing, no attempt is made in this study to prescribe ethical conduct or to delineate "wrong" from "right" judgements. It is important to establish that various cultural values across countries do not imply or justify individual ethnic or cultural stereotypes.

CHAPTER 2
LITERATURE REVIEW

In Chapter 1 it was shown that accounting is a socio-technical activity in which the values and judgements of preparers and users of financial information are important. An understanding of the similarities and differences in judgements of professional accountants across nations should improve the quality and comparability of international accounting information, systems and procedures.

Cross-cultural research is increasingly being recognised as an important area in accounting. This is reflected in an increasing number of studies which have examined the influence of culture on various dependent variables including management control systems design (Harrison, McKinnon, Panchapakesan, & Leung, 1994; Chow et al., 1994, 1999), external auditors' independence (Agacer & Doupnik, 1991; Yamamura et al., 1996; Patel & Psaros, 2000), professional ethics (Cohen et al., 1995) and aspects of international comparative accounting (Bloom & Naciri, 1989; Jaggi & Low, 2000; Chui, Lloyd, & Kwok, 2002; Hope, 2003; Doupknik & Richer, 2004; Chand, Patel, & Patel, 2005). Many of the cross-cultural studies in accounting have examined the linkage between selected dimensions of culture and preferences for, or responses to, various aspects of management planning, control and performance evaluation systems. These studies, referred to here as cross-cultural management accounting research, were reviewed by Harrison and McKinnon (1999).[1] Saudagaran and Diga (1999) provided an evaluation of the contingency-based approach in comparative international accounting and Chanchani and MacGregor (1999) examined cross-cultural issues on topics ranging from management accounting to a discussion of cultural relativism in accounting. Additionally, Prather-Kinsey and Rueschhoff (2004) provided a timely synopsis of international accounting research journals and their international research content. Moreover, some useful analyses and suggestions related to cross-cultural accounting studies are included in Doupnik and Tsakumis (2004).

This chapter makes a contribution by providing a discussion of various theoretical and methodological issues that have not been fully addressed in the cross-cultural accounting literature. Examples of such issues that are likely to enhance the quality of cross-cultural accounting research include the importance of Confucianism and Hinduism in providing insight into the *core*[2] cultural features of subjects of Chinese and Indian ethnic backgrounds, respectively, and the importance of invoking relevant historical, psychological and philosophical literature to understand *core* cultural values.

The focus of this study is located within the area of international financial accounting and auditing, with particular reference to cross-cultural studies on accountants' values and judgements. As such the literature review presented in this chapter does not cover all cross-cultural studies in financial accounting and auditing.[3] Rather, it is restricted to cross-cultural studies of professional accountant and auditor values, perceptions and judgements that have provided some original contribution to the literature. Publications that are largely replications have been ignored in this analysis.

The main objective is to identify the theoretical and methodological strengths and limitations of previous research with a view to informing and guiding both the theoretical specification and treatment of culture and its operationalisation and methodology. It is hoped that the suggestions included in this paper may provide some useful guidance to future cross-cultural studies' researchers.

The chapter is organised as follows. The first section reviews and evaluates studies that did not fully operationalise the conception of culture or that may be said to have operationalised culture as a "black-box". While these studies provided useful insights into perceptual differences across the nations selected, those insights may be limited because the studies treated culture as a convenient "catch-all" explanatory variable. The second section reviews and evaluates studies that invoked Hofstede's (1980) and Hofstede and Bond's (1988) five dimensional cultural taxonomyin theory development and hypotheses formulation. These studies are discussed under the following headings: (i) Empirical Support for Gray's (1988) Framework; (ii) Audit judgements; (iii) Ethical Perceptions; (iv) Organisational culture in accounting firms and (v) whistle-blowing as an internal control mechanism. The final section presents the conclusions and recommendations for improving cross-cultural research in auditing and financial accounting with particular reference to studies on professional accounting and auditor values, perceptions and judgements. This section also describes how this study addresses some of the theoretical and methodological limitations identified in the review of the relevant literatures.

The studies reviewed in this chapter are listed in Tables 1A, 1B and 2 in the appendix to this chapter. Specifically Table 1A lists nine national comparative studies in financial accounting and auditing related to professional accountant and auditor values, perceptions and judgements that did not fully operationalise the conception of culture. The table shows, for each study, the country(ies) at issue and, where applicable, the sample size and nature of subjects in the study, the method used and the dependent variables examined. Table 1B lists 18 studies which used the five-dimensional cultural taxonomy, showing the same details for each study as in Table 1A, but adding details of the cultural dimension(s) drawn on. Table 1B has three panels classifying the 18 studies into categories of Audit and Financial Reporting judgements (Panel A), Ethics judgements (Panel B) and Organisational Culture in Accounting Firms (Panel C). (The one study in the fifth category of whistle-blowing as an internal control mechanism, and the only such study in this category (Schultz et al., 1993), is shown in Panel B). Table 2 shows the same 27 studies as Tables 1A and B, but organises them in terms of their dependent variables and includes details as to whether they developed a priori directional hypotheses as well as classifying them in terms of whether their results provided support or no support for culture or whether the results were mixed.

STUDIES THAT OPERATIONALISED CULTURE AS A "BLACK-BOX"

Financial accounting and auditing studies that operationalised culture as a "black-box" (Table 1A) were the first attempts to examine the influence of culture on various dependent variables, ranging from perceptions of external auditors' independence to various meanings of accounting concepts. Many of these studies made little attempt to determine what culture is, or to determine what it is about culture that produced the claimed effects. That is, "the employment of the culture concept has been an excuse for intellectual laziness, whereby "culture" has often served simply as a synonym for "nation" without any further theoretical grounding" (Child, 1981, p. 304). This is partly understandable because culture is perhaps the most "elusive term in the generally rather fluid vocabulary of the social sciences" (Johoda, 1984, p. 140). As a result, earlier cross-cultural accounting researchers were satisfied with "an omnibus, unpackaged referent" (Rohner, 1984, p. 134), and little attempt was made to "unwrap the packaged construct culture" (Rohner, 1984, p. 111). A summary of studies that failed to "unpackage" the conception of culture and simply operationalised culture as an unspecified independent variable follows, commencing with studies in the financial accounting and auditing areas.[4]

One of the first cross-cultural studies in financial accounting by Ferris, Dillard, and Nethercott (1980) compared perceptual differences between auditors in Australia and the USA on their personal values, motivational levels and work environment. The study found significant similarities and therefore concluded that, "accountants from linguistically, culturally, and economically similar countries tend to have similar personal value structures and work environment perceptions" (p. 367). While providing useful insight, Ferris et al. (1980) did not fully explain what attributes or dimensions of culture were similar between Australia and the US. Directional a priori hypotheses were not formulated and culture was operationalised as a "black box"; that is, as an unspecified independent variable to explain the results of the study.

Using similar reasoning to Ferris et al. (1980), Americ, Kanungo, and Aranya (1983) identified significant cross-cultural differences in work-related values between Anglophone and Francophone professional accountants in Quebec, Canada. They concluded that "culture has a significant effect on certain professional and work values of professional accountants", but that other "cultural work values appeared to be minimized by the process of becoming a professional accountant" (Americ et al., 1983, p. 190). This study provided some discussion of differences between Anglophone and Francophone accountants in terms of the importance placed on certain work-related values and formulated a priori directional hypotheses. However, the study was largely atheoretic about the cultural work values on which it drew, and culture was essentially operationalised as an unspecified independent variable.

Another study that did not fully "unpackage" culture was that by Welton and Davis (1990). They compared the results of American and New Zealand college students' perceptions of various issues relating to accountants' professional ethics. Comparisons of ethical perceptions were made between the groups stratified by those who had been exposed to ethics in the formal curriculum versus those who had no ethics exposure. The study found significant perceptual differences in nine out of eighteen cases between students in the US and New Zealand who were not given formal instructions in ethics. These differences were reduced to only two cases for students with formal ethics instruction. The study concluded that "the need to bring about similar behavior regarding professional ethics in the international business environment may be accomplished through the formal education process, at least where the cultures have similar backgrounds such as those of the United States and New Zealand" (p. 268). This study made an important contribution to ethics research but did not explain what aspects of the national cultures of New Zealand and the US were similar. In that respect, the study would have been improved by the formulation of directional a priori hypothesis, and by an explanation of the specific attributes of culture that accounted for the perceptual similarities and differences between New Zealand and US respondents.

In another study, Belkaoui and Picur (1991) compared perceptual differences among managers and partners from one of the big-six accounting firms in each of Canada, the USA and Great Britain in respect of a set of fundamental accounting assumptions and principles including the accounting entity assumption and the conservatism principle. The authors argued that "the cultural relativism thesis provided the research hypotheses on the relationship between cultural membership and concept perception" (p. 118). After finding certain perceptual differences, post-hoc rationalisation led the authors to argue that "the main difference in the subjects that may influence their perception of accounting concepts was the difference in their *national culture*" (Belkaoui & Picur, 1991, p. 120, emphasis added). Compared to the studies described above, Belkaoui and Picur (1991) provided additional insight into national cultures. Specifically, the study concluded that the differences among subjects' perceptions of conservatism were consistent with their scores on Hofstede's (1980) cultural dimension of Uncertainty Avoidance Hofstede (1980). However, the three nations selected for study had similar Uncertainty Avoidance levels as scored by Hofstede (1980).[5] While this study did invoke Uncertainty Avoidance as a post-hoc possible reason for national perceptual differences on the principle of conservatism, it did not provide a clear theoretical linkage between other dimensions of culture and the dependent variables. Their conclusion that "these findings support the contention that accountants from different cultures differ in their perceptions of accounting concepts" (p. 118), while useful, may have been further supported and explained by providing a theoretical linkage between relevant cultural dimensions and perceptions of accounting concepts.

Another study that did not fully operationalise culture was Agacer and Doupnik (1991). They compared perceptions of external auditors' independence among professional accountants from the USA, the Philippines and West Germany. Directional a priori hypotheses were not formulated. The results showed that West German accountants perceived higher risk of impairment of independence than subjects from the USA and the Philippines. While the authors concluded that "perception of auditor independence is indeed sensitive to cultural differences" (p. 234), they did not provide explanation of this sensitivity.

In the study by Lyons and Tong (1992), bank lending officers in Hong Kong were surveyed to establish whether they had more confidence in audited financial statements prepared by auditors who also provided management advisory services. Their results were found to be contrary to those found in Anglo-American countries (for example, Schulte, 1965). That is, bank officers in Hong Kong did not consider that auditors' independence was jeopardised by the provision of management advisory services. They concluded that "clearly a significant reason for this may be culture context" (Lyons & Tong, 1992, p. 99). Again, while providing useful insights, the study did not "unbundle" the various components that comprised their concept of "culture context"; such "unbundling" may have allowed further insight into their finding.

Lindsay (1992) investigated the perceptions of the financial community in Australia and Canada with respect to auditor–client conflict resolution. In accordance with previous intra-country studies (for example, Farmer, Rittenberg, & Trompeter, 1987; Knapp, 1985; Ettredge, 1988), he found that the nature of the accounting issues, the extent to which management consulting services were provided, the degree of competition within the profession and the size of the audit firm were perceived to be significant determinants of audit firm behaviour. The reasons for selecting Australian and Canadian subjects were not explained and whether the study expected similarities or differences in perceptions was not stated. In addition, the study did not discuss similarities/differences in cultural attributes between Canada and Australia.

In a similar vein, Patel (1992) failed to find any significant difference between professional accountants in Fiji and New Zealand in their perceptions of external auditors' independence. The study concluded that the results show that "perceptions of external auditors' independence is not sensitive to cultural difference" (Patel, 1992, p. 413). Post-hoc rationalisation led to the conclusion that the similarities in perceptions could be the result of the close historical ties between the two countries. In particular, the result was argued as traceable to New Zealand's influence on the formal curricula at secondary and tertiary education levels in Fiji, and the close professional ties between the Fiji Society of Accountants and the New Zealand Society of Accountants. While the study set out to examine the influence of culture on perceptions of external auditors' independence, the concept of culture was not operationalised or invoked in theory development, and a priori directional hypotheses were not formulated.

Bagranoff, Houghton, and Hronsky (1994) also failed to operationalise culture adequately in their study. They investigated whether there were differences in judgements between North American and Australian professional accountants in relation to factors involving the classification in financial statements of an item as either "extraordinary" or "ordinary". After finding significant perceptual differences, the study concluded that "results indicate that cross-cultural differences are likely to influence the meaning of accounting concepts and that future research in this area is warranted" (1994, p. 35). However, Bagranoff et al. (1994) did not examine or explain what those differences were and, again therefore may be seen to have treated culture as the "omnibus, unpackaged referent" referred to by Rohner (1984, p. 134).

Despite the limitations outlined, the above studies contributed to cross-cultural accounting research by showing that judgements in accounting are not neutral and value-free, and that culture is an important variable that needs further investigation in accounting contexts. However, the studies also show that research as early as 1992 and 1994 in the case of Lyons and Tong, Lindsay, Patel, and Bragranoff et al. has lacked explicit analysis of specific dimensions of culture. Studies such as these, which attribute but do not theoretically link perceptual similarities or differences to culture, while useful, do not enhance our understanding of those cross-cultural similarities and differences.

Culture is a complex, multi-faceted concept (Child, 1981; Jahoda, 1984), and a more rigorous analysis and operationalisation of the concept (than is present in the studies reviewed to this point) is a necessary condition for further theoretical advances in cross-cultural accounting research. In particular, a better understanding of culture requires providing a theoretical linkage between specific dimensions of culture and the particular dependent variable(s) under examination in such research (Child, 1981, p. 330; Berry, Poortinga, Segall, & Dasen, 1992, p. 224). Of the nine studies listed in Table 1A, only one study (Americ et al., 1983) formulated a priori directional hypotheses. This is shown in Table 2 which summarises the findings not only of the nine studies reviewed in the chapter to date, but also 18 other studies (specifically, Soeters & Schreuder, 1988; Karnes, Sterner, Welker, & Wu, 1989; Gul & Tsui, 1993; Pratt et al., 1993; Schultz et al., 1993; Cohen et al., 1995; Salter & Niswander, 1995; Patel, Psaros, & Roberts, 1996; Eddie, 1996; Patel & Psaros, 2000; Yamamura et al., 1996; Kachelemeier & Shehata, 1997; Johns, Smith, & Strand, 1999; Cable & Patel, 2000; Jaggi & Low, 2000; Chui et al., 2002; Hope 2003; Doupnik & Richer, 2004).

These latter 18 are distinguished from the nine studies reviewed to date in that, unlike those nine, they operationalised culture mainly by relying on the five-dimensional cultural taxonomy of Hofstede (1980) and Hofstede and Bond (1988). One of these 18 studies (Chui et al., 2002) used Schwartz's

(1994) cultural values and Hope (2003) invoked a combination of both Schwartz (1994) and Hofstede (1980). Table 2 also shows that these 18 are further distinguished from the former nine in that all but two of these (the exceptions being Soeters & Schreuder, 1988, and Cohen et al., 1995) developed a priori hypotheses which provided linkages between selected cultural dimensions as the independent variables(s) and various accounting issues as the dependent variables.

STUDIES THAT APPLIED HOFSTEDE'S CULTURAL DIMENSION(S) IN THEORY DEVELOPMENT

The broad and complex aspects of social meanings, values, beliefs and customs associated with culture require researchers to thoroughly analyse the specific components of culture relevant to their studies. This has led to the call for the conception of culture to be "unpackaged" (Rohner, 1984, p. 111). For social psychologists, this "unpackaging" takes the form of identifying constructs that relate to judgements and behaviour, such as values, motivations, beliefs, expectancies for reinforcement and personality traits (Whiting, 1976; Smith & Bond, 1993, p. 221).

This concept of culture, based solely on the structural functionalist perspective, uses societal norms and values. Of the values-based conceptions of culture, one of the most important and useful for empirical research is that of Geert Hofstede (Bhagat & McQuaid, 1983; Triandis et al., 1993; Smith et al., 1996). Hofstede's contribution is that he unbundled culture into dimensions, or norm values and hence provided a potentially rich starting point for the development of theory and hypotheses relating to cross-cultural differences in accounting practice. Consequently, as shown in the following section, Hofstede's taxonomy has been extensively applied in cross-cultural accounting research.

It should be acknowledged at this point that norms and values are only one aspect of culture (Triandis, 1994). Consequently, this structural functionalist perspective fails to link culture to other important aspects of society, such as the relationship between culture and power, culture and conflict, culture and the maintenance of the status quo in a society and culture and the distribution of wealth. Insight into such complex issues is better provided by other perspectives such as the "interpretive" and "critical" approaches (see Chua, 1986 for details). Despite this limitation, a values-based approach in operationalising culture has provided useful insight into the influence of culture on various accounting issues.

The remainder of this section reviews the cross-cultural research on professional accountant and auditor values, perceptions and judgements which have used Hofstede's (1980) and Hofstede and Bond's (1988) five dimensional cultural taxonomy. The review is organised under the heading: (i) Empirical Support for Gray's (1988) Framework, (ii) Audit judgements, (iii) Ethical Perceptions, (iv) Organisational Cultures in Accounting Firms and (v) whistle-blowing as an internal control mechanism. Among other things, the review shows that several of the criticisms identified by Harrison and McKinnon (1998), in their review of cross-cultural research in management control systems design, are also applicable to the cross-cultural research in financial accounting and auditing.

Patel (2004) and Harrison and McKinnon (1998) identified a number of criticisms of accounting cross-cultural studies. Two of the major criticisms are: (i) a tendency for the research they reviewed to rely on one or a limited number of the five cultural dimensions and not to consider all five dimensions constituting the totality of national cultures and (ii) a tendency to treat the dimensions as if they were equally important across nations with a corresponding failure to consider the more complex issue of the differential centrality or intensity of cultural norms and values across societies.

EMPIRICAL SUPPORT FOR GRAY'S FRAMEWORK

Discussion of two studies, namely Salter and Niswander (1995) and Eddie (1996), that drew on Hofstede's five-dimensional cultural taxonomy and which provided empirical evidence to support Gray's (1998) framework, follows. Studies that have tested only one of Gray's four hypotheses (secrecy versus transparency) include Jaggi and Low (2000) and Hope (2003). These studies (Salter & Niswander, 1995; Eddie, 1996; Jaggi & Low, 2000) are summarised in Panel A of Table 1B.

The previous chapter provided a framework based on work by Hofstede (1980) and Gray (1988) which is applied in the study to examine the influence of cultural values on professional judgements. With reference to this framework, Salter and Niswander's (1995) study is important because they operationalised Gray's (1988) model and showed a significant relationship between financial reporting practices and Hofstede's (1980) cultural dimensions. Specifically, based on financial reporting practices from 29 countries,[6] Salter and Niswander (1995, p. 391) found that "the relationship is strongest in explaining the level of (financial) information provided and the level of de jure uniformity where more than 50% of the variance is explained".

Another study which operationalised Gray's (1988) model and provided empirical evidence to show the relationship between Hofstede's (1980) cultural dimensions and financial reporting practices was Eddie (1996). This study developed a disclosure index that contained 101 items to measure the extent of consolidation disclosure in the annual reports of 184 corporations in Australia, Hong Kong, Indonesia, Japan, Korea, Malaysia, Philippines, Singapore, Taiwan and Thailand. The results from Eddie's (1996) study showed a significant relationship between Hofstede's cultural dimensions and the extent of consolidation disclosure.

Besides providing empirical evidence to support Gray's (1988) framework, both the studies by Salter and Niswander (1995) and Eddie (1996) are relevant because they examined two of the three countries selected for examination in this study (these are Australia and Malaysia).

AUDIT JUDGEMENTS

Discussion of those studies that have relied solely on Hofstede's five-dimensional cultural taxonomy and which are related to the dependent variable of interest in this study, namely, auditor–client conflict resolution, follows. These studies (summarised in Panel B of Table 1B) are discussed in greater detail compared to the earlier group because of their theoretical relevance to the current study.

Gul and Tsui (1993) examined the influence of the cultural dimension of Uncertainty Avoidance on Hong Kong and Australian auditors' perceptions of the "subject to" audit qualification. The study hypothesised and found support that auditors in a weak Uncertainty Avoidance society (Hong Kong) were likely to feel more secure and less threatened by the risk of losing clients and therefore would show a higher preference for the "subject to" qualification than auditors in a strong Uncertainty Avoidance society (i.e., Australia).

Of particular importance to this review is the statement in Gul and Tsui (1993, p. 359), "The 18 local Hong Kong (Chinese) auditors classified by Hofstede (1980) as weak uncertainty avoiders…". No attempt was made in the study to measure Uncertainty Avoidance to verify whether Hofstede's (1980) results were still applicable to Australian and Hong Kong auditors in 1993. Evidence suggests that this may not be the case.[7] It is therefore suggested that studies that rely on Hofstede's cultural dimension(s) need to measure the relevant dimensions to confirm whether the scores are still applicable to the specific sample selected for study in the 1990s.

A second limitation of the Gul and Tsui (1993) study was a failure to consider all five cultural dimensions that relate to the totality of the national cultures. That is, assuming Hofstede's taxonomy, the national cultures comprise the dimensions of Power Distance, Collectivism, Uncertainty Avoidance, Masculinity and Long/Short-term Orientation. If any of these dimensions is not used in theory development, then the study needs to explain the reason(s) for the omission, and also to discuss the theoretical implications of any omitted cultural dimension(s).

Gul and Tsui (1993) assumed that Uncertainty Avoidance was the core cultural dimension that differentiated Hong Kong and Australian auditors. However, empirical evidence shows that Uncertainty Avoidance may not be a relevant dimension for comparing Asian and Anglo-American countries because this dimension was not found in two other important studies, namely, The Chinese Culture Connection (1987) and Smith et al. (1996) (this issue is elaborated on in Chapter 3). Therefore, the theoretical exposition drawn by Gul and Tsui (1993), based solely on differences in Hofstede's (1980) ranking of Uncertainty Avoidance for Australia and Hong Kong, is open to criticism.

In another study, Patel et al. (1996) and Patel and Psaros (2000) examined the competing cultural and acculturational influences on perceptions of external auditors' independence by final-year undergraduate accounting students in Britain, Australia, India and Malaysia. Only Individualism was invoked in the theory development. The study failed to find support for the cultural hypothesis which stated that subjects from countries that rank higher on measures of Individualism (Britain and Australia) are more likely to have greater differences (i.e., larger variations) in their perceptions, compared to subjects from countries that rank lower in terms of Individualism (India and Malaysia). Instead, the study found support for the acculturation hypothesis, which stated that subjects from countries with greater political, economic and socio-cultural interactions (Australia and Britain) are more likely to have greater similarities (i.e., less variations) in their perceptions, compared to subjects that have lesser acculturational influences (India and Malaysia).

Consistent with the study by Gul and Tsui (1993), Patel et al. (1996) and Patel and Psaros (2000) failed to consider all relevant cultural dimensions in the formulation of the cultural hypothesis. Evidence shows that Individualism, Power Distance and Confucian Dynamism are the relevant dimensions for comparing decision making among subjects from Asian and western countries (this issue is discussed in Chapter 3). By developing the cultural hypothesis solely on the Individualism dimension, Patel et al. (1996) and Patel and Psaros (2000) assumed that Power Distance and Confucian Dynamism do not influence perceptions of external auditors' independence.

Since Power Distance and Confucian Dynamism are not used in the theory development, the study needed to explain the reason(s) for their omission. In addition, no attempt was made to verify whether Hofstede's (1980) results were still applicable to the specific sample of Australian, Indian, British and Malaysian students in 1996.

A study by Yamamura et al. (1996) examined differences in audit decision making between senior audit staff selected from big-six firms in Japan and the US. Specifically, based on Rank Consciousness (Power Distance),[8] the study hypothesised that US auditors would be more questioning of senior management judgements, and as a result would assess inherent risk higher and would require more audit procedures than Japanese auditors. Based on Group Orientation (Individualism),[9] it was hypothesised that, compared to US auditors, Japanese auditors were expected to select fewer audit procedures that required approaching clients directly, and to rank direct procedures lower in importance. Only partial support was found for these hypotheses. The mean number of audit procedures required by US auditors significantly exceeded the mean number required by Japanese auditors in each of the three cases that were used in the study. Therefore, as hypothesised, evidence showed that US auditors were less accepting of management judgements than Japanese auditors. However, Japanese auditors were significantly more questioning of management in the case involving bad debts, while US auditors were more questioning in the case involving a construction project. The study concluded that the differences between the US and Japanese auditors could be explained by "environmental factors rather than the theorized effect of cultural differences" (p. 347). An example of the "environmental factors" was the massive bad debt losses during the early 1990s, which could explain the cautious stand taken by Japanese auditors when auditing doubtful receivables.

While providing useful insight into the influence of Rank Consciousness and Group Orientation on auditors' judgements, the study has a number of limitations similar to those of the previous studies reviewed. First, while Yamamura et al. (1996) invoked Rank Consciousness to support one of their hypotheses and Group Orientation to support the other, they did not provide theoretical explanation for this choice. Nor did they consider theoretically whether each cultural dimension might have had implications for the other hypothesis or whether other cultural dimensions, not invoked in their study, might also have had theoretical relevance. And, like many other studies in this area, Yamamura et al. (1996) did not measure Rank Consciousness (Power Distance in Hofstede's terms) or Group Orientation (Individualism) to corroborate whether Hofstede's (1980) scores were applicable to the sample and the countries in the 1990s.

In another study, based on differences between the USA and Hong Kong on cultural dimensions of Power Distance, Individualism and Confucian Dynamism, Tsui (1996) found that Hong Kong auditors had lower *P* scores (a measure of "ethical reasoning" based on scores from a "Defining Issues Test") than USA auditors.[10] That is, subjects in a country with large Power Distance, low Individualism and Long-term Orientation were found to possess lower "ethical reasoning" than their counterparts in Anglo-American countries. However, this is an example of a study that used a research instrument (specifically, the DIT of ethical reasoning), developed from the societal values of industrialised western nations, to evaluate ethical reasoning of individuals from other nations and cultures where societal values may differ.

The DIT developed by Rest (1979) measures an individual's level of ethical reasoning based on Kohlberg's (1969) theory of Cognitive Moral Development. This six-stage sequence theory assumes that the stages are applicable in all countries. That is, the DIT assumes that the ethical values being measured have equal uniformity and intensity in all societies. For example, stage three is "interpersonal concordance", stage four is "law and duty to the social order", and stage five is "societal cooperation" (Ponemon, 1992, p. 241). To assume that these stages are equally important and valued in all societies may be argued to be simplistic. Stage six of Kohlberg's (1969) theory is "nonarbitrary social cooperation: how rational and impartial people would organise cooperation". The focus is on fairness of the law or rules derived from general principles of justice as determined by rational people (Ponemon, 1992, p. 241). "Rational", "impartial", "fairness" and "justice" are conceptions that are dependent on the values that are cherished in a society (Triandis, 1994). It is therefore not surprising that the DIT has been criticised for cultural biases (Gibbs, 1977; Murphy & Gilligan, 1980; Ma & Cheung, 1996).

Triandis (1994, p. 53) notes that values found in some Asian societies, such as communal sharing, collective happiness, non-violence, purity, chastity, filial piety and community responsibility are missing from the scoring manual of the DIT. The theory used in developing the DIT is individualistic because it assumes that people are autonomous and that morality is purely individual. The values chosen in the test, such as individual property, human life and individual conscience refer to values cherished in individualistic societies (Triandis, 1994, p. 53). Thus, the results of the study of Tsui (1996) may be explained by the potentially theoretical irrelevance of measuring ethical reasoning with the DIT in Asian and other developing countries.

A critical analysis of a more recent study by Doupnik and Richer (2004) further highlights some of the theoretical and methodological problems in cross-cultural accounting studies. This study examined the influence of national cultures of USA and Germany on judgements of professional accountants on selected "in-context" probability expressions such as likely, probable, virtually certain, etc. The study concluded that in most cases, German accountants were more conservative than American accountants.

The entire cultural theoretical underpinning in Doupnik and Richer (2004) is based on Hofstede's (1980) and Hofstede and Bond's (1988) cultural value index scores and ranks for the US and Germany. The study needs to convince the readers that these scores are still applicable in the current period. Note that Hofstede (1980) collected his data around the mid-1970s. Importantly, Hofstede (1994a) developed the "Values Survey Module" to enable researchers to measure the five cultural dimensions to address the issue of whether the cultural scores are still applicable to their specific samples in the current period. Completing the Hofstede's Values Survey Module of 1994 takes about 10 minutes.

While the five-dimensional culture model is useful, it must be acknowledged that this quantified approach is only one measure of culture (Triandis, 1994). An almost exclusive reliance on the five-dimensional model has resulted in a failure to examine other perspectives to understand the richness and complexity of cultural differences and similarities.

Doupnik and Richer (2004, p. 16) need to convincingly support the validity of their conclusion that, "This study provides evidence that differences in cultural values affect the interpretation of IAS probability expressions by German and US accountants". Importantly, the findings in a cross-cultural study should clearly be attributable to cultural values and not to other confounding factors such as the historical roles and objectives of accounting in Germany and the US. In other words, the study needs to explain why accountants from the US and Germany are selected for examination. Research related to both subjective and empirical classifications of countries in relation to the development, role and objectives of accounting practices and systems and concepts show differences between Germany and the US. For example, in Germany, the professional accountant's role has historically been concerned primarily with the implementation of relatively prescriptive and detailed legal requirements. As such, accountants in Germany historically had very little experience in exercising their professional judgement (Radebaugh & Gray, 2002). In contrast, exercise of accountant's professional judgement is an important and integral aspect of accounting in the US. These differences in accounting practices between Germany and the US are likely to have confounded the results of the study.

The study fails to control differences in organisational cultures of accounting firms in the US and Germany. As such, Doupnik and Richer

(2004) have not clearly established that the findings are clearly attributable to cultural values and not to other confounding factors such as differences in organisational cultures of the firms in the two countries (see Gernon, 1993 for additional examples). Culture is a complex and multi-faceted concept (Triandis, 1994; Smith et al., 1996), and a more rigorous analysis and operationalisation of the concept (than is present in this study) is a necessary condition for any further advances in cross-cultural accounting research. In particular, a better understanding of culture requires a theoretical linkage between specific dimensions of culture and the particular dependent variable(s) under examination in such research.

A summary of studies discussed in this section under audit judgements (Gul & Tsui, 1993; Patel et al., 1996; Patel & Psaros, 2000; Yamamura et al., 1996; Tsui, 1996; Doupnik & Richer, 2004), together with another seven studies (Kachelemeier & Shehata, 1997; Johns et al., 1999; Cable & Patel, 2000; Jaggi & Low, 2000; Chui et al., 2002; Hope, 2003) is presented in Table 1B Panel A.

STUDIES ON CROSS-CULTURAL ETHICAL PERCEPTIONS

Three studies that have made some original contributions, namely Karnes, Sterner, Welker, and Wu (1990); Cohen et al. (1995); and Schultz et al. (1993) on cross-cultural ethical perceptions are listed on Table 1B, Panel B. A critical analysis of these three studies with the objective of highlighting their theoretical and methodological limitations follows.

Karnes et al. (1990) found some support for differences between Taiwanese and USA public accountants' perceptions of the risks and benefits associated with committing an unethical business practice. Specifically, they found some evidence that Taiwanese accountants tended to perceive a smaller degree of risk associated with unethical business practices that impact on a "close in-group in a beneficial manner" (p. 60). Conversely, Taiwanese accountants tended to perceive a larger degree of risk being associated with those unethical business practices that impacted on "close in-groups in a harmful manner" (p. 60). The study concluded that, "public accountants appear to view unethical business practices through a national culture filter" (p. 60).

The cultural dimension of Individualism which differentiates between in-groups and out-groups was the only dimension invoked by Karnes et al. (1990) in their theory development. However, Power Distance and Confucian Dynamism may also be relevant dimensions in examining some of the issues covered in the scenarios that were used in the Karnes et al. (1990) study. Indeed, some of the insignificant results found in that study may be explained by invoking Power Distance.[11] Compared to the US, Taiwanese accountants not only differentiated between the in-group and the out-group, but also placed greater emphasis on maintaining the organisational status quo (which is a characteristic of Power Distance) and also took into account the long-term consequences of unethical practices on their organisations (a characteristic of Confucian Dynamism). This concern for maintenance of the status quo and Long-term Orientation may have overridden the Taiwanese accountants' concern for immediate "financial gain" in six of the eight cases that were used in their study (see Karnes et al., 1990, Table IV, p. 58).

A second limitation may be the possible confounding effect of the influence of organisational culture. US accountants were selected from multinational accounting firms (big-eight), whereas Taiwanese firms were local. Evidence suggests that multinational accounting firms have a distinct organisational culture (Soeters & Schreuder, 1988).[12] No attempt was made in the Karnes et al. (1990) study to discuss or control for these differences in organisational cultures.

A further issue arising from the Karnes et al. (1990) study, and one of particular importance to cross-cultural research, is that of content equivalence. Content equivalence refers to the equivalence of rules and concepts at issue among the countries being studied, and is a pre-requisite for cross-cultural theory development and hypotheses formulation (Gernon, 1993). In the case of Karnes et al. (1990), they did not establish or demonstrate that the concepts and rules of insider trading (as one of their instances of unethical business practices) are similar (have content equivalence) in the US and Taiwan. This lack of content equivalence may have affected the results of their study. For example, if there are any differences in the concepts and rules of insider trading between the US and Taiwan (such as what constitutes a "related party"), then the difference found in accountants' perceptions of the risks of committing an unethical business practice associated with insider trading between these countries may have been attributed to the lack of content equivalence rather than to national culture. On the other hand, establishing content equivalence in relation to insider trading between the US and Taiwan would have provided greater assurance that the perceptual differences found in the study were attributable to national cultural differences.

Thus, the establishment of content equivalence is important in cross-cultural studies because it enables a study to rule out some confounding explanations for differences found in subjects' perceptions and judgements among the countries that are examined. This reinforces the importance of establishing content equivalence in this and other future cross-cultural studies in accounting and auditing. The way in which this research monograph deals with this issue is discussed in Chapter 4.

In another important study, Cohen et al. (1995) examined differences in the ethical decision making of auditors from Latin American countries, Japan and the United States. Theory development was based on Hofstede's (1980) cultural dimensions but an a priori directional hypothesis was not provided. The hypothesis tested simply stated that there would be significant differences among auditors in the three countries in their ethical decision making. Subjects were presented with eight scenarios, each describing a possibly questionable action related to public accounting practice. The authors report that "the results confirm that differences exist in ethical decision making among the US, Japanese and Latin American respondents", and that "the strongest differences emerged in the Latin–US comparisons" (p. 56). A major contribution of this research is the evidence that across all countries examined, respondents reported that they would act more ethically than their peers. This is called "social desirability response bias" (SDRB) and cannot be ignored in cross-cultural accounting research.[13]

While the study provided useful insight, the results reported need to be interpreted with caution for the following reasons. First, as noted above, Cohen et al. (1995) did not formulate directional hypotheses. They justified this by arguing that to do so would considerably reduce the reliability of the study because, "in order to use the five dimensions to generate directional hypotheses, it is necessary to specify ex ante for each vignette the direction and strength of the relationship between differences on *each* of the five dimensions and differences in ethical evaluations. Thus the researchers would have to provide five judgements for each of eight vignettes" (p. 45). This justification for not developing the directional hypotheses may be open to criticism, in that the study could potentially have identified the theoretical relevance or irrelevance of the five cultural dimensions as they applied to each country and each questionable act. Cohen et al. (1995) assumed that there would be consistent differences among Latin American, Japanese and US auditors on their ethical judgements on the following issues; "collectability of receivables, confidentiality, conflict of interest, bidding for a risky client, lowballing, favours for a client, underreporting billable hours and underperforming the audit" (p. 52). Each of these eight questionable acts is complex, but it would have been possible for Cohen et al. to examine the pre-existing theoretical and empirical evidence as it related to each of these questionable acts.

After examining that evidence and identifying the important issues that might affect judgements on each of the eight questionable acts selected for study, Cohen et al. (1995) could have then proceeded to identify the core and peripheral values in the cultures being compared. For example, Uncertainty Avoidance may not be a core value in comparing the Asian (Japan) and Western (the US) subjects (The Chinese Culture Connection, 1987; Smith et al., 1996). After identifying the core cultural values in the nations selected for study, it would have been possible to proceed to the theory development and hypotheses formulation stages of the research. The result of this process might well have been that no consistent directional hypotheses could be formulated for all eight vignettes, such that the authors would not have proceeded on the assumption that there would be persistent similarities or differences among accountants from the US, Japan and Latin countries on a wide range of ethical issues in accounting. The important outcome of the weakness of the Cohen et al. (1995) study in failing to seek to formulate hypotheses, and the above discussion of how such a weakness could have been overcome, is that this study (and other future studies in similar areas) needs to ensure that each issue is examined separately taking into account the relevant theoretical and empirical evidence.

As in the discussion of the Karnes et al. (1990) study earlier in this section, the ethical constructs under examination in Cohen et al. (1995) might also suffer the content equivalence limitation. For example, vignette one dealt with issues related to revenue recognition; however, Cohen et al. (1995) did not establish that the concept and rules of revenue recognition had content equivalence in the nations examined. This lack of content equivalence may have confounded the results of their study. For example, differences in ethical decision making among auditors from Latin American countries, Japan and the US may be the result of differences in rules of revenue recognition (such as when and how to recognise revenue) rather than their national cultures. Similarly, Jaggi and Low (2000), Chui et al. (2002), Hope (2003) and Doupnik and Richer (2004) failed to establish content equivalence in their studies. For example, Doupnik and Richer (2004) failed to establish that the verbal probability expressions used in their study have content equivalence in Germany and in the USA. Again, this reinforces the importance of establishing content equivalence in cross-cultural studies in accounting and auditing.

Again, like many other studies in this area including the more recent ones such as Jaggi and Low (2000), Hope (2003), Doupnik and Richer (2004), and Cohen et al. (1995) did not measure the cultural dimensions to corroborate whether Hofstede's (1980) scores were applicable to their samples and countries in the 1990s. Furthermore, Venezuela, Colombia, Chile, Ecuador, Honduras and Panama were grouped as "Latin countries". The grouping of six countries into one "Latin countries" was not supported by empirical evidence. However, Cohen et al.'s (1995) clustering may have been justified by using Hofstede's Values Survey Module of 1994 or some other relevant instrument, to measure the cultural dimensions in each of the nations comprising "Latin countries".

ORGANISATIONAL CULTURES IN ACCOUNTING FIRMS

Two cross-cultural studies on organisational cultures in accounting firms that are relevant to the current study are Soeters and Schreuder (1988) and Pratt et al. (1993).

Soeters and Schreuder (1988) examined whether there were cultural differences between local Dutch and international accounting firms operating in the Netherlands. They conducted interviews with Dutch partners of international accounting firms to confirm that these firms had strong US orientation in their organisational philosophies and policies. Specifically, their research question was whether it was possible to detect the influence of the US culture on the international firms in the Netherlands. If so, this might explain any differences between measurements of work-related values of employees in international and Dutch firms. The study used Hofstede's (1980) instrument to measure differences in organisational cultures. The results showed that there were significant differences between the Dutch and international firms in some of the questions that measured Power Distance, Uncertainty Avoidance, Individualism and Masculinity. The study concluded that self-selection of workers, in combination with the selection policies of international accounting firms, was "probably the best explanation for the US oriented culture in these organizations" (Soeters & Schreuder, 1988, p. 82).

Pratt et al. (1993) extended Soeters and Schreuder's (1988) work by examining the differences in work-related values among professional accountants from Australia, Britain and the US who were categorised into three groups. In group one were British accountants working in British firms and Australian accountants in Australian firms. In group two were British accountants working in US firms and Australian accountants working in US firms and in group three were US accountants working in US firms. The study found partial support for the hypothesis that the scores on each of

Hofstede's (1980) four cultural dimensions for group two would be between the scores of groups one and three. Specifically, the results showed that British accountants working in the US firms operating in Britain "reflected the cultural values of US accountants" (p. 626), but no such relationships were found for Australian accountants in the US firms in Australia.

Of importance to this study is that the two studies provide some evidence, albeit qualified, that there are similarities in organisational cultures of international accounting firms. The importance for this study is that these similarities allow some comfort that organisational culture is controlled for in the cross-cultural comparison. This is returned to, and elaborated on, in the Method chapter (Chapter 4).

WHISTLE-BLOWING AS AN INTERNAL CONTROL MECHANISM

Schultz et al. (1993) is the only cross-cultural study on whistle-blowing. The study investigated whether "managers and professional staff" from France, Norway and the United States differed in their attitudes towards reporting of "questionable acts".[14] A questionable act was defined as an action that violated a standard of justice, honesty or economy. The authors argued that the relatively higher scores for the French on Hofstede's (1980) cultural dimensions of Power Distance and Uncertainty Avoidance could lead to French organisations being more authoritarian, more bureaucratic and less participative. Accordingly, the study hypothesised and found some support that French subjects would have lower tendencies to report "questionable acts" than other nationalities. The authors concluded that their "study supports the claim by Hofstede, Neuijen, Ohayv, and Sanders (1990) and Hofstede (1989) that national culture dominates organizational culture in matters involving value judgements" (Schultz et al., 1993, p. 96). Based on this finding, the study concluded that multinational enterprises which aim to achieve similar levels of reliability in their accounting systems across divisions located in various countries need to implement control systems that are compatible with national cultural values.

The Schultz et al. (1993) study may be criticised on the following two grounds. First, the study did not control for organisational culture. The US and Norwegian companies were publicly owned but the French were wholly owned subsidiaries of US companies. The organisational culture of the US parent is likely to filter to the subsidiaries and this may have confounded the results (or the lack thereof) found in the study (Gernon, 1993).

Second, research related to both subjective and empirical classifications of countries in relation to the development, role and objectives of accounting practices, systems and concepts show differences among the USA, France and Norway (Choi & Mueller, 1992; Choi & Meek, 2005). These differences in the objectives of accounting are likely to have confounded the results of the study. Once again, the Schultz et al. (1993) study highlights the need to ensure content equivalence for the accounting constructs/issues that are examined. For example, one case in the Schultz et al. (1993) study involved a US revenue recognition problem; however, the study failed to examine whether the revenue recognition rules are identical across the three countries. In a similar manner, Gernon (1993, p. 109) noted that another case in the Schultz et al. (1993) study assumed that quality control inspections are equally important in the US, France and Norway.

An overarching issue applicable to all the studies reviewed in this section which have relied on Hofstede's (1980) and Hofstede and Bond's (1988) five-dimensional model of culture is that almost no attempt has been made to complement and enrich the selected cultural dimensions with theoretical and empirical support from other disciplines such as sociology and psychology. This issue is not restricted to cross-cultural studies of professional accounting and auditor values, perceptions and judgements. Harrison and McKinnon (1999), in their review of cross-cultural management accounting research, also stressed a potential over-reliance on the five-dimensional, values-based model of Hofstede (1980) and Hofstede and Bond (1988). While this model is a useful starting point for theory development and hypotheses formulation, it is not sufficient. It is strongly suggested that future cross-cultural studies in accounting should seek to complement and enrich the five-dimensional approach to culture with other perspectives including those available in the sociological, historical and psychological literatures.

It is of interest to note that some of the earlier international accounting studies, such as Briston (1978) and McKinnon (1984), which were conducted prior to the dissemination of Hofstede's cultural dimensions, drew on the historical, sociological and psychological literatures to explore the national cultures at issue in their studies. McKinnon (1984), for example, in her study of cultural constraints on auditor independence in Japan drew extensively on historical and sociological literatures to provide a richer insight into Japanese culture and to illustrate the "culture inconsistency" of auditor independence in Japan, and the associated need for a greater reliance on institutional controls to ensure compliance with legislative reporting provisions and a structured maintenance of auditor independence.

It would seem that the development of cross-cultural research in accounting is at a point where the strengths of the five-dimensional Hofstede's model and of the sociological, psychological and historical literatures could be usefully drawn together to enhance future research.

CONCLUSION AND RECOMMENDATIONS

This chapter has reviewed 27 cross-cultural studies in financial accounting and auditing relevant to this study. The purpose of the review was to identify the theoretical and methodological strengths and weaknesses of previous research in these areas with a view to informing and guiding both the theoretical specification and treatment of culture and the study's operationalisation and methodology. This final section of the chapter first summarises important considerations relevant to the theoretical specification of this study arising from the review and then summarises important considerations relevant to the method.

CONCLUSIONS WITH RESPECT TO THEORY

The summary in Table 1A shows that in nine studies, culture was simply operationalised as a "black-box". That is, culture was operationalised as an unspecified independent variable to explain the results of the studies. While these studies provide useful insights into differences in accounting and audit judgements across countries, those insights may be limited. Culture is a complex and multi-faceted concept, and a better understanding of it requires providing a clear linkage between the core dimensions of culture in the nations concerned and the dependent variable(s) under examination. The five-dimensional or componential model of culture, developed by Hofstede (1980) and Hofstede and Bond (1988), has proved useful in unpackaging the cultural "black-box". Consequently, most of the cross-cultural studies in accounting have extensively applied this taxonomy.

The componential studies in accounting have relied almost totally on either one or a limited number of Hofstede's cultural dimensions in theory development and hypotheses formulation. For example, 14 of the 20 cross-cultural studies of management control system design, reviewed by Harrison and McKinnon (1999), relied almost exclusively on one or more of Hofstede's cultural dimensions. In addition, 10 studies in audit and financial accounting judgements (with particular reference to studies on professional accounting and auditor values, perceptions and judgements) shown in Table 1B operationalised culture by invoking either one or more cultural dimensions. This simplistic treatment of culture, which relies on one or a limited number of cultural dimensions and does not consider all five dimensions constituting the totality of national cultures, has tended to limit theoretical advances in cross-cultural accounting research. If any of the five dimensions is not applied in theory development, then the study needs to explain the reason(s) for the omission, and needs also to discuss the theoretical implications of the omitted cultural dimension(s). Studies by Karnes et al. (1989), Gul and Tsui (1993), Patel et al. (1996), Patel and Psaros (2000), Kachelemeier and Shehata (1997), and Johns et al. (1999) relied only on one dimension and Schultz et al. (1993) and Yamamura et al. (1996) on two dimensions in their hypotheses formulation. Similarly, Jaggi and Low (2000) and Doupnik and Richer (2004) used four of the five cultural dimensions.

None of the studies in Table 1B provided any discussion of the implications of the omitted cultural dimensions. This "pick and choose" approach to selection of relevant cultural dimensions may limit our understanding of the influence of culture on various accounting constructs selected for study. Consequently, this study (and other future studies in this area) needs to pay attention to developing a more comprehensive and holistic perspective on cultural differences and similarities.

Another associated problem in a number of cross-cultural studies is the assumption that Hofstede's (1980) scores for the cultural dimensions were still applicable during the period of the study. Only three of the 18 studies in Table 1B computed the cultural scores. It is indeed surprising to note that recent studies published in good-quality journals such as Jaggi and Low (2000), Hope (2003) and Doupnik and Richer (2004) also fall in this category. It is suggested that studies relying on Hofstede's cultural dimension(s) need to measure those dimensions to confirm whether the scores are still applicable to their specific samples in the period of the study.

While the five-dimensional culture model is useful, it must be acknowledged that norms and values are only one measure of culture (Triandis, 1994, p. 133). An almost exclusive reliance on norms and values has resulted in a failure to examine other perspectives to understand the richness and complexity of cultural differences and similarities. As an example relevant to the current study, India and Malaysia are both low on measures of Individualism; however, a complete reliance on this similarity in theory development is likely to provide a narrow insight and may lead to discarding other important aspects of cultural differences between these societies. For example, the caste system is an important determinant in defining the "in-group" and the "out-group" in India (Sinha & Sinha, 1990), whereas, among the Chinese in Malaysia, *Ren Qin* (relationship orientation) is an important factor (Cheung, 1986, p. 185).[15] Therefore, simply relying on Hofstede's measures of low Individualism in India and in Chinese-based societies in theory development may provide only a limited insight into the cultures of these societies.

Another related problem is the failure in a number of cross-cultural studies to formulate a priori directional hypotheses. Table 2 reveals that almost one third of the studies did not formulate such hypotheses. Earlier exploratory studies in cross-cultural research in accounting, and the increase in theoretical and empirical evidence from other disciplines, should enable accounting researchers to formulate a priori directional hypotheses.

To address some of the limitations of the simplistic values-based approach in cross-cultural research, it is suggested that this approach be complemented by historical, sociological, psychological and other relevant literatures. This combination of the five-dimensional cultural model and the supporting literatures from other disciplines would also identify and provide an understanding of the core and the peripheral values in a given society. Theory development and hypotheses formulation can then proceed driven largely by the differences in core cultural values. Such is the approach taken in this study.

To further enrich understanding of cultural values in a nation, it may be useful to conduct interviews with selected subjects with an interest in culture to obtain additional evidence on attributes of culture that are of importance to the accounting profession and the particular dependent variables that are examined in the particular study. Conducting such interviews provides additional insight into core cultural norms and values that may impact on the dependent variables. Any relevant aspects of professional accounting subcultures in a country could also be identified by personal interviews. Again, such is the approach adopted in this study.

CONCLUSIONS WITH RESPECT TO METHOD

The review of the cross-cultural studies in this chapter also identified several important considerations with respect to guiding the methodology of this study.

First is the importance in cross-cultural accounting and auditing research of the need to establish content equivalence in the accounting constructs or issues being examined. The reviews of the Karnes et al. (1990), Schultz et al.

(1993), Cohen et al. (1995), Jaggi and Low (2000), Chui et al. (2002), Hope (2003), and Doupnik and Richer (2004) all indicated the importance of establishing content equivalence as a prerequisite for cross-cultural theory development and hypotheses formulation. It was suggested that the failure to establish content equivalence in cross-national studies might confound their findings because the differences found in subjects' perceptions and judgements between and across nations may be the result of differences in the rules and concepts at issue (such as when and how to recognise revenue), rather than in national culture. This study provides some assurance about content equivalence by selecting Australia, India and Malaysia as nations for study because they belong to the British Commonwealth model of accounting development (Mueller, 1968; Mueller et al., 1991; Nobes & Parker, 2004). These three countries were colonised by the British who were also responsible for the development of accounting and corporate legislation. In each country the objective of accounting is generally based on the concept of "decision usefulness" which is principally oriented towards the decision needs of investors. This issue is elaborated on in Chapter 4.

A second methodological consideration to emerge from the review conducted in this chapter is that SDRB cannot be ignored in cross-cultural research. Identified specifically from the Cohen et al. (1995) study, this study takes steps to provide some control over this bias. These steps are outlined in Chapter 4.

APPENDIX II

Table 1A. Summary of Selected Cross-Cultural Studies.

Study	Country (Sample Size) (Subjects)	Method	Dependent Variables	Cultural Dimensions
Ferris et al. (1980)	Australia (45) US (45) Auditors	Survey questionnaire	• 12 job-related outcomes (e.g., responsibility, security advancement) • Performance measured by supervisory ratings and salary levels • Personal evaluation of performance	Culture as a 'black-box'
Americ et al. (1983)	Canada (Francophone 132) (Anglophone 130) Professional accountants	Survey questionnaire	• Importance of job context factors (13 items) • Importance of job content factors (13 items) • Professional commitment (15 items)	Culture as a 'black-box'
Welton and Davis (1990)	With ethics exposure: US (149) NZ (99) Without ethics exposure: US (119) NZ (283) Accounting students	Survey questionnaire	Ethical perceptions	Culture as a 'black-box'

Belkaoui and Picur (1991)	US (47) UK (21) Canada (19) Professional accountants	Survey questionnaire	Going concern, entity, stable monetary unit, periodicity, cost principle, relevance principle, matching, objectivity, consistency, full disclosure, materiality, conservatism	Culture as a 'black-box'
Agacer and Doupnik (1991)	US (119) West Germany (85) Philippines (108) Professional accountants	Survey questionnaire	Perceptions of external auditors' independence	Culture as a 'black-box'
Lyons and Tong (1992)	Hong Kong (22) Bank lending officers	Survey questionnaire	Provision of management advisory services (yes or no)	Culture as a 'black-box'
Lindsay (1992)	Canada (94; 80) Australia (69; 49) Analysts and bankers respectively	Survey questionnaire	• Nature of accounting standard • Provision of management consulting services • Competition • Audit firm size	Cultural attributes were not discussed
Patel (1992)	Fiji (20) NZ (19) Professional accountants	Survey questionnaire	Perceptions of external auditors' independence	Culture as a 'black-box'
Bagranoff et al. (1994)	US (84) Australia (96) Professional accountants	Survey questionnaire	Classification of extraordinary items	Culture as a 'black-box'

Table 1B

Study	Country (Sample Size) (Subjects)	Method	Dependent Variables	Cultural Dimensions
Panel A: Audit and Financial Reporting judgements				
Gul and Tsui (1993)	Hong Kong (18) Australia (17) Auditors	Survey questionnaire	Perceptions of 'subject to' audit qualification	Uncertainty avoidance
Salter and Niswander (1995)	29 countries	Statistical analysis	Audit perspective Professional self-regulation Professionalism Inter-company consistency Conservatism Optimism Broad index of disclosure Index of disclosure	Uncertainty avoidance Individualism Power distance Masculinity
Eddie (1996)	Australia, Hong Kong, Indonesia, Japan, Korea, Malaysia, Philippines	Statistical analysis	Consolidation disclosure index (101 items)	Uncertainty avoidance Individualism Power distance Long-term orientation
Patel et al. (1996) Patel and Psaros (2000)	Australia (94) UK (60) India (66) Malaysia (78) University accounting students	Survey questionnaire	Perceptions of external auditors' independence	Individualism
Yamamura et al. (1996)	US (170) Japan (57) Professional accountants	Survey questionnaire	• Inherent risk assessments • Number of audit procedures selected	Rank consciousness (power distance) Group orientation (individualism)
Kachelemeier and Shehata (1997)	Canada (80) Hong Kong (80) China (80) University business students	Between subjects experiment	• Voluntary revelation of private information • Voluntary cooperation • Demand for auditing	Individualism
Johns et al. (1999)	US (50) Non-US (28) Organisational members (details not provided)	Survey questionnaire	Frequency of use of group support software	Individualism

Patel et al. (1999)	Australia (72) India (84) Malaysia (92) Senior professional accountants	Survey questionnaire and interviews	judgements related to auditor client conflict resolution	Individualism, power distance and long-term orientation
Cable and Patel (2000)	China (40) Australia (21) University accounting students	Survey questionnaire	judgements related to aggressive financial reporting practices	Confucianism for Chinese culture and sociological literature for Australian culture
Jaggi and Low (2000)	Canada (40) France (64) Germany (52) Japan (96) UK (83) USA (274)	Statistical analysis	Financial disclosures	Uncertainty avoidance Individualism Power distance Masculinity
Chui et al. (2002)	22 countries	Statistical analysis	Capital structure	Schwartz (1994) cultural vales of conservatism, intellectual and affective autonomy, hierarchy, mastery, egalitarian commitment and harmony
Hope (2003)	39 countries	Statistical analysis	Financial disclosures	Uncertainty avoidance Individualism Power distance Masculinity Schwartz (1994) cultural vales of conservatism, intellectual and affective autonomy, hierarchy, mastery, egalitarian commitment and harmony
Doupnik and Richer (2004)	USA (143) Germany (88 in German language and 49 in English)	Survey questionnaire	In-context verbal probability expressions	Uncertainty avoidance Individualism Masculinity Long-term orientation
Panel B: Ethics judgements				
Karnes et al. (1990)	US (24) Taiwan (33) Professional accountants	Survey questionnaire	Risks and benefits to commit Unethical business practice	Individualism
Cohen et al. (1995)	US (62) Japan (38) Latin America (38) Auditors	Survey questionnaire	• Ethical perceptions • Likelihood that they and their colleagues would perform the action	Description of five dimensions but these are not invoked in theory development

Table 1B. (continued).

Study	Country (Sample Size) (Subjects)	Method	Dependent Variables	Cultural Dimensions
Schultz et al. (1993)	France (44) Norway (41) US (60) Professional and Managerial staff	Survey questionnaire	• Likelihood of reporting questionable acts • Responsibility to report • Seriousness of the issue • Personal cost to report	Power distance Uncertainty avoidance
Panel C: Organisational Culture in Accounting Firms				
Soeters and Schreuder (1988)	Netherlands 3 local firms (523) 3 international (116) Professional accountants	Hofstede's (1980) instrument	Nil. Cultural scores computed	Uncertainty avoidance Masculinity
Pratt et al. (1993)	British in UK firms (23) British in US firms (139) Americans in US firms (66) Aust. in Aust. firms (27) Aust. in US firms (59) Americans in US firms (189)	Hofstede's (1980) instrument	Nil. Cultural scores computed	Power distance Individualism

Table 2. Summary of Findings.

Dependent Variables	A priori Directional Hypothesis(es)	Support for Influence of Culture	Mixed or Equivocal Results	No Support for Influence of Culture
• 12 job-related outcomes (egs. responsibility, security, advancement) • Performance measured by supervisory ratings and salary levels • Personal evaluation of performance	No	Ferris et al. (1980)		
• Importance of job context factors (13 items) • Importance of job content factors (13 items) • Professional commitment (15 items)	Yes		Americ et al. (1983)	
Hofstede's (1980) instrument	No	Soeters and Schreuder (1988)		
Risks and benefits to commit unethical business practice	Yes	Karnes et al. (1990)		
Ethical perceptions	No		Welton and Davis (1990)	
Going concern, entity, stable monetary unit, periodicity, cost principle, relevance principle,	No	Belkaoui and Picur (1991)		

Table 2. (continued).

Dependent Variables	A priori Directional Hypothesis(es)	Support for Influence of Culture	Mixed or Equivocal Results	No Support for Influence of Culture
matching, objectivity, consistency, full disclosure, materiality, conservatism				
Perceptions of external auditor's independence	No	Agacer and Doupnik (1991)		
Provision of management advisory services	No	Lyons and Tong (1992)		
• Nature of accounting standard • Provision of management consulting services • Competition • Audit firm size	Yes but not cultural			Lindsay (1992)
Perceptions of external auditors' independence	No			Patel (1992)
Classification of extraordinary items	No	Bagranoff et al. (1994)		
Perception of 'subject to' audit qualification	Yes	Gul and Tsui (1993)		
Hofstede's (1980) instrument	Yes		Pratt et al. (1993)	
• Likelihood of reporting questionable acts • Responsibility to report • Seriousness of the issue	Yes	Schultz et al. (1993)		

Table 2. (continued).

Dependent Variables	A priori Directional Hypothesis(es)	Support for Influence of Culture	Mixed or Equivocal Results	No Support for Influence of Culture
• Personal cost to report				
• Ethical perceptions	No	Cohen et al. (1995)		
• Likelihood that they and their colleagues would perform the action				
• Audit perspective	Yes	Salter and Niswander (1995)		
• Professional self-regulation				
• Professionalism				
• Inter-company consistency				
• Conservatism				
• Optimism				
• Broad index of disclosure				
• Index of disclosure				
Consolidation disclosure index	Yes	Eddie (1996)		
Perceptions of external auditors' independence	Yes	Patel et al. (1996)		
• Inherent risk assessments	Yes		Yamamura et al. (1996)	
• Number of audit procedures selected				
• Voluntary revelation of private information	Yes	Kachelemeier and Shehata (1997)		
• Voluntary cooperation				

Table 2. (continued).

Dependent Variables	A priori Directional Hypothesis(es)	Support for Influence of Culture	Mixed or Equivocal Results	No Support for Influence of Culture
• Demand for auditing				
Frequency of use of group decision support software	Yes	Johns et al. (1999)		
judgements related to auditor–client conflict resolution	Yes	Patel et al. (1999)		
judgements related to aggressive financial reporting practices	Yes	Cable and Patel (2000)		
Financial disclosures	Yes		Jaggi and Low (2000) for code law countries	Jaggi and Low (2000) for common law countries
Capital structure	Yes	Chui et al. (2002)		
Financial disclosures	Yes	Hope (2003)		
judgements related to in-context verbal probability expressions	Yes	Doupnik and Richer (2004)		

CHAPTER 3
THEORY DEVELOPMENT AND HYPOTHESES FORMULATION

As shown in Chapter 2, most cross-cultural studies in accounting have relied extensively on the five-dimensional model of culture, identified by Hofstede (1980) and Hofstede and Bond (1988), to examine various accounting issues such as management control systems design, ethical judgements, standard setting practices and organisational culture in accounting firms. While these studies demonstrated the importance of culture, their insights may be limited because most of the studies neglected findings from other disciplines, such as the sociological, psychological and historical literatures, specifically that the form and nature of cultural dimensions may be different among various nations. As a result, most cross-cultural studies in accounting provide only a limited insight into the depth, richness and complexity of cultural differences, and have tended to invoke Hofstede's aggregated dimensions, and ignored important core differences and nuances in culture and tended to draw inappropriate and simplistic conclusions.

While it is useful to classify culture into distinct dimensions, a more holistic approach is needed for this study to provide an insight into the specific nature of the cultural dimensions applicable to Indians, Chinese Malaysians and Australians. One of the objectives of this chapter is, therefore, to supplement the five-dimensional model of culture in each of the three countries by incorporating relevant evidence from other disciplines such as that contributed by the sociological, psychological and historical literatures. This evidence, as well as the five-dimensional model is drawn on in developing the theory and formulating the hypotheses for testing.

The chapter proceeds as follows. The first section provides reasons for selecting the cultural dimensions of Power Distance, Individualism and Long-term Orientation, and for the exclusion of Uncertainty Avoidance and Masculinity dimensions in the theory development and hypotheses formulation. This section also discusses the location of Australia, India and Malaysia on each of Hofstede's cultural dimensions of Power Distance, Individualism and

Long-term Orientation, and classifies Indians and Chinese Malaysians in one cluster (comprising large Power Distance, low Individualism and Long-term Orientation) and Australians in another cluster (comprising small Power Distance, high Individualism and Short-term Orientation). This section then goes on to summarise important features of cultural differences between the two clusters based largely on Hofstede's cultural dimensions.

The second section provides insight into the specific nature of cultural dimensions that are applicable to Chinese Malaysians and Indians by drawing on the relevant features of Confucianism and Hinduism respectively. Additionally, relevant historical and sociological literatures are summarised to provide insight into those aspects of Australian culture that are particularly applicable to the issues examined in this study. The third section draws out various relevant features of cultural differences between Indians and Chinese Malaysians in one cluster and Australians in another cluster, to formulate hypotheses on auditor–client conflict resolution, and whistle-blowing as an internal control mechanism.

SELECTION OF RELEVANT HOFSTEDE'S CULTURAL DIMENSIONS

The following four reasons justify the inclusion of the cultural dimensions of Power Distance, Individualism and Long-term Orientation, and the exclusion of Uncertainty Avoidance and Masculinity in the theory development and hypotheses formulation.

First, the dimensions of Uncertainty Avoidance and Masculinity were excluded based on the results of the studies of the The Chinese Culture Connection (1987) and of Smith et al. (1996). The purpose of The Chinese Culture Connection (1987) study was to compare cultural dimensions by designing an Eastern questionnaire based on Chinese traditions and correlating results from its use with those derived from the use of Western questionnaires. Overlapping cultural dimensions would show that the dimensions were applicable to both the Chinese and Western cultural perspectives. The results of The Chinese Culture Connection (1987) provided evidence that Uncertainty Avoidance is not a meaningful cultural dimension for East–West comparisons because the study failed to find a cultural dimension that was related to Uncertainty Avoidance (Hofstede & Bond, 1988). Uncertainty Avoidance is associated with the "search for Truth" and "the Chinese do not believe this to be an essential issue" (Hofstede & Bond, 1988, p. 16). In the East (represented by Confucianism, Buddhism and Hinduism), the focus is not on the search for, or attainment of a, "single and absolute truth"; rather the assumption that a person can "possess an objective truth is absent" (Hofstede, 1994b, p. 8). In contrast, an essential element of Western thinking (represented by Judeo-Christian tradition) is the search for an objective truth (Hofstede, 1994b, p. 8).[1]

Turning to Smith et al. (1996), this study surveyed 8,841 managers and other organisational employees from 43 countries with the objective of establishing interrelationships among the cultural dimensions found in Hofstede (1980); The Chinese Culture Connection (1987) and Schwartz (1990, 1994). Smith et al. (1996) found substantial evidence of replicability of the results of previous studies with respect to providing support for the existence of the cultural dimensions of Individualism, Power Distance and Long-term Orientation. However, the study did not find evidence of the cultural dimensions of Uncertainty Avoidance or Masculinity.

Second, and adding to the support found by Smith et al. (1996) for the general existence and relevance of the dimensions of Power Distance, Individualism and Long-term Orientation, is the specific support provided for these dimensions in Cohen et al.'s (1996b) study examining cross-cultural ethical differences. In this study, 11 academic experts in cross-cultural research in accounting and business disciplines were asked to identify the usefulness of Hofstede's five dimensions of culture to predict cross-cultural differences in ethical sensitivity. The study demonstrated that Power Distance, Individualism and Long-term Orientation were consistently related to ethical judgements in a series of eight accounting-related ethical scenarios (Cohen et al., 1996b).

Finally, further evidence for the inclusion of the cultural dimensions of Power Distance, Individualism and Long-term Orientation, and the exclusion of Uncertainty Avoidance and Masculinity dimensions in the theory development and hypotheses formulation in this study is obtained from an analysis of the cultural indices reported by Hofstede (1980).

Hofstede (1980) provides the indices and ranking of 50 countries on each of the four dimensions of Individualism, Power Distance, Uncertainty Avoidance and Masculinity. The Uncertainty Avoidance indices reported by Hofstede (1980) were (on a range from 6 to 112 representing low to high): Malaysia 36, rank 8; India 40, rank 9 and Australia 51, rank 17. The Masculinity/Femininity indices were (on a range from 5 to 95 representing Femininity to Masculinity): Malaysia 50, rank 26–27; India 56, rank 30–31 and Australia 61, rank 35. Consequently, the fact that these nations do not differ substantially on the Uncertainty Avoidance and Masculinity dimensions means that these dimensions are unlikely to be implicated in the cross-cultural comparisons in this study.

By contrast, the location of Australia, India and Malaysia on Hofstede's Cultural Dimensions of Individualism, Power Distance and Long-term

Orientation provides additional support for the inclusion of these dimensions in the theory development and hypotheses formulation. The Individualism indices reported by Hofstede (1980) were (on a range from 3 to 91, from low to high): Malaysia 26, rank 17; India 43, rank 30 and Australia 90, rank 49. Of the 50 countries examined by Hofstede (1980), Australia is second only to the USA on Individualism, while Malaysia and India are ranked lower on Individualism with their rankings of 17 and 30 respectively. The Power Distance indices reported by Hofstede (1980) were (on a range from 11 to 104, from low to high): Australia 36, rank 13; India 77, rank 42; and Malaysia 104, rank 50. Malaysia was therefore, the largest Power Distance nation, both overall and among the three countries selected in this study, followed by India with a rank of 42. Australia, with a rank of 13, was classified as a small Power Distance nation. Australia, India and Malaysia were in two distinct clusters on the cultural dimensions of Individualism and Power Distance, with Australia high in Individualism and small on Power Distance, and Malaysia and India low in Individualism and large on Power Distance.

In terms of Long-term Orientation, India, with an index value of 61 (as scored by Hofstede (1994b, p. 166)), was classified as a Long-term Orientation nation, and Australia, with a score of 31 was classified as a Short-term Orientation nation.

A score for Malaysia is not available for Long-term Orientation. However, the clustering of the other four cultural dimensions shows Malaysia clustering fairly closely with other Chinese dominant societies such as Hong Kong and Singapore.[2] It is therefore likely that Malaysia could be classified as a Long-term Orientation nation (this classification will also be tested in the empirics of this study in Chapter 5). In addition, later in the chapter, Confucianism is invoked to provide further support for arguing that Chinese Malaysians have a Long-term Orientation.

The cultural dimensions of Individualism, Power Distance and Long-term Orientation and their comparative measures and assessments across the three nations are summarised in Table 3.1.

Interpreting Hofstede's cultural indices for India and Australia is not likely to be a problem because the ethnic groups in these countries are not as diverse as that of Malaysia. Hindu Indians comprise approximately 81% of India's total population and Europeans (Caucasians) comprise about 92% of Australia's population (http://www.cia.gov/cia/publications/factbook/geos/as.html#People). Consequently, it is likely that Hofstede's (1980) subjects in India and Australia were largely drawn from the dominant ethnic groups in each nation. However, interpreting Hofstede's cultural indices for Malaysia may be problematic, because Malaysia is a multi-ethnic country

Table 3.1. Summary of Relevant Cultural Indices.

	Individualism	Power Distance	Long-Term Orientation
Australia	90 (High)	36 (Small)	31 (Short)
India	43 (Low)	77 (Large)	61 (long)
Malaysia	26 (Low)	104 (Large)	Not available (but imputed as long)

Source: Hofstede (1980) and Hofstede and Bond (1988).

where Malays, Chinese and Indians respectively comprise 51%, 24% and 7% of the total population (http://www.cia.gov/cia/publications/factbook/geos/my.html#People). However, during the period that data were collected in Malaysia, it is likely that most of Hofstede's subjects were Chinese Malaysians, given that the data were collected from a private sector business organisation. (Recall that Hofstede's data were collected through a survey of employees in national subsidiaries of IBM.) Even today Chinese Malaysians comprise the majority of the professional staff in the private sector. Furthermore, earlier it was stated that the clusterings of the cultural dimensions of Power Distance, Individualism, Uncertainty Avoidance and Masculinity show Malaysia clustering fairly closely with other Chinese dominant societies such as Singapore and Hong Kong. Consequently, it is likely that Hofstede's (1980) cultural scores relate to Chinese Malaysians. Importantly, this study measures cultural scores of Australians, Indians and Chinese Malaysians using data from a sample of senior professional accountants. Recall that only 3 of the 18 studies in Table 1B in Chapter 2 computed the cultural scores. It was suggested that studies relying on Hofstede's cultural dimension(s) need to measure those dimensions to confirm whether the scores are still applicable to their specific samples in the period of study.

Although it was noted earlier that The Chinese Culture Connection (1987) differed from Hofstede's (1980) original findings in that it did not find evidence of the Uncertainty Avoidance dimension, and found, instead, the Long-term Orientation dimension, there was a strong commonality between the two studies with respect to the other dimensions of Individualism, Power Distance and Masculinity. This commonality, together with the replication support provided by Smith et al. (1996) for Individualism, Power Distance and Long-term Orientation (also noted previously), indicates a substantial robustness to these dimensions, particularly given that the studies used different questionnaires, on different population samples, and at different points in time.

These commonalities provide one basis for the use of these three dimensions in the theory development and hypotheses formulation in this study.

However, the critical reason for the choice of these dimensions is their theoretical relevance to the issues in the study, and the theoretical irrelevance of Uncertainty Avoidance and Masculinity. The irrelevance of these latter dimensions was noted earlier in this section. Inclusion and exclusion of the dimensions on the grounds of their theoretical relevance and irrelevance is important in overcoming the limitations of the "pick and choose" approach to the selection of relevant cultural dimensions which has characterised many prior studies. For example, as noted in the last chapter, studies by Karnes et al. (1989), Gul and Tsui (1993), Patel et al. (1996), Patel and Psaros (2000), Kachelemeier and Shehata (1997) and Johns et al. (1999) relied only on one dimension, and Schultz et al. (1993) and Yamamura et al. (1996) on two dimensions in their hypotheses formulation. Similarly Jaggi and Low (2000) and Doupnik and Richer (2004) used four of the five cultural dimensions. This "pick and choose" approach to selection of relevant cultural dimensions may limit our understanding of the influence of culture on accounting.

Based on the above discussion, this study broadly classifies Australians on the one hand, and Indians and Chinese Malaysians on the other, into two cultural clusters. The first cluster comprising cultures such as Australian is classified as small Power Distance, high Individualism and Short-term Orientation, and the second comprising cultures such as Indian and Chinese Malaysian is classified as large Power Distance, low Individualism and Long-term Orientation.

The next section summarises important features of Hofstede's (1980) and Hofstede and Bond's (1988) cultural differences that are relevant in examining comparative differences in judgements among professional accountants in the two clusters.

RELEVANT FEATURES OF HOFSTEDE'S CULTURAL DIMENSIONS DIFFERENTIATING CHINESE MALAYSIAN/INDIAN AND AUSTRALIAN CULTURES

Drawing on Hofstede (1980, p. 235), the connotations of low Individualism among Chinese Malaysians and Indians would suggest that they are more likely to show, "Emotional dependence of individuals on organisations and institutions; greater emphasis on belonging to organisations and social importance of organisational membership; private life invaded by organisations and clans to which one belongs; opinions that are predetermined; expertise, order, duty, security are provided by organisation or clan; belief in in-group decisions; and value standards that differ for in-groups and out-groups". In contrast, more highly individualistic Australians are likely to be motivated by their own preferences, needs and rights, giving priority to personal rather than to group goals (Triandis, 1995). In addition, Australians are more likely to show "emotional independence of individuals from organisations or institutions; greater emphasis on individual initiative and achievement; greater value for autonomy, variety, and pleasure" (Hofstede, 1980, p. 235). Since individual decisions are valued in high individualistic societies, there is a belief that, "value standards should apply to all irrespective of their position or wealth" (Hofstede, 1980, p. 235).

The connotations of large Power Distance among Chinese Malaysians and Indians suggest that organisational members are more likely to see "power as a basic fact of society which antedates good or evil and its legitimacy is irrelevant" (Hofstede, 1980, p. 119). Moreover, "power-holders are entitled to special privileges and the stress is on coercive and referent power; other people are a potential threat to one's power and rarely can be trusted" (Hofstede, 1980, p. 119). Therefore, in large Power Distance societies, "might prevails over right; whoever holds the power is right and good" (Hofstede, 1994b, p. 43). Leaders are also more likely to make decisions autocratically and paternalistically, and subordinates generally show preference for this type of managerial decision-making style. Subordinates are further expected to be told what to do and not to question authority figures. As a result, employees are generally fearful of authority figures and not likely to disagree with them (Hofstede, 1980, p. 119). This is particularly applicable to Chinese- and Indian-based organisations with their emphasis on higher degrees of authoritarianism and rigid hierarchies (Bond, 1991; Sinha & Sinha, 1990).

In contrast, in Australia which is a small Power Distance society, "the use of power should be legitimate and is subject to judgement between good and evil; all should have equal rights; powerful people are expected to look less powerful than they are; stress is on reward, legitimate and expert power; and people at various levels feel less threatened and more prepared to trust people" (Hofstede, 1980, p. 122).

Leaders are generally expected to make decisions after consulting affected parties, and subordinates are more likely to show preference for managers' decision-making style centred on a consultative and give-and-take approach. Consequently, employees are generally not afraid of disagreeing with their superiors, and authority figures are expected to show greater consideration (Hofstede, 1980).[3]

Social stability of large Power Distance and low Individualism nations is based on "unequal" relationships between people (Bond & Hwang, 1986). Mutual and complementary obligations are the key features in which a junior partner owes the senior respect and obedience; the senior owes the junior partner protection and consideration (Hofstede & Bond, 1988). In an organisational context, harmonious and stable hierarchy and complementarity of roles are essential features of low Individualism and large Power Distance nations (Hofstede, 1994b). Consequently, actions of superiors and the powerful are not questioned by subordinates. In the sections that follow, it will be shown that, in respect of Chinese Malaysians and Indians, concern for acceptance of hierarchy and harmony is linked to aspects of Confucian and Hindu values that emphasise commitment and loyalty to one's superiors and organisation.

Long-term Oriented cultures such as Indian and Chinese tend to place greater emphasis on "virtue than on truth" (Lu, 1983, p. 66). For example, "the Chinese Value Survey demonstrated the strategic advantage of cultures that can practise virtue without a concern for truth" (Hofstede, 1994b, p. 172). Consequently, the Long-term Oriented cultures are more likely to apply ethical values which are based more on "practical non-religious systems" (Hofstede, 1994ba, p. 172). Eastern philosophies in countries such as India and China are less concerned with "the truth" and more with "practical" ethics (Zimmerman & Unnithan, 1975, p. 42). In contrast, in Western religions such as Christianity and Judaism, "ethical rules tend to be derived from religion: virtue from truth" (Hofstede, 1994b, p. 172). Individual ethical reasoning is therefore an important feature of cultures derived from Christianity and Judaism.

While it is useful for comparative purposes to classify Australia, India and Malaysia into two cultural clusters based on the cultural dimensions identified by Hofstede (1980) and Hofstede and Bond (1988), a richer and a more holistic approach is needed to provide an insight into the specific nature of the cultural dimensions in each of the three nations. To provide this richer insight, discussion of relevant literatures, which complement Hofstede's five-dimensional model as they apply to Chinese Malaysians, Indians and Australians respectively, follows. Only those cultural characteristics that are relevant in examining differences in judgements among professional accountants from the three nations are discussed.

RELEVANT ASPECTS OF CHINESE MALAYSIAN CULTURE

Malaysia is a multi-ethnic country where Malays and Chinese play dominant roles in politics and business respectively. The political structure in Malaysia is based on demarking constituencies based on ethnicity (Hu, 1993).[4] As a result, to win votes during elections, candidates exploit racial issues and sensitivities, causing polarisation in the process Federal Territory MCA Liaison Committee, 1982; The Economist, 25 August 2005).

Today, as on many occasions in the past, the Chinese community remain concerned about their future in the country, "They ask if they will continue to have a rightful place in Malaysia. Will their children be able to share the same opportunities as other children? Will they and their children be able to live with dignity and self-respect in the future?" (Federal Territory MCA Liaison Committee, 1982, p. vii).[5]

Of the three major ethnic groups, Chinese Malaysians are economically the most successful. This success has created ethnic divisions and a long tradition of anti-Chinese legal discrimination.[6] The Chinese Malaysians see themselves as a besieged minority, surviving by their wits, and especially by their hard work (Strauch, 1981; Redding & Wong, 1986; http://www.jihadwatch.org/dhimmiwatch/archives/000821.php).

Greater insight into the specific nature of cultural values among the Chinese Malaysians is gained by examining relevant aspects of Confucianism. Confucianism is important and relevant in understanding the Chinese culture, including the overseas Chinese in countries such as Singapore, Malaysia, Taiwan and Hong Kong (Kao, 1993; Bond, 1991; Lu, 1983; Kahn, 1979; Zimmerman & Unnithan, 1975; Lang, 1968). For example, Kahn (1979) proposed the post-Confucian hypothesis which postulated that the sources of economic growth of overseas Chinese rested on the notion of a common cultural heritage of Confucianism (also see Redding & Wong, 1986). Furthermore, Confucianism's importance is reflected in the incorporation of its philosophy into the curricula for secondary students in Singapore (Lu, 1983). Confucian philosophy is also part of the curricula in schools in Malaysia organised by the Chinese community (Hong, 1982; Hu, 1993). The shared Confucian tradition among the overseas Chinese, operating in a "network of family and clan", has been referred to as the "Chinese Commonwealth" (Kao, 1993, p. 24) and the "overseas Chinese global tribe" (Chang, 1995, p. 967). As a result, irrespective of the countries to which Chinese people have migrated, Confucian values persist in the character of Chinese civilisation (Brindley, 1989, 1990; Kao, 1993).

Confucian philosophy derives from the teachings of Chung-ni-K'ung (551–479 BC) (known in the West as Confucius), a Chinese politician, philosopher and a social reformer. The teachings of Confucius permeated the philosophical literature of the Chinese empire, its fiction and poetry as well as the laws of the successive imperial dynasties (Lang, 1968; Bond & Hwang, 1986). Confucian teachings occupy the centre stage in almost all approaches to Chinese social behaviour (Bond & Hwang, 1986).[7] Confucianism has some religious features in its teaching, but in essence, it is not a religion but a system of political and ethical philosophy.

Confucius' fundamental concern was to create an orderly society to replace the feudal chaos of the China of his time (Bond & Hwang, 1986). The new Chinese state was to be ruled by what he called "chun-tze" (the perfect gentleman). A perfect gentleman is "distinguished by love of humanity and piety towards his parents and superiors; he meticulously observes the prescribed rites" (Lang, 1968, p. 9). One of the most important aspects of Confucianism in creating "chun-tze" was teaching people complete subordination by expressing "love and piety towards superiors, as well as observance of rites and rules of propriety" (Lang, 1968, p. 9). Complete subordination was expected not only from public officials but from common people as well.

Confucius' emphasis on complete subordination may explain Hofstede's (1980) classification of large Power Distance in Chinese societies. The fundamental Confucian assumption is that man exists in relationship to others (Bond & Hwang, 1986). Confucius' teachings focus on people accepting a hierarchical order in which everybody has a rightful place that needs no further justification. For example, Confucius advocated "let the ruler be a ruler, the minister be a minister, the father be a father, and the son be a son" (Confucian Analects in Lu, 1983, p. 101). Consequently, "the ruler would be pleased with the social and political stability that might result from such an order" (Confucian Analects in Lu, 1983, p. 101). Familial, social and political stability remained the ultimate aim of Confucianism (Lu, 1983; King & Bond, 1985; Liu, 1986).

It is therefore not surprising that Confucius' philosophy has been criticised for merely serving the interests of the ruling class (the powerful and influential people), and not the interests of the ordinary people (Feng You-lan, in Lu, 1983, p. 115). Such famous Confucian literature as the "Four Books" and the "Five Classics", which emphasised complete subordination to superiors, were studied diligently in the past by the prospective Confucian power elite for the purpose of passing the civil service examination (Lu, 1983). Furthermore, it has been argued that Confucius was placed on "a pedestal for worship by the powerful and influential" (Lu, 1983, p. 109).[8]

Confucius and his disciples extended and intensified the rules governing domination and subordination by regulating the organisation of the family (Lang, 1968, p. 10).[9] A Confucian model of an authoritarian family was constructed by prescribing strict rules and rites that should govern the patriarchal and patrilineal Chinese society. A typical Chinese family is generally a tightly knit social unit in which individuals could expect their relatives, clan, or other family members to look after them in exchange for unquestioning loyalty. Authority ranking among family members provides some insight into the concept of Power Distance among Chinese families. For example, in the traditional Chinese family, the grandfather eats first, selecting the pieces he likes best, then the oldest son, then other sons eat according to age. After the sons have made their choices, the oldest female can choose, followed by the other females in descending order of age (Triandis, 1995).

Further insight into the causes of large Power Distance and low Individualism in Chinese societies can be traced to the importance placed on "filial piety". Filial piety requires "subordination of personal desires to a hierarchy of deference that reaches up to the father, back to the ancestors, and up to heaven" (Cornberg, 1994, p. 138). Bond and Hwang (1986, p. 228) noted that an emphasis on filial piety leads inevitably to a culture of large Power Distance, and dependency orientation. Filial piety is "the root of all virtues" (Wu, 1927, p. 316), and is the essence of the concept of "ren".[10] Confucius extended the virtue of filial piety to rules governing domination and subordination by insisting that, "Few of those who are filial sons and respectful brothers will show disrespect to superiors, and there has never been a man who is not disrespectful to superiors and yet creates disorder" (Lu, 1983, p. 6).

To a Confucian, the family unit is important because it is the training ground for morality, and filial piety is important because it is the "root of morality" (Lu, 1983, p. 92). In fact, Confucius believed that the primary moral duty of filial piety must be upheld even at the expense of other secondary moral obligations such as social justice (Chan, 1963). As a result, the decision about what is ethical or unethical is not an individual choice but is contextual, depending on the status and relationships among the people involved. For example, the peculiarity of Confucian filial piety can be illustrated by the following story in the Confucian Analects:

> One feudal prince proudly told Confucius, "In my country there is an upright man. When his father stole a sheep, he bore witness against him." Confucius said: "The upright men in my community are different from this. The father conceals the misconduct of the son and the son the misconduct of the father. Uprightness is to be found in this" (Lu, 1983, p. 66).

Confucius demanded unreserved obedience and devotion of the son to his father, of the younger to the elder, and of the subject to the ruler. Of the five cardinal human relationships (wu lun) mentioned by Confucius, three are family relationships (father–son, husband–wife, elder brother–younger brother). Family relationships are followed by friendship, which forms the transition from family life to public life. However, the most important "wu lun" is that of "prince and minister (subject), which crowns the successful work of the family and insures peace in the state" (Lang, 1968, p. 10).

The avoidance of conflict and maintenance of equilibrium are the cardinal virtues in the Chinese culture (Cheung et al., 1996). Harmony could only be realised if each member of the society was conscientious in following the requirements of his or her role (Bond & Hwang, 1986, p. 215). That is, harmony and equilibrium are maintained when, " ...a centripetal family gathers in its forces by demanding the primary loyalty of its members and mobilizing their labor power, political, and psychological allegiances on behalf of kinsmen" (Salaff, 1981, p. 8, in Redding & Wong, 1986, p. 284).

Confucius stressed his adherence to tradition and taught his followers to consider traditionalism as fundamental in their thinking. Despite the stress on tradition, Confucian doctrine and practice were characterised by realism and flexibility. In everyday life this doctrine manifested itself in a tendency to do things in a "more or less" (ch'a-pu-to) way and to solve every conflict by compromise (Lang, 1968, p. 11). Flexibility in making judgements is "the heart of the art of moral experience of the Chinese" (Cornberg, 1994, p. 147). Consequently, flexibility and adaptability, not consistency, becomes a focal issue in considering Chinese character (Bond & Hwang, 1986, p. 216). It has also been argued that flexibility and compromise are the major source of the strength of Confucianism that has allowed the doctrine to survive for over two thousand years in China, and in the various nations where the Chinese have migrated (Lang, 1968; Chang, 1992).[11] It is posited in this study that the concept of "ch'a-pu-to" and the importance placed on flexibility and adaptability in Chinese cultures is likely to lead to an emphasis on *context* rather than *content* in judgements regarding what is ethical or unethical.

THE CONCEPT OF FACE

Most of the features of Confucianism, discussed earlier, stress the importance of familial and social harmony. One of the important behaviour modification techniques used in maintaining societal harmony is the Chinese concept of "face or to save face" (Hu, 1944).[12,13] The concept of "face" provides additional insight into the large Power Distance and low Individualism of Chinese societies.

The concept of "face" has two aspects. The first is "mien-tzu", which stands for a reputation achieved in life through success and ostentation. For this kind of recognition, one's ego is dependent at all times on one's external environment (Hu, 1944, p. 45). The second is the concept of "lien". "Lien" is the respect of a group for, "A man with a good moral reputation: the man who will fulfil his obligations regardless of hardships involved, who under all circumstances shows himself a decent human being. It represents the confidence of society in the integrity of ego's moral character (moral character does not refer to character structure, but to the opinion that society forms of ego), the loss of which makes it impossible for him to function properly within the community" (Hu, 1944, p. 45).[14]

Both the concepts of "mien-tzu" and "lien" rely on the forces of social sanctions for enforcing moral standards. A violation of "mien-tzu" or "lien" is described by the words "tau-lien" (to lose lien). "Tau-lien" is a condemnation by the society for immoral or socially disagreeable behaviour. It is a serious infraction of the moral code of society, which, once brought to the notice of the public, is a blemish on the character of the individual and his or her family, and excites a great deal of comment" (Hu, 1944, p. 46).

Hofstede's (1980) cultural dimension of Power Distance is implicated in the concept of "lien". For example, subordinates who have failed to carry out successfully the orders of their superiors feel that "they have no lien" (Hu, 1944, p. 54). Also, a higher social standing of a person is associated with maintaining greater dignity, and as a result, his or her "lien" is more vulnerable (Ho, 1976, p. 867).

The notion that in Chinese culture, "an amorphous society is constantly supervising the conduct of an individual's ego, relentlessly condemning every breach of morals and punishing with ridicule, has bred extreme sensitivity in some people" (Ho, 1976, p. 868). As a result, individuals learn from an early age that infringement of the social code will bring shame not only to the individual concerned, but also to the extended family, including those who educated and promoted the individual (Hu, 1944; Bond & Hwang, 1986). From an early age, children are admonished, "don't lose lien for us" (Hu, 1944, p. 46). This not only implants in the mind of the young person the concept of lien, but gives him or her the consciousness of the collective responsibility which the family bears in regard to his or her behaviour. An individual is taught that his or her character should befit the standing of the family (Hu, 1944; Redding & Wong, 1986).

The Western concept of an anomic individual is alien to the Chinese culture. "Man" in Chinese culture is seen "as a relational being, socially situated and defined within an interactive context" (Bond & Hwang, 1986, p. 215). Individual initiative and development are not considered important in Chinese societies. This is largely derived from the philosophy that human nature is originally evil. As the evil nature cannot be responsible for initiating moral standards, to cultivate moral values is a matter of imposing them upon humans from an external source (Xun Zi, in Lu, 1983, p. 16).

The concept of an individual possessing a unique "ego" is also absent among the Chinese.[15] The concept of "ego" in a Chinese society is a collective, which always belongs to a closely integrated group on which is reflected some of the individual's glory or shame.[16] The family, the wider community of friends, and superiors, all have an interest in an individual's advancement or setbacks (Bond & Hwang, 1986). Public disgrace or ridicule not only affect the individual concerned, but also the reputation of the extended family. As a result, a person does not simply "lose his own face" (Hu, 1944, p. 50), but also loses "lien" of the extended family. Since structural harmony within a group is emphasised, every person has to concern himself or herself with "right conduct in maintaining one's place in a hierarchical order" (Stover, 1974, p. 246).

The emphasis on societal sanctions in Chinese societies for enforcing moral standards has resulted in individual ethical judgements that are not internalised and unique to an individual, but are largely determined by the external environment and the context (Brindley, 1989). In such a context, multiple standards of morality operate and are seen as perfectly acceptable. In Confucian ethics, "there is no abstract standard by which to resolve the conflict of values" (Hsieh, 1967, p. 32 in Redding & Wong, 1986, p. 285). Thus the application of multiple standards in dealing with people is morally acceptable (Brindley, 1989).

In summary, the preoccupation with "cultural concern for harmony-within-hierarchy" can be used to explain Chinese social behaviour (Bond & Hwang, 1986, p. 213). The essential aspects of Confucianism in constructing Chinese cultural values are: an individual exists through, and is defined by his or her relationship to others; these relationships are structured hierarchically; and social harmony is ensured through each individual honouring the requirements in the role relationships. That is, Chinese cultural values lead to, "submission to social expectations, social conformity, worry about external opinions, and non-offensive strategy in an attempt to achieve one or more of the purposes of reward attainment, harmony maintenance, impression management, face protection, social acceptance, and avoidance of punishment, embarrassment, conflict, rejection, ridicule, and retaliation in a social situation" (Yang, 1981, p. 161).

RELEVANT ASPECTS OF INDIAN CULTURE

This section highlights the important aspects of Hinduism, which are essential in understanding Indian cultural values. Only those aspects of

Hinduism that provide a richer insight into the specific nature of Indian cultural values, and are of particular relevance to the issues selected for examination in the study, are examined.

India, the world's largest democracy with an estimated population of 1.08 billion in 2005 (http://washingtontimes.com/upi-breaking/20040818-105443-7992r.htm), was a British colony till independence in 1947. Hindus comprise about 80% of the total population. This land of tremendous contrasts is organised so that "every individual in India is always linked to the rest of the social body by a network of incredibly diversified ties, with the result that no one in this gigantic country....could ever be completely abandoned" (Lapierre, 1986, p. 56).

The teachings of Hinduism and Confucianism have a number of common features. Both have some religious features in their teachings, but in essence, neither are religions in terms of the Judaeo–Christian traditions (Lu, 1983; Bharati, 1985). Both are essentially systems of political and ethical philosophy the objectives of which are to create familial, social and political stability (Bharati, 1985; Brindley, 1989; Kangayappan, 1992; Kao, 1993). The cultural concern for "harmony-within-hierarchy" dominates both Hinduism and Confucianism, and provides insight into the specific nature of low Individualism and large Power Distance in Indian and Chinese cultures. Bond and Hwang (1986) provide details of the importance of "harmony-within-hierarchy" in Chinese culture, and Sinha and Sinha (1990) and Kangayappan (1992) provide insight into its importance in Indian culture.

Similar to Confucianism, Hinduism also regards filial piety as one of the most important virtues (Zimmerman & Unnithan, 1975). Aspects of filial piety discussed earlier in relation to Chinese culture are also important in maintaining familial and social harmony in India. Another cultural characteristic common to Chinese and Indian cultures is the concept of "face" in modifying behaviour (Kapadia, 1966). Both the concepts of filial piety and face may be of greater significance in India than in Chinese society, because, as will be shown in sections that follow, rigid "social stratification" is a tenet of Hinduism.[17]

It is largely the caste system of social stratification that has glued Indian society since the arrival of Aryans in the Indus valley around 1500 BC (Kangayappan, 1992).[18] The word "caste" is derived from the Portuguese, "casta", a word used by early Portuguese sailors to describe the social stratification in India (Sinha, 1995, p. 28). Caste is a form of closed social stratification in that it is determined by birth on grounds over which people have no control (Edgar, Earle, & Fopp, 1993). An examination of the caste system provides some insight into the cultural values of low Individualism and large Power Distance in India.

Hinduism has allowed the apartheid of the caste system to survive Muslim invasions, British colonialism and even 50 years of democracy. Ghurye (1969, p. 23) noted that, "On the whole, the British rulers of India, who professed to be the trustees of the welfare of the country, never seem to have given much thought to the problem of caste, in so far as it affected the nationhood of India". Hinduism's tenet that "a person is condemned to his[19] caste determines whether he becomes a doctor or a scavenger, whom he marries, which village well he drinks from, and his social standing in a complex, ordered hierarchy, all by his actions in a past life" (Ahmed, Ganguly, Belaur, & Bhagwan, 1997, p. 34).

The above reference to "past life" is the Hindu belief in reincarnation. Reincarnation is the belief that humans are born with a blueprint of character, mainly prepared by their actions in previous lives based on the law of "karma" (cause and effect): "Even as a person casts off worn-out clothes and puts on others that are new, so the embodied soul casts off worn-out bodies and enters into others that are new" (Nikhilananda, 1968, p. 62).

"Karma" in previous life determines in a hierarchical order whether one is born as a human (which is the result of satisfactory scores on one's karma), or as any other living organism (a result of unsatisfactory scores on one's karma) (Nikhilananda, 1968, pp. 47–68). Hofstede and Bond's (1988) cultural dimension of Long-term Orientation is implicated in the Hindu concept of reincarnation. The belief in reincarnation provides the ultimate Long-term Orientation among the Hindus (Bharati, 1985).

Bhagavad Gita, the holy Hindu scriptures, states that "Never must one give up the work for which one is born" (Bharati, 1985, p. 48).[20] Bhagavad Gita further states that "it is better to do one's own inborn work well than trying to do another one's (inborn) work" (Bharati, 1985, p. 48). Defenders of the caste system cite a verse from the Upanishads, Hinduism's ancient sacred texts, to justify the practice of the caste system, "Those whose conduct on earth has given pleasure can hope to enter a pleasant womb, that is, princely class. But those whose conduct on earth has been foul can expect to enter a foul and stinking womb, that is the womb of a bitch, or a pig, or an outcaste" (Ahmed et al., 1997, p. 47).[21]

A hymn from the sacred Hindu scriptures, "Rig Veda", describes how this human stratification came about: "a cosmic giant, Purusha, sacrificed parts of his body to create mankind. His mouth became the Brahman (the priests), his arms were made into the Warrior (Kshatriya), his thighs the People (Vaishiya) and from his feet the Servants (Shudra) were born" (Ahmed et al., 1997, p. 34). Through the centuries, these four main divisions (called varnas) were subdivided into more than 3,000 sub-castes, based on the purity of their profession. For example, "a goldsmith is higher up the ladder than a blacksmith, and a priestly Brahman, whose rituals bring him in touch with the gods, is highest of all. The untouchables, however, are off the ladder completely. By origin, many were India's dark-skinned first inhabitants, conquered by Aryans and assigned such awful tasks as burning bodies, skinning carcasses and removing 'night soil' – human excrement from latrines. For thousands of years, outcastes were burdened with these denigrating chores" (Ahmed et al., 1997, p. 34).

Even among the Dalits (the "untouchables"), strong caste rivalries exist. For example, one study discovered 900 Dalit "sub-castes" in the country (Ahmed et al., 1997, p. 37). Some Dalits have tried to escape caste fetters by converting from Hinduism to Christianity, Islam and Buddhism, which preach that all men are equal before God (Bharati, 1985, p. 204). However, evidence shows that the caste system has crept into other religions, so that a "Dalit convert is not treated as well as, say, a Brahman or a Kshatriya. Religious conversion is not an escape" (Ahmed et al., 1997, p. 38). Thus in India there is institutionalisation of inequality by canonical decree (http://www.dalits.org/default.htm).

The Hindu practice of the caste system with its emphasis on the concept of reincarnation provides a good example of a large Power Distance, low Individualism and Long-term Orientation society, from which there can be no escape. Religious and social duties are regarded in India as a "debt contracted through coming into existence in the community and remaining in it as a member" (Zimmer, 1951, p. 31). The debt is to be paid to the "gods who protect and favor us, the ancestors to whom we owe our existence, and our fellow creatures, with whom we share life's joys and sorrows. The virtuous fulfilment of one's life-role (dharma) is all important" (Zimmer, 1951, p. 31).

Social stratification along the lines defined by caste is also a strong feature of organisational behaviour in India (Phegade, 1997). For example, evidence shows that employees have used caste connections to pressurise personnel managers not to dismiss workers of their own caste, even in cases of serious misconduct (Sinha & Sinha, 1990; http://countrystudies.us/india/89.htm). Even large Indian multinationals, such as the Aditya Birla Group have tended to hire fellow members of their Marwari business sub-caste for key positions (Elliot, 1997, p. 48). The importance placed on caste has resulted in a "soft-work culture" where the professed goals and objectives of an organisation are compromised to accommodate social habits and values (Sinha & Sinha, 1990, p. 707). An Indian is generally not sensitive to the goals of work and productivity, but shows greater concern for "the unfolding of emotional affinity" (Sinha & Sinha, 1990, p. 707). Members of organisations in India enter them with a set of values stressing caste bonds, a sensitivity to interpersonal harmony, and a sense of social hierarchy. Hierarchy in social systems is a universal phenomenon, but the extent to which "Indians are disposed to structure all relationships hierarchically is phenomenal" (Sinha & Sinha, 1990, p. 707). Indian social systems are steeply hierarchical and Indians are highly status conscious (Dumont, 1970; Roland, 1984; Palkhivala, 1997; http://countrystudies.us/india/89.htm).

The traditional view of work in India is of a duty that should be performed either in the family or within the intra-caste framework. Indians prefer personalised relationships based on strict rules which govern superior and subordinate relationships (Trompenaars, 1993, p. 42). The pattern of superior and subordinate relationships dictated by the caste system has also affected power relations in Indian organisations (Selvadurai, 1997). Even large public companies in India are run "like personal fiefdoms".[22] Superiors expect loyalty, compliance, and total submission by the subordinates (Phegade, 1997). Employees feel easier when working in superior–subordinate roles, rather than with equals. Peer group relationships induce anxiety until the peers are "ranked on some real or imaginary dimension" (Sinha & Sinha, 1990, p. 709). Once a hierarchical structuring of relationships is established, "juniors yield to seniors on every conceivable on-the-job or off-the-job occasion" (Sinha & Sinha, 1990, p. 709).

Hindu scriptures provide further insight into superiors and subordinates relationships, "abandoning all commendable acts, seek shelter with me alone, I will liberate you from all sins; do not worry at all" (Bhagavad Gita, chapter 18, verse 66). Subordinates who yield to power are bestowed with all kinds of undue favours, while those who do not are distanced and discriminated. This reward/punishment behaviour modification technique has resulted in subordinates' unquestioning loyalty to superiors (Kangayappan, 1992). The relationship is characterised by "sneh" (affection) for the subordinate and "shradha" (deference) for the superior. Thus an Indian organisation consists of a network of "affection reciprocity" (Roland, 1984, p. 21), wherein the avoidance of conflict and maintenance of hierarchical equilibrium are the cardinal rules (Triandis, 1994, pp. 4–8). This has also been referred to as "cultural coexistence" (Schulberg, 1968, p. 17).

"Affection reciprocity" has been seen as partly responsible for the massive official corruption in India. For example, India is ranked 88th out of 158 countries listed in 2005 Corruption Perceptions Index (http://www.transparency.org/cpi/2005/cpi2005.sources.en.html). Venkataraman (2002, p. 1) concluded that, "The most disquieting aspect of the widespread corruption in India is the fact that it is not anymore confined to politicians or the government machinery alone. It is prevalent amongst almost every section of the society at every level". The relations built on power, the bestowal of favours, and punishment produce what Phegade (1997, p. 78) has described as an "unholy union of businessmen, bureaucracy and politicians (which) has prompted bribery, violations of rules, black-money and unfair practices".

The importance of "affection reciprocity" and "cultural coexistence" in India is also reflected in the Hindu concept of a "collective ego". The concept of a "collective ego" is different from the "empirical self" as conceived by the majority of Western thinkers (Shils, 1961, p. 119). For example, when asked to identify themselves, typical Hindus would give their names, the name of the village where they originally came from, and their caste. If they are a south Indian Brahman, they would introduce themselves with a Sanskrit formula, which translates: "Of the gotra (seer's lineage), of the Rigveda (or Samaveda, whichever Veda his family belongs to), born in the house of X (his remembered agnatic ancestor), grandson of so and so, son of so and so; I am Mr Srinvasa Iyer" (Bharati, 1985, p. 211). Unlike the Western notion of self, the "empirical ego comes last in this formula" (Bharati, 1985, p. 211). For the Hindu, self-representation is firstly a representation in social, then secondarily a representation in occupational terms. The reversal of the identification order between the West and India is important because it signifies a polarisation between the "fixed, immutable self of the westerner, and the mutable self of the Hindu" (Bharati, 1985, p. 212). Consequently, one's personal ego is not as important as maintenance of hierarchical order and harmonious interpersonal relationships in a relatively stable social order (Marriott, 1976; Sinha & Sinha, 1990).

The difference between the Hindu and Western concept of self provides an insight into how individuals in these societies are likely to differ in their judgements. Individuals, according to Western social and psychological theories, are seen as "separate, indivisible bounded units" (Marriott, 1976, p. 111). By contrast, anthropologists suggest that the Indian self is "not an individual, but a 'dividual' self" (Bharati, 1985, p. 196). That is, Indians assign different meaning to different layers of selfhood, "one's true, permanent self, is quite different from the self that he produced and proffered within society" (Bharati, 1985, p. 196). There are so many layers of self, that what appears to be contradictory to Western eyes is seen as acceptable to Hindus.[23] Consequently, among Indians there is no "cognitive dissonance" in judgements because if one has multiple views of self, different ones could be called on to self-justify multiple standards of morality (Triandis, 1994). Therefore, similar to the Chinese culture, multiple standards of morality operate and are seen as acceptable in India (Bredemeier, 1978; Triandis, 1994).

Bharati (1985, p. 210) provided an interesting example of "cognitive dissonance". She reported that "it used to rouse my ire when perfectly literate Hindus made statements like, 'I am a vegetarian and I am a meat-eater'". While the statement is a contradiction from a Western perspective, to an Indian, this statement means that as far as the relationships in the family and caste are concerned, the individual is a vegetarian. However, outside the prying eyes of the family and the caste, the individual would eat meat, as long as this was kept a secret from family and caste members. If this secret was revealed to caste members, the individual could be ostracised and this would affect the family's status in the society. It may even become difficult for parents to find suitable spouses for their children (this interpretation was provided to the author by an academic in Pune University, India). India is a "pragmatic culture that concentrates on what works" (Triandis, 1994, p. 191).

The concept of an individual seen as a separate person having the choice to decide what is ethical or unethical is generally absent among the Indians. An individual is part of a collective which decides the rules of acceptable behaviour (Triandis, 1994). People are more concerned about acting appropriately than about doing what they consider right or wrong (Trompenaars, 1993; Triandis, 1995). Therefore, judgements related to what is considered ethical or unethical are dependent on the people and the context concerned (Trompenaars, 1993). Issues related to family, friendship, caste reputation and preservation of harmony, are of greater importance than what is considered ethical or unethical (Trompenaars, 1993).[24] As a result, "contradictory actions do not pose a cognitive conflict in their simultaneous and/or collective occurrence" (Bharati, 1985).

The next section of the chapter describes relevant Australian cultural values with the objective of comparing Australian cultural values with those of Chinese Malaysian and Indian values.

RELEVANT ASPECTS OF AUSTRALIAN CULTURAL VALUES

In the earlier sections of the chapter, insight into Chinese Malaysian and Indian cultures was gained by examining respectively the major features of Confucianism and Hinduism. Unlike the Chinese Malaysian and Indian cultures, no single religion or philosophy can provide an adequate explanation of the specific nature of high Individualism, small Power Distance and Short-term Orientation in Australian culture. Traditionally, the predominant religion in Australia is Christianity (68% of the population [http://www.cia.gov/cia/publications/factbook/geos/as.html]). However, Christianity does not have as significant influence over everyday life in Australia as Confucianism and Hinduism in Chinese Malaysian and Indian cultures. In addition, unlike the literature on Chinese Malaysian and Indian cultural values where aspects of Confucianism and Hinduism respectively are extensively discussed, the literature on Australian cultural values does not discuss the influence of Christianity in much detail. Nonetheless, despite the relatively lesser importance of religion in influencing cultural values, some of the precepts of Christianity can be seen as supportive of, and consistent with, many of the Australian cultural values discussed in the section that follows. Therefore, the section that follows relies on historical and sociological literatures to provide insight into those aspects of Australian culture that are particularly relevant to the issues examined in the current study.

Australia's colonisation began in 1788 to take the overflow from Britain's cramped penitentiaries. Along with the convicts, Australia's earliest immigrants came mostly from Britain and Ireland. The earlier migrants to Australia have been described as "those fortunate members of the lower orders who had broken loose from British hierarchy and were exercising their own choices about their style of life" (Bolton, 1984, p. 176). For example, Bryce (1921, p. 181) noted that: "If any country and its government were selected as showing the course which a self-governing people pursues free from all external influences and little trammelled by intellectual influences descending from the past, Australia would be that country". Consequently, on a number of important issues, it was difficult for members of Britain's ruling class and intellectuals to accept the legitimacy of some of the choices made by the early Australians (Bolton, 1984).

Freedom from the then prevailing rigid class divisions in Britain, combined with the hostile features of the Australian landscape, provides an historical insight into the high Individualism that was cherished by the early settlers (Goodnow, Burns, & Russell, 1989).[25] Australia's massive and hostile landscape has historically encouraged belief in the value of "going it alone", reduced the possibility of developing social networks, and thereby weakened community controls on the way family life proceeded (Goodnow et al., 1989, p. 40). Self-reliance and high Individualism, both cognitively and physically, became an important survival tool (Borrie, 1989).

Historically, Australian society has shown the capacity to tolerate and absorb ethnic and cultural differences (Edgar et al., 1993). People of different backgrounds, cultures, education levels and values have come to Australia and survived together, with a low level of hostility and conflict. Despite examples of racial and ethnic prejudice and discrimination,[26]

Australia has not suffered the divisions of European nations,[27] or the strong religious differences that are common in some countries, such as India and Malaysia.

In per capita terms Australia, along with Israel, has maintained the highest migration rates of the developed countries (Withers, 1989, pp. 8–9). Since migrants tend to be more individualistic than those opting not to migrate, even the recent immigrants to Australia are expected to be more individualistic than their counterparts in their respective countries. In addition, each year 30% of the population change their residence and 20% change their city (Withers, 1989, p. 3). It is likely that greater population mobility in Australia is associated with high Individualism.

In 2005, the ethnic composition of Australia is estimated as follows: Caucasian 92%, Asian 7% and Aboriginal and others 1% (http://www.cia.gov/cia/publications/factbook/geos/as.html). While 68% of the Australian population profess to be Christians and 4% non-Christians, the remainder category (comprising "no religion" 15% and "not stated" 13% showed the most increase over the last 10 years. Unlike India and Malaysia, organised religion is not a major issue in Australian society. For example, it is estimated that only one in two Australians attend a religious service more than once a year (apart from weddings, funerals or baptisms). Australian society has been described as "secular, but tolerant" (Withers, 1989, p. 12). Individual rights and freedom are of greater importance than religious doctrines.

Unlike the importance of the extended families in Indian and Chinese cultures where several generations may live together under one roof, and children after marriage may bring their spouses to live with their parents, nuclear families where parents and children live together in one household, have been the historical pattern in Australia (Edgar et al., 1993). A number of historians have been impressed by the extent to which the lives of men and women in Australia are separated from one another, both in the workplace and within families (Goodnow et al., 1989). Explanations offered are generally in terms of the early disproportion in the number of men and women,[28] and the influence of the individualistic nature of the Irish heritage (Goodnow et al., 1989). However, family patterns in Australia are changing rapidly and there are claims that "if we continue to dismantle the family at accelerating pace since 1965, there will not be a single family left by the year 2008" (Goodnow et al., 1989, p. 27).[29] This trend towards higher Individualism in Australia is also reflected in statistics which showed that more than 10% of the adult population now live alone and almost a quarter of all households now consist of one person, and estimated that approximately

40% of marriages will end in divorce, and that 20% of women in Australia will remain childless throughout their lives.

These moves towards the exercise of greater individual choices and the breakdown in traditional nuclear families in Australia have resulted in greater isolation and alienation for individuals (Gunn, 1997). Loneliness, a product of excessive individualism,[30] is largely the result of the breakdown of the traditional nuclear family, and what has become to be known as the "loss of social capital – an undermining of the network, neighbourliness and co-operation that holds a community together" (Gunn, 1997). Loss of social capital may perhaps account for the fact that since 1997, 1 in 14 young Australians tried to commit suicide.

Indian and Chinese families tend to be patriarchical where greater social power is assigned to the male. In contrast, Australian families tend to be egalitarian, in which power is generally shared by both spouses (Edgar et al., 1993).[31] It has been argued that freedom and equality in all works of life are cherished to a greater degree in Australia than in almost any other country (Withers, 1989).

Two values that reflect Australian ideals are "equalitarianism" and "egalitarianism" (Waters, 1990, p. 24). These values are evident in areas of social policy such as multiculturalism and through norms such as the insistence on a "fair go", and through greeting statements such as "gidday mate" (Edgar et al., 1993, p. 254). The importance of *equalitarianism* and *egalitarianism* provides some insight into the nature of Power Distance in Australian society.[32] A discussion of issues that are relevant in understanding small Power Distance in Australia follows.

Australians have a tradition of taking great pride in their country's egalitarian values (Withers, 1989). Since folk stories of a culture often reveal the central preoccupation which informs social behaviour (Bond & Hwang, 1986), the following story is narrated because it touches a responsive chord in many Australians and provides some insight into the importance of egalitarian values in the country:

> Field Marshal Sir William Slim was well-liked as Australia's Governor-General (from 1953–1960). On one outback tour he drove into a small town, leapt in full uniform from his car, and strode up to a stockman: I'm Slim', said the Governor-General, thrusting his hand forward in greeting. The hand was amiably grasped, accompanied by the laconic query: 'G'day Slim. Slim who?' (Withers, 1989, p. 1).[33]

The importance of egalitarianism is also reflected in the Australian tradition of "cutting down its tall poppies" (Withers, 1989, p. 14).[34] Australian heroes are generally common men and women who display "individual achievement that can clearly be ascribed to those rare and admirable talents that owe little or nothing to family, fortune or friends, or to the fate of others" (Withers, 1989, p. 14). Furthermore, the widespread distribution of land and home ownership (Australia has one of the highest percentages of home ownership in the world), the early social experimentation that laid the foundations for the welfare state, and the extensive worker protection via arbitration, tariffs and unions, created a history that sees Australia as different from other countries in its commitment to egalitarianism. Prominent visitors to Australia have found that "in speech, dress and manner, Australians are not nearly as easily distinguishable from each other as in other countries" (Withers, 1989, p. 16). Unlike India, travellers to Australia today soon learn to sit in front of the taxi next to the driver.

Australia, like many other Western countries, is industrialised, capitalist, and dominated by economic factors consistent with industrialisation and capitalism. The pattern of development of the advanced Western industrial societies is based on high Individualism which allows people to develop their individual motivations, skills and competence in ways best suited to them (Edgar et al., 1993; Hofstede & Hofstede, 2005). A main purpose of socialisation in Western cultures, such as Australia, is the development of individual identity, the learning of individual cognitive skills and self-control, and the internalisation of moral standards (Edgar et al., 1993). In contrast, one of the major purposes of socialisation in Indian and Chinese cultures, discussed earlier in the chapter, is the maintenance of harmonious interpersonal relationships and acting in a manner appropriate to one's position in a hierarchical social order.

Compared to the Indian and Chinese cultures, Australians place greater importance on individualism and independence. This is reflected in the vocabularies of educational psychology and sociology that echo the needs of the individual: "developmental tasks, individual differences, self-actualisation,[35] the autonomous self, discovery learning, equal opportunity, free competition, reward for merit, skill learning, and taking responsibility for one's own learning" (Edgar et al., 1993). The ultimate objective in human development in Western nations is the development of a "competent self: a view of oneself as being effective, able to control one's own life and make one's own way in it, as opposed to feeling ineffectual, powerless, controlled by others and having to conform to rules one has no chance of changing" (Brewster-Smith, 1968, p. 161). That is, unlike the cultural features of Indians and Chinese Malaysians described earlier, the aim in Australian culture is to develop self-directed behaviour rather than to rely on external incentives such as familial harmony and social prestige. Meritocracy, which suggests that the individual and not the individual's family or background is in control of his or her destiny, forms the basis of Australian society (Edgar et al., 1993).

Earlier in the chapter it was suggested that another important feature of social reality in Chinese and Indian cultures in maintaining the social network is the concept of "face". The importance of "face" is the consequence of living in a society that is very concerned with relationships and social contexts. These values support interrelatedness through sensitivity to social contacts. The Australian mentality, deeply ingrained with the values of individualism, finds it difficult to understand the concept of "face". For "face" is not a purely individual concept. It does not make sense to speak of the 'face' of an individual as something cognitively lodged within the person. It is meaningful only when "face" is considered in relation to that of others in the social network (Ho, 1976).

Stover (1974) took the cocktail party as an example for illustrating the Western individualistic game of "one-upmanship", and compared it with the Chinese game of "face":

> In the typical western cocktail party, everyone plays the game of 'one-upmanship' using the polite boasting and free-floating expressions of sentiment that go with elevating oneself as a means of establishing a positive image. They joke about this and that, jostling for position while gradually revealing something of their personality and feelings. At the Chinese dinner party, on the other hand, rank is fixed by the seating plan, everyone knows his standing relative to everybody else. They are all expected to follow 'li', doing the proper things with the right people, bowing and gesturing in verbal ritual, and paying respect to others (in Bond & Hwang, 1986, p. 244).

Both the relevant features of Hofstede's cultural dimensions discussed earlier and the more holistic approach adopted later in the chapter which drew on relevant features of philosophical, sociological, psychological and historical literatures have established significant differences between Indians and Chinese Malaysians in one cluster, and Australians in another. The next section draws on the cultural differences between the two clusters discussed in the earlier sections, to formulate the hypotheses of the study with respect to resolution of auditor–client conflict, and whistle-blowing as an internal control mechanism.

HYPOTHESIS 1: RESOLUTION OF AUDITOR–CLIENT CONFLICTS

The cultural differences between the clusters identified in the chapter were based on two sources, which complemented each other. The first source was the five-dimensional cultural taxonomy developed by Hofstede (1980) and Hofstede and Bond (1988). Based on this cultural taxonomy, Indians and Chinese Malaysians were categorised in the cluster comprising large Power Distance, low Individualism and Long-term Orientation, and Australians were grouped in another cluster comprising small Power Distance, high Individualism and Short-term Orientation. The second source for clustering nations was a more holistic approach, which provided insight into Chinese Malaysian and Indian cultures by examining respectively the major features of Confucianism and Hinduism. Insight into Australian culture was gained by relying on relevant historical and sociological literatures. This section summarises the cultural differences between Chinese Malaysians and Indians on the one hand, and Australians on the other, that are likely to lead to differences in judgements in relation to auditor–client conflict resolution. The following section does the same for whistle-blowing as an internal control mechanism.

In the context of auditor–client conflict, a client has a greater bargaining power and is a more "powerful" party because a client has an option of switching auditors. In addition, the current audit market in each of the three nations at issue is characterised by a large number of auditing firms that are aggressively pursuing expansion programmes (Lindsay, 1992; Andersen, 1995; Bloom & Schirm, 2005).[36] In such a competitive environment, accounting firms are often forced to consider "other factors" (for example, economic and power factors) besides relevant technical issues in resolving conflicts with their clients (Knapp, 1985; Lindsay, 1992; Lehman, 1992; O'Malley, 1993; The Future of the Accounting Profession: Auditor Concentration, 2005). Consequently, the economic incentive to accede to client pressures would be present in each of the three nations. However, this thesis hypothesises (and tests) that cultural differences between Indians and Chinese Malaysians, on the one hand, and Australians, on the other, may produce differences in judgements related to the likelihood and acceptance of resolving audit conflicts by acceding to clients.

The cultural characteristics discussed in the chapter suggest that Indian and Chinese Malaysian professional accountants are less likely to confront "powerful" audit clients in resolving conflicts because their cultures are more concerned with cultivating harmonious interpersonal relationships, maintaining the organisational status quo and a stable hierarchy, and acting in a manner appropriate to one's position in a rigid hierarchical social order. In Indian and Chinese cultures, subordinates and other less powerful people "yield to their seniors on every conceivable on-the-job or off-the-job occasion" (Sinha & Sinha, 1990, p. 709). Running organisations as if they were their "personal fiefdoms"' is common among Indian and Chinese managers. Superiors expect loyalty, compliance and total submission by subordinates and other less powerful people with whom they have business dealings.

The cultural concern for "harmony-within-hierarchy" at all costs among Indians and Chinese Malaysians is an important factor in their resolution of conflicts. The social mechanisms which maintain harmony are so rigid that an "escape from the network is not an option, and the network must stay intact" (Redding & Wong, 1986, p. 285). As a general rule, conflict and confrontation are avoided as there is greater concern for personal relationships and social harmony. Evidence shows that avoidance of conflict and maintenance of hierarchical equilibrium are the cardinal rules in Indian and Chinese organisations. The cultural concern for maintaining harmony at all costs becomes of even greater importance if one of the parties concerned is a power-holder. Power-holders in Chinese and Indian cultures are given special privileges and decisions made by powerful people are not likely to be questioned. Consequently, in such a cultural context, professional accountants are likely to accede to client pressures rather than to resolve conflicts through confrontation.

Another related factor that is important in resolving conflicts is how Indian and Chinese cultures view the relationship between an individual and others in their family, organisation and the society in general. In these cultures an individual exists through, and is defined by, his or her relationship to others (these relationships are structured hierarchically). An individual is part of a collective which decides the rules of acceptable behaviour. People are more concerned with acting appropriately against those collective rules than with acting in a manner that they personally might consider acceptable (ethical or unethical) behaviour. An individual is part of a "collective ego" which has established societal norms governing individual behaviour on issues such as how conflicts are to be resolved. Harmony is maintained by ensuring that each member is conscientious in following the requirements of his or her societal duty.

As a result, in Indian and Chinese cultures, judgements related to what is considered ethical or unethical is not an individual choice but is contextual, depending on the status and relationships among the people involved. Multiple standards of morality are seen as acceptable because there are no absolute standards by which to resolve conflict of values. In resolving conflicts, the ultimate objective in Indian and Chinese cultures is the application of pragmatic ethical rules which emphasise the importance of maintaining "face" and acting in a manner appropriate to one's position in a hierarchical organisational and social order. Again, these cultural values among Indian and Chinese Malaysian professional accountants are likely to be supportive of them acceding to pressures by powerful clients in resolving conflicts.

In contrast, the literature suggests that Australian cultural values are not consistent with professional accountants resolving conflicts by bowing to pressures from powerful clients. Cultural values discussed earlier in the chapter suggest that the major concern in Australian society is on setting high values on individualism and independence. Australians are likely to be motivated by their own needs, rights and preferences, giving priority to personal rather than group, organisational, or societal goals. As such, there is much greater emotional independence of individuals from organisations. Greater value in organisations and society is attached to individual initiative, achievement and autonomy. Maintaining "harmony-within-hierarchy" is not an important cultural trait in Australia. On the contrary, the high value placed in Australia on self-reliance, individual initiative and on individual freedom of choice, is generally consistent with the cultural value that a certain amount of conflict (although not excessive) is essential in resolving personal differences both within families and in organisations.[37] As a general rule, appropriate use of conflict and confrontation are seen as viable means of resolving personal differences. Consequently, in such a cultural context, professional accountants are likely to confront their clients to resolve conflicts rather than acceding to pressures by powerful clients.

Compared to Indians and Chinese Malaysians, Australians are less likely to be threatened by powerful clients because the cultural values of equalitarianism and egalitarianism suggest that value standards should apply to all irrespective of their position or wealth. Power-holders in Australian culture are generally not given special privileges, and decisions made by powerful people are likely to be questioned, challenged and criticised. Furthermore, unlike Indian and Chinese cultures where decisions made by superiors and powerful people are unchallenged, Australia has a tradition of "cutting down its tall poppies" (Withers, 1989, p. 14).

Therefore, consistent with the Australian cultural values of equalitarianism and egalitarianism, confrontation, adversarial forms of debate, and direct approaches may be seen as acceptable ways of resolving conflicts. In addition, these approaches to resolving conflicts are likely not to be dependent on the social or economic status of parties, or on the relationships among the people involved. These direct approaches to resolving conflicts are also consistent with the high value placed in Australia on attainment of self-actualisation and the development of a "competent-self". An important aim in Australian culture is to develop self-directed behaviour rather than to rely on externally imposed societal norms. For example, to be effective, individuals are socialised to control one's own life and make one's own way in it. In contrast, in Indian and Chinese cultures, individuals feel ineffectual, powerless, controlled by others, and they have to conform to rules they have no chance of changing. Western culture shows a greater concern for the "truth" than for acceptable behaviour (Triandis, 1994, p. 191). Unlike the cultural features of Indians and Chinese described earlier, the aim in Western cultures such as Australia is for individuals to develop unique and internalised moral judgements, rather than to rely on external incentives such as maintaining "face" or organisational hierarchy and harmony. Again, these Australian cultural values are not supportive of professional accountants acceding to pressures by powerful clients.

As a result, other things being equal, cultural differences between Indians and Chinese Malaysians, on the one hand, and Australians on the other, are expected to produce differences in judgements related to the likelihood and acceptance of resolving audit conflicts by acceding to clients. Consequently, the first hypothesis (one is behavioural and one attitudinal) stated in directional form is as follows:

H1a: Australian professional accountants are less likely to resolve audit conflicts by acceding to clients than Indian and Chinese Malaysian professional accountants.

H1b: Australian professional accountants are less accepting of resolving audit conflicts by acceding to clients than Indian and Chinese Malaysian professional accountants.

HYPOTHESIS 2: WHISTLE-BLOWING AS AN INTERNAL CONTROL MECHANISM

Recall that the definition of whistle-blowing adopted in this study includes the option of reporting a superior's wrongdoing to parties either inside or outside an organisation. Since the definition involves reporting of a superior's wrongdoing, a whistle-blower is always the less powerful party. The less powerful whistle-blowers in all cultures may have a certain degree of reluctance to engage in whistle-blowing. However, as for the auditor–client conflict situation, this study suggests (and tests) that cultural differences between Indians and Chinese Malaysians, and Australians, may be a determinant of differences in judgements related to the likelihood and acceptance of engaging in whistle-blowing as an internal control mechanism.

The reporting of a superior's unethical practices by a whistle-blower to parties either inside or outside an organisation, by its nature creates confrontation and conflict. Since the main issues in whistle-blowing involve power relations and the use of confrontation to resolve conflicts, the previous discussions on the cultural differences between Indians and Chinese Malaysians compared to Australians, as those differences related to audit–client conflict resolution, are also relevant here.

The earlier discussions suggest that, compared to Australians, Chinese and Indians are more likely to avoid organisational conflict and confrontation, and to show greater concern for maintaining "face", organisational hierarchy, and harmony. Autocratic and paternalistic leadership styles are accepted among Indians and Chinese because laws and rules differ for superiors and subordinates. Since hierarchical order is common and unchallenged in families and organisations, it is expected that superiors' actions would require less justification in their cultures. These cultural differences, together with Indian and Chinese cultural values summarised in earlier sections, are consistent with less acceptance and less likelihood of subordinates using whistle-blowing to resolve conflicts with their superiors.

Another related concept is the greater pressure on a subordinate to cover up a supervisor's unethical action in Indian and Chinese cultures. For example, evidence suggests that individuals in low Individualism cultures may willingly participate in a cover-up for "communitarian motives – to save face and protect the reputation of the group" (Cohen, Pant, & Sharp, 1992, p. 691). Evidence also shows that both formal as well as informal organisational structures in low Individualism and large Power Distance societies provide less chance through conventional channels for subordinates to question superiors' actions (Schultz et al., 1993, p. 81). This evidence is consistent with the findings that there are lower rates of whistle-blowing in cultures which favour more authoritarian and less participative organisations (such as Indian and Chinese Malaysian cultures) (Miceli & Near, 1992; Jha, 2005). In addition, the earlier discussion on Indian and Chinese cultures, which suggests the existence of multiple standards of morality and the pragmatic nature of ethical rules (particularly when dealing with powerful people), is also not consistent with the use of whistle-blowing to expose superiors' wrongdoings.

In contrast, Australians are less likely to be threatened by organisational superiors because one's position or wealth does not provide special privileges. The importance placed on egalitarianism and equalitarianism would suggest that rules and regulations should apply to everyone equally. Employees are generally not afraid of questioning their superiors' actions, and greater employee participation is the preferred style of management. Cultural values in Australia are not likely to encourage individuals to cover up a superior's unethical action for "communitarian motives".

In addition, evidence suggests that there should be higher rates of whistle-blowing in cultures which favour greater organisational participation and less authoritarian styles of leadership (such as the Australian culture) (Miceli & Near, 1992). As discussed earlier, Australian cultural values, with insistence on a *fair go* and on *meritocracy*, are again not compatible with covering up a superior's unethical practices. The emphasis on "truth" in determining what is right or wrong without reference to the context and people involved is also a relevant factor in the acceptance of whistle-blowing. Compared to Indian and Chinese cultures, greater emphasis is placed in Australian culture on consistency between what is "inside" the person and that person's behaviour. In summary, these Australian cultural values, together with the discussions presented earlier in the hypotheses formulation section of this chapter, are consistent with greater acceptance and greater likelihood of subordinates using whistle-blowing to expose their superiors' wrongdoings.

As a result, other things being equal, cultural differences between Indians and Chinese Malaysians, on the one hand, and Australians, on the other, are expected to produce differences in judgements related to the likelihood and acceptance of engaging in whistle-blowing as an internal control mechanism. Consequently, the second hypothesis (one is behavioural and one attitudinal) stated in directional form is as follows.

H2a: Australian professional accountants are more likely to engage in whistle-blowing as an internal control mechanism than Chinese Malaysian and Indian professional accountants.

H2b: Australian professional accountants are more accepting of engaging in whistle-blowing as an internal control mechanism than Chinese Malaysian and Indian professional accountants.

CHAPTER 4
RESEARCH METHOD

This chapter outlines the research method used in the study, and explains the strategies employed to enhance the reliability and validity of the results.

The data used to test the hypotheses developed in Chapter 3 were collected using a survey questionnaire administered to a sample of senior professional accountants from big-five accounting firms in India, Malaysia and Australia.[1] The sample comprised 84, 92 and 72 respondents from India, Malaysia and Australia respectively. Additionally, interviews were conducted with 11 university academics in India, nine in Malaysia and 10 in Australia, with an interest in culture. These interviews were designed to supplement relevant psychological, sociological and historical literatures for the three nations, and thereby provide a more holistic and richer understanding of the cultural values in each of the countries.

The chapter is organised as follows. The first section explains the reasons for selecting Australia, India and Malaysia as the nations for study. The second section describes the selection of the organisations and respondents used for the survey questionnaire. The third section explains the choice and the details of the survey questionnaire used to measure the variables including Hofstede's Values Survey Module (1994). This section also describes the use of the Multidimensional Ethics Measure, a research instrument consisting of eight bipolar scales divided into three dimensions (Moral Equity, Relativism and Contractualism), to examine the various complex influences on cross-cultural ethical judgements. An explanation of the steps taken to control for the potential for SDRB in the questionnaire is also provided, together with an explanation of the distribution and collection of the questionnaires. The fifth section discusses the results of the pilot testing of the survey questionnaire. The sixth section describes the purpose and the details of the questions used in the personal interviews of university academics. The final section provides a summary of the chapter.

SELECTION OF COUNTRIES FOR STUDY

It was shown in Chapter 2 that most of the studies in cross-cultural behavioural research in accounting may be described as ex-cathedra propositions without adequate analysis. Two main reasons for this criticism are as follows. First, as shown in Chapter 2, a significant number of studies particularly in the cross-cultural financial accounting and auditing literature have simply treated culture as a "black box", and have not clearly explained the specific nature of the cultural differences that are associated with observed differences in accounting and auditing practices. Second, it appears that countries are often selected for cross-cultural research because of the ease of collecting data without a thorough analysis of the countries' cultural and accounting environments.

For example, Agacer and Doupnik (1991) used data from the US, West Germany and the Philippines to identify cross-cultural differences in perceptions of external auditors' independence. Karnes et al. (1989) selected the US and Taiwan for examining cross-cultural perceptual ethical differences. Schultz et al. (1993) used subjects from France, Norway and the US to examine ethical sensitivity, and Cohen et al. (1995), in their study of ethical differences, selected subjects from Japan, the US, and Latin America (countries grouped under Latin America included Venezuela, Colombia, Chile, Ecuador, Honduras, Panama and eight others). Johns et al. (1999) selected US and non-US and Doupnik and Richer (2004) selected US and Germany.[2]

While these studies provide useful insights into perceptual differences across the nations selected, those insights may be limited because of differences in the way accounting has evolved in particular countries.[3] An important consideration in such studies is to establish that the particular accounting concept under examination has "content equivalence" in the countries being studied for the effect of cultural differences.

Content equivalence refers to similarities in the accounting rules, procedures and concepts. For example, Schultz et al. (1993) compared perceptual differences among managers and professional staff from France, Norway and the US on certain ethical issues. One of their research cases involved a revenue recognition problem. Establishing content equivalence would involve showing that the rules and their application for revenue recognition are similar in these countries. Evidence shows that this is not the case. Rather, revenue recognition is a controversial issue in both the US and Anglo-American countries, requiring the exercise of professional judgement (Psaros & Patel, 2003). In comparison, historically "the uniquely French emphasis on uniformity, and its application through the standardized national code of accounting, the Plan Comptable General" (Radebaugh & Gray, 1993, p. 96), means that decisions do not require the exercise of professional judgement.[4] Also in France, tax laws tended to override the accounting rules to the extent that charges deductible for tax purposes must be recorded in the accounts if the tax benefit is to be claimed. Consequently, revenue recognition rules are strongly influenced by the tax laws. Therefore, it is likely that revenue recognition rules and their application do not have content equivalence in France and the US. As a result, comparing judgements of professional accountants in France and the US on revenue recognition may not provide meaningful information.

Both theoretical and empirical classifications of countries in relation to the development and role of accounting practices, systems and concepts, show differences among countries such as the US, West Germany, the Philippines, Taiwan, France, Norway, Japan and Brazil (see Choi & Mueller, 1992; Radebaugh & Gray, 2002; and Nobes & Parker, 2004). However, research also shows some commonalities across countries in terms of the historical, cultural and socio-economic factors that have influenced both accounting systems and the accounting principles underlying financial measurement and reporting in different countries and regions. Prior studies such as Mueller (1968), a report by the AAA (1977), Nobes and Parker (1981) and Mueller, Gernon, and Meek (1994), point to a number of "zones of influence" that cluster nations with respect to their patterns of accounting development.[5]

Using the zones of influence criteria for selecting countries for this study should therefore facilitate the establishment of content equivalence of the accounting issues under examination. Specifically India, Malaysia and Australia have been selected in the current study because:

- These countries are classified in the British Commonwealth model of accounting development (see Mueller, 1968; Mueller et al., 1991; Radebaugh & Gray, 2002; Roberts et al., 2005 for details). All were colonised by the British who were also responsible for the development of accounting and corporate legislation. The concept of the "true and fair view" of financial affairs of a business has been an important principle in accounting development in these three countries. In each case the objective of accounting is generally based on the concept of "decision usefulness" which is principally oriented towards the decision needs of investors. In the British Commonwealth model of accounting development, accounting standards allow for flexibility in accordance with the perceived circumstances of individual companies (Radebaugh & Gray, 2002; Patel, 2004). Consequently, the exercise of professional judgement remains an integral aspect of financial accounting in Australia, India and Malaysia.

- Accounting ethics in these countries have developed by focusing on the interaction of ethics and professionalism and by emphasising the importance of "self-regulation". In contrast to greater public regulation and statutory control in countries with Franco–Spanish–Portuguese influence, the accounting profession in the British Commonwealth model is largely self-regulated. That is, professional accountants through their membership of their respect professional accounting bodies remain influential in the development of accounting standards in the three countries selected for study.[6]
- In each of the three countries, a conceptual framework (CF) project had been mounted, with the stated expectation that this would result in reporting requirements becoming more consistent and logical because they will stem from an orderly set of concepts.
- Over the last few years there has been a significant increase in the acceptance of International Accounting Standards (IASs) and International Financial Reporting Standards (IFRSs) which are issued by the IASB. The forces of globalisation and political expediency are forcing many countries to adopt IASs/IFRSs, resulting in an optimistic future for the international convergence and harmonisation of IASB standards. Convergence with IFRSs issued by the IASB is a major objective of financial reporting in each of these countries in recent years. For example, Australia, adopted the IASs/IFRSs from January 2005; the Financial Reporting Foundation and the Malaysian Accounting Standards Board (MASB) have changed the nomenclature of MASB standards. Beginning from 1 January 2005, existing MASB standards will be renamed Financial Reporting Standards (FRSs), and the numbers will change to correspond to those of the international standards (http://www.iasplus.com/country/malaysia.htm); and India is moving quickly towards convergence (http://indiabudget.nic.in/es2001-02/chapt2002/chap36.pdf).
- In each country the professional bodies are well established and accountants enjoy a prestigious status. The founding date (dates of earliest predecessor bodies are shown in brackets) of the Australian Society of Certified Practising Accountants was 1952 (1887), and the Institute of Chartered Accountants in Australia was 1928 (1886) (Nobes & Parker, 1995, p. 4). The Malaysian Institute of Accountants (Institut Akauntan Malaysia) was established in 1967, and the Malaysian Association of Certified Public Accountants (Institut Akauntan Umum Malaysia) in 1958 (Tay, 1993, p. 240). The Institute of Chartered Accountants in India was set up in 1947.

- Membership of the accounting profession in the three countries is limited to university accounting graduates who are required to pass additional examinations conducted by the professional bodies and are required to possess at least three years of relevant experience before gaining full professional membership (Tay, 1993).

The above six commonalities in the development and role of accounting in India, Malaysia and Australia provide some confidence about the content equivalence of the accounting issues examined in this study.

Notwithstanding the similarities in accounting development, there are significant cultural differences among these countries. As was shown in Chapter 4, India and Malaysia are clustered within the cultural dimension cells of high Collectivism, large Power Distance and Long-term Orientation, whereas Australia is classified as high Individualism, small Power Distance and Short-term Orientation. For theory testing purposes, a higher explanatory power can be achieved by sampling from countries whose cultural differences are large. That is, if a theory predicts a larger difference in ethical sensitivity between countries A and B than between C and D, then the same explanatory power can be achieved with a smaller sample size from A and B than from C and D.

SELECTION OF ORGANISATIONS AND RESPONDENTS FOR THE SURVEY QUESTIONNAIRE

In order to enable differences in judgements among accountants from the three nations to be attributable to cultural differences, control of the potentially confounding factors of organisational culture and level of seniority is needed. To control for these variables in this study, only staff of the rank of supervisor or higher from the big-five, multinational accounting firms were selected as subjects. Respondents were drawn from four of the big-five firms in Malaysia, and from three firms each in India and Australia. The names of the firms that participated in this study in each nation cannot be disclosed because they were assured that their anonymity would be protected.

Evidence shows that there are many similarities in organisational culture in the larger multinational accounting firms (Kinney, 1986; Wheeler, Felsig, & Reilly, 1987; Soeters & Schreuder, 1988; Pratt & Beaulieu, 1992; Ponemon, 1992; The Future of the Accounting Profession: Auditor Concentration, 2005). This is largely the result of self-selection and socialisation. Self-selection is the process by which individuals make themselves available for recruitment in organisations that are compatible with their organisational commitment, satisfaction and aspirations. Socialisation refers to the process by which values of organisational members are made compatible with those of the organisation. For example, Ponemon (1992, p. 244) notes that large multinational accounting firms have a similar organisational culture since they, "have an 'up or out philosophy' during the promotion process. Firm management may implicitly screen employees who do not share compatible traits, beliefs or ethical values. Accountants selected for promotion within the firm, therefore, will possess ethical reasoning capacities consistent with firm management".

Similarities in organisational culture arise largely because of the standardisation of activities such as the audit process, hiring and promotion criteria, and the implementation of a firm's code of professional conduct. Furthermore, empirical evidence from cross-sectional, longitudinal and experimental studies corroborates the existence of a similar socialisation phenomenon in larger public accounting firms. New employees follow certain rites of passage. They are likely to be indoctrinated as to what is considered to be important in the organisation, what standards of conduct are upheld, and what kind of humour is acceptable. For example, an earlier study related to an examination of the interaction between national and organisational cultures of three of the big-six international accounting firms and three other firms, which were Dutch in origin and organisation, showed that self-selection of employees of the international firms, in combination with the deliberate selection policies of the firms themselves, was the best explanation for their distinct organisational culture (Soeters & Schreuder, 1988). Indeed, an examination of the reports emerging on the demise of Arthur Anderson and other scandals surrounding the big-four accounting firms clearly shows the power and influence of organisational culture on ethical reasoning abilities of organisational participants.

In summary, the similarities in organisational cultures of big-five accounting firms, and the selection of senior respondents, provides confidence that differences in judgements among respondents can be attributed to cultural differences.

Selection of Respondents

Respondents were selected from the cities of Sydney and Newcastle in Australia, Kuala Lumpur in Malaysia, and Bombay and New Delhi in India. All of these cities, except Newcastle, are the most important commercial centres in their respective countries. Newcastle was included because the researcher had personal contacts with firms in that city.

Individual respondents for the survey questionnaire were randomly selected by partners of the firms, in conformity with the stated criteria that respondents should at least be the rank of supervisor.[7] The individual identities of respondents to the survey questionnaire were not known, however, various demographic data on gender, age, highest academic qualification, years of professional work experience, and their organisational position were obtained. The data on respondents' positions in the firms confirmed the selection of appropriate respondents.

THE SURVEY QUESTIONNAIRE

The purposes of this section are firstly, to explain the choice of a survey questionnaire to collect the data to test the hypotheses, secondly to outline the design of the survey questionnaire and thirdly, to explain how the survey was distributed and collected.

Choice of Survey Questionnaire

This section justifies the use of survey research and explains how this study sought to address the major limitations of the survey research method.

Survey research methods are the techniques used in obtaining information directly from a group of individuals in some specific context. The major strength of survey research is its suitability for studying "naturally occurring phenomena", particularly when external validity is at a premium (Brownell, 1995, p. 31). Compared to experiments, the survey method enhances the external validity of studies. That is, by eliciting from respondents certain facts, beliefs and behavioural descriptions relating to their own organisational experiences, survey methods can produce results with greater generalisability, compared to their experimental counterpart.

The survey research method was selected in this study for its cost effectiveness in collecting data from 258 professional accountants located in five cities in three countries. In addition, the external validity of the results is an important aspect of this study, which seeks to draw conclusions on cultural influences on ethical judgements generally in the countries studied, and potentially beyond to countries with similar mixes of cultural dimensions. While cost effectiveness and external validity favour the use of survey research, it is also important that a number of strategies should be adopted to overcome its major limitations. Consequently, the following steps were taken to address the limitations of survey research.

One of the first rules of survey research is a clear formulation of a priori hypotheses. Surveys can be used for exploratory research, but not with any degree of efficiency (Dane, 1990). Consistent with this rule, this study deals with four a priori hypotheses, formulated from the relevant literature in accounting, psychology, sociology and history.[8] Secondly, Dane (1990, p. 127) also notes that pre-testing survey instruments "is the most important phase of survey research". Again, consistent with this approach, five stages of an extensive pilot testing of the research instruments were used in this study. These stages are discussed later in the chapter.

Compared to experiments, survey research exposes studies to internal validity threats, that is, to the possibility that there may be rival explanations for the observed results. The following features of this study should reduce the threats to internal validity.

- As discussed earlier, Australia, India and Malaysia belong to the British Commonwealth model of accounting development. This provides reasonable assurance of the content equivalence of the accounting concepts examined in the study.
- Again, as discussed earlier, senior staff from the big-five international accounting firms were selected as subjects in the study. This was designed to ensure that subjects have similar rank and are influenced by similar organisational culture.
- A number of steps were taken to minimise the threat to cross-cultural studies from SDRB. These aspects are discussed later in the chapter in the section on controlling errors in measurement.

In summary, the survey research method was selected as the most appropriate method for this study, with a number of steps being taken to overcome the limitations associated with this method.

Questionnaire Design

The purpose of the survey questionnaire was to measure the independent variables (national cultures of India, Malaysia and Australia) and the dependent variables (judgements of accountants in relation to whistle-blowing and auditor–client conflict resolution). The choice of Hofstede's (1994a) updated version of the Value Survey Module to measure the national cultures of the three nations was discussed in Chapters 1 and 3.

The Values Survey Module (1994) is a modified version of Hofstede's (1980) survey module. The Values Survey Module (1994) consists of 26 items, of which four items each relate to the calculation of Power Distance,

Individualism and Long/Short-term Orientation indices (the details are provided in Chapter 5).

The Values Survey Module (1994) provides two criteria that must be satisfied before its use. The first criterion states that the minimum number of respondents from each country must be 20. The second criterion states that respondents should always be based on samples that are matched, as well as possible, on all aspects other than nationality. Both these criteria were met in this study. The sample in this study comprised 84, 92 and 72 senior professional accountants from big-five, multinational accounting firms from India, Malaysia and Australia respectively. Selection of senior staff from big-five firms ensured that respondents had similar rank and were influenced by similar organisational culture.

Additionally, Hofstede's dimensions of culture are supplemented by interviews with university academics in each of the three countries. These are discussed later in this chapter in the section on interviews.

To measure judgements of accountants, the Multidimensional Ethics Measure was used. This measure was applied to three accounting scenarios contained in the questionnaire. This section first discusses the importance of using scenarios in examining judgements of respondents. This is followed by a description of the three accounting scenarios used in the study. The first scenario deals with auditor–client conflict resolution and the remaining two cover whistle-blowing as an internal control mechanism. The next section describes the Multidimensional Ethics Measure used to measure judgements of accountants. The final section outlines how this study dealt with the potential for social desirability bias in respondents' answers to the questionnaire. The complete survey questionnaire is shown as an appendix at the end of this chapter.

Accounting Scenarios

This study uses scenarios which are defined as "short descriptions of a person or a social situation which contain precise references to what are thought to be the most important factors in the decision-making or judgement-making processes of respondents" (Alexander & Becker, 1978, p. 94). Scenarios allow studies to frame the research questions to incorporate complex and multidimensional issues reflecting decision making in the real world (Cavanagh & Fritzsche, 1985). This allows empirical researchers using scenarios to elicit from respondents their beliefs, preferences, intentions, reasoning, judgement, or intended behaviour regarding ethical issues (Weber, 1992, p. 137).

Recent studies in ethical research in accounting utilising the cognitive-developmental theories show that scenarios, in contrast to questions about a code of professional conduct, lead to a richer explanation of differences in ethical decision making among professional accountants. The use of scenarios as contexts in accounting allows the researcher to introduce a more realistic and richer context than other approaches to data gathering techniques (Reidenbach & Robin, 1990). Flory et al. (1992) and Tsui (1996) provide evidence to suggest that complex and multifaceted dynamics of decision making regarding ethical issues in accounting can be best captured with scenarios that on average use 200 words,[9] and which retain the essential complexity of a realistic ethical problem. The superiority of using scenarios to understand ethical decision making in accounting is reflected in an increasing number of studies that use scenarios rather than obtaining accountants' perceptions on various aspects of their professional code of ethics. Some original examples of accounting research using scenarios include Flory et al. (1992); Shaub, Finn, and Munter (1993); Schultz et al. (1993) and Cohen et al. (1995, 1996a).

To be useful, scenarios must possess "construct validity". The ethical evaluation of a situation is an abstract, complex concept which cannot be measured directly. Such concepts are called "constructs", and researchers have developed indirect methods for measuring them. Studies in the social sciences rarely regard a measure as completely valid in every circumstance, but rather consider the process of validation to be unending. Consequently, such complex constructs as ethics must be tested in a variety of settings and with different groups to confirm that the initial results are not related to a particular group or setting. That is, "repeated use of the same measurement items by different individuals to evaluate different situations or applications is an important test of the construct's validity" (Nunnally, 1978, p. 94). As discussed in the next section, the three scenarios selected in the study have been used in a number of prior research studies with various groups and settings. Their extensive use in prior studies lends comfort to their construct validity. Each of the three scenarios is outlined below.

SCENARIO ONE: AUDITOR–CLIENT CONFLICT RESOLUTION

The auditor–client conflict situation used in this study is based on a scenario originally developed and pilot tested by Knapp (1985). The scenario describes a dispute that has arisen between the auditor-in-charge and the management of a large company over the materiality of certain unrecorded liabilities discovered during the audit. The management argues that the total amount of unrecorded liabilities is immaterial and therefore it is unnecessary to make adjusting entries in the financial statements. On the other hand, the auditor-in-charge feels that the amount is material and that the financial statements should be adjusted accordingly. In addition, the company is an important client contributing significantly to the total audit revenue of the audit firm, and the audit market is characterised by a large number of auditing firms that are aggressively pursuing expansion programmes. The auditor-in-charge eventually decides that the unrecorded liabilities would be ignored for purposes of financial statements as well as the auditor's report. Respondents are asked to evaluate the action of the auditor-in-charge. The way in which respondents were asked to evaluate this action is discussed later under the heading, Multidimensional Ethics Measure.

Knapp's (1985) scenario has been used a number of times. For example, Gul (1991) examined the perceptions of 49 senior bank lending officers from New Zealand regarding various aspects of auditor–client conflict resolution. The study showed that there was a "need to strengthen auditors' position in audit conflict situations and to improve third-party perceptions of the auditors' ability to resist management pressure" (Gul, 1991, p. 169).

Next, after extensive pilot testing, Tsui and Gul (1994) used the scenario to examine the interaction effects of ethical reasoning and locus of control on the behaviour of auditors in an audit conflict situation. Respondents were experienced auditors from a sample of large and small accounting firms in Hong Kong. The study found that ethical reasoning is an important determinant of auditors' behaviour and that it can dominate personality variables such as locus of control. The scenario provides useful insight into the various cognitive variables that influence auditor–client conflict resolution.

SCENARIOS TWO AND THREE: WHISTLE-BLOWING AS AN INTERNAL CONTROL MECHANISM

Empirical research suggests that the nature and extent of retaliation imposed by management against whistle-blowers is one of the most significant determinants of behaviour (Greenberger et al., 1987; Near & Miceli, 1986). For this reason, it was considered desirable to include two levels of management retaliation in the whistle-blowing scenarios. In one scenario, the potential whistle-blower's chances of promotion could be greatly reduced if he questioned the general manager's authority and reported the questionable activity to the chairperson of the board of directors. In the other scenario, the potential whistle-blower was told by the director of internal audit that he would be "fired" if he decided to pursue the matter any further. These two scenarios (scenarios two and three) are discussed in turn.

Scenario two describes an internal auditor in a large company whose work involves reviewing expense accounts. When reviewing the expense account of the marketing manager, he found reimbursement requests for items such as a moderately expensive necklace, and a bill for his wife's personal secretary. These items were not reimbursable according to the company policy. When questioned, the marketing manager was upset and showed the general manager's signature authorising the payment. The internal auditor knew that the general manager was a close friend of the marketing manager and that the internal auditor's promotion chances could be greatly reduced if he questioned the general manager's authority. After thinking about the issue for a few days, the internal auditor decided not to report the matter to the chairperson of the board. Respondents are asked to evaluate the action of the internal auditor.

The above scenario is based on an incident that was reported in the US and was extensively pilot tested in the US, Norway and France by Schultz et al. (1993). The scenario enabled Schultz et al. (1993) to measure the various variables that are important in whistle-blowing. In particular, the scenario allowed Schultz et al. (1993) to show the importance of national culture on value judgements, with the French stressing personal responsibility for whistle-blowing more than Norwegian or American subjects. Thus, the study provided an important insight into the influence of national culture on whistle-blowers' behaviour.

Scenario three describes an internal auditor with an organisation that is a primary contractor for the government. During the current audit, the internal auditor discovered a series of bogus invoices to customers that had already been paid. He reported this finding to the director of internal audit. The director said that he would report it to authorities within the company. But after a few days, the director told the internal auditor to "forget about it". When the internal auditor persisted, the director shouted that if he pursued this any further, he would be fired. The internal auditor is aware that with his qualifications, he was not likely to find another such well-paid position in the current economic climate. After thinking about this for a few days, the internal auditor decided not to report the matter to the next higher level of management. Respondents are asked to evaluate the action of the internal auditor.

The above scenario is based on an incident that was reported in the US by Meier and Rittenberg (1986). This was developed into a scenario and extensively pilot tested by Arnold and Ponemon (1991). They used the scenario to examine American internal auditors' perceptions and the influence of ethical reasoning on whistle-blowing. The findings revealed that internal auditors with relatively low levels of ethical reasoning were unlikely to use whistle-blowing as a means for disclosing wrongdoing. More importantly, the scenario captured the various factors that may influence whistle-blowing. A modified version of this scenario which included a change of context, was further validated by Schultz et al. (1993) to examine the influence of the national cultures of the US, France and Norway on various aspects of whistle-blowing.

MULTIDIMENSIONAL ETHICS MEASURE

A contribution of this study is that it examines the complex influences on judgements of professional accountants from Australia, India and Malaysia by means of a Multidimensional Ethics Measure rather than a unidimensional measure. The problem with asking a single item question for a construct as complex as ethics is that the validity of the measure is highly suspect (Cohen et al., 1993). Indeed, the superiority of multiple item scales over single item scales is rarely questioned in social science research.

By contrast, much of the cross-cultural ethics accounting research has used a single item bipolar Likert scale to capture perceptions on various accounting constructs. For example, Agacer and Doupnik (1991) used a single item Likert scale ranging from 1 (very low risk) to 9 (very high risk) to measure the risk of the external auditors compromising their independence under certain situations. Cohen et al. (1995) asked respondents to evaluate the action described in their scenarios by indicating on a Likert scale, ranging from 1 (ethical) to 7 (unethical).

Complex and multi-faceted dynamics of professional judgements, particularly in relation to ethical issues in accounting, cannot be adequately captured on a single item bipolar Likert scale. Evidence suggests that single item measures may be less reliable than multiple item measures, and consequently more error laden (Kerlinger, 1986; Nunnally, 1967) and of suspect validity (Cohen et al., 1993b). Thus, the results of research using single item measures of ethical evaluation may be limited.

A second aspect of the single item measurement problem is that it does not provide insight into the dynamics of ethical evaluation. A single item scale makes it virtually impossible to understand the ethical perspective(s) that is (or are) invoked in making the evaluation. That is, "if we are to improve our understanding of the evaluation process and to make positive reactions to situations which warrant a reaction, it is important to address the problems inherent in the pluralistic nature of ethical theory and its measurement" (Reidenbach & Robin, 1988, p. 872).

Individuals use more than one rationale in arriving at complex ethical judgements. These rationales are a function of the situation faced by the individual, and "each rationale used represents a necessary dimension in any measure that expects to capture a true sense of that ethical judgement" (Reidenbach & Robin, 1990, p. 640). The use of a Multidimensional Ethics Measure allows a researcher to go beyond a simplistic understanding of "what" respondents believe and begins the process of understanding "why" they believe it.[10]

This research uses the Multidimensional Ethics Measure designed by Reidenbach and Robin (1988, 1990) and tested for validity and reliability in an accounting context by Flory et al. (1992) and Cohen et al. (1993b, 1996a), to examine previously unexplored dynamics of cross-cultural judgements. In addition, however, the study also uses the single item measure (ethical/unethical). The use of both the uni-dimensional and multidimensional measures enables the study to provide empirical evidence on the proposition that the explanatory power of the Multidimensional Ethics Measure is greater than that of the univariate (ethical/unethical) measure. The issue is elaborated on in Chapter 6.

The Multidimensional Ethics Measure consists of eight bipolar scales and was based on the theoretical importance of the following three dimensions: Moral Equity, Relativism and Contractualism. Additionally, various items in each of the three dimensions are also arranged in terms of their theoretical importance. Each dimension is explained in turn.

MORAL EQUITY DIMENSION

This dimension is the most complex of the three comprising the Multidimensional Ethics Measure because it is concerned with controversial normative beliefs about what is fair/unfair, just/unjust, and morally right/not morally right in human conduct. The ideas behind the Moral Equity Dimension are expressed through such general terms as "good", "bad", "virtuous", "praiseworthy", "right", "ought" and "blameworthy" (Beauchamp, 1982, p. 5). The Moral Equity Dimension is largely derived from the ethical philosophy of justice theory. A brief discussion of two relevant aspects of justice theory, namely distributive justice and procedural justice, follows.

Most of the influential and fundamental concepts of justice theory come from the writings of Aristotle. He provided guidance on translating notions of justice into societal practices and developed six principles of distributive justice which would explain "how to proportion when people or performances are unequal" (in Reidenbach & Robin, 1990, p. 650). The principles include: (1) to each person an equal share; (2) to each person according to individual need; (3) to each person according to that person's rights; (4) to each person according to individual effort; (5) to each person according to societal contribution and (6) to each person according to merit (Beauchamp & Bowie, 1983). It is not necessary that a society adopts one principle of distributive justice and excludes the others. For example, in Australia, welfare payments to the poor and unemployed are based on some measure of need, while promotions at work may be based on merit.

A second aspect of the Moral Equity Dimension and of justice theory is the concept of procedural justice, which aims to develop rules or procedures that result in fair or just outcomes. Forms of procedural justice include "perfect" and "imperfect" outcomes (Reidenbach & Robin, 1990, p. 651). Perfect procedural justice aims to achieve a fair result in every case, while in imperfect procedural justice, the rules represent the best attempt to produce fair results but sometimes the outcomes are unjust. Of greater importance to a society is the value placed by that society on achieving perfect procedural justice.

Prior research suggests that a broad-based Moral Equity Dimension is almost a fundamental decision rule for evaluating the moral content of business situations (see for example, Tsalikis & Nwachukwu, 1989; Reidenbach & Robin, 1988, 1990; Flory et al., 1992, Cohen et al., 1993b, 1996a). In this regard, Reidenbach and Robin (1990, p. 646) note:

> Decisions are evaluated essentially in terms of their inherent fairness, justice, goodness and rightness. Moreover, this dimension incorporates the idea of family acceptance. This dimension relies heavily on lessons from our early training that we receive in the home regarding fairness, right and wrong as communicated through childhood lessons of sharing, religious training, morals from fairy tales and fables.

In view of this evidence, the study incorporates the following four items (arranged in the order of their theoretical importance by Reidenbach & Robin, 1988, 1990) which comprise the Moral Equity Dimension of the Multidimensional Ethics Measure:

- Fair/unfair
- Just/unjust
- Morally right/not morally right
- Acceptable to my family/unacceptable to my family

Fair/unfair, just/unjust and morally right/not morally right, measure ethical evaluation based on how an individual understands and applies these concepts. The item, acceptable to my family/unacceptable to my family, measures ethical evaluation from the perspective of an individual's family.

RELATIVISM DIMENSION

The Relativism dimension in the Multidimensional Ethics Measure comprises the following two items arranged in the order of their theoretical importance:

- Culturally acceptable/unacceptable
- Traditionally acceptable/unacceptable

The essence of Relativism is that all values are a function of culture, and as a result, there are no universal ethical rules. That is, cultural values are important in defining individual ethical beliefs. Since ethical rules are relative to a specific culture, the values and behaviour of people in one culture need not dictate the conduct of people in another culture.

For example, evidence shows that the principles of distributive justice (discussed earlier in the section, Moral Equity Dimension) are influenced by cultural values. For example, cultures that are high on measures of Individualism are more likely to employ equity or fairness rather than equality, and need principles when making decisions regarding distribution of resources (Leung & Bond, 1984; Leung & Iwawaki, 1988). Consequently, the influence of culture cannot be ignored in any discussion of ethical issues.

Managers have used the Relativism dimension, that is, the cultural differences in methods of doing business, as a defence against alleged unethical behaviour in international settings. For instance, "baksheesh" (bribery) appears to be an acceptable behaviour in certain parts of the world. For example, Spitzer (1979, p. 69) in describing his experiences in India concluded that, "Almost any matter, official or otherwise, could be expedited by a bribe". Indeed, India is ranked 88th out of 158 countries listed in 2005 Corruption Perceptions Index (http://www.transparency.org/cpi/2005/cpi2005.sources.en.html).

To gain better understanding of cross-cultural differences in ethical judgements and behaviours, the Relativism dimension is particularly beneficial. Moreover, Western cultural biases are likely to be minimised when cultural relativism is invoked in explaining ethical differences among cultures.

CONTRACTUALISM DIMENSION

The Contractualism dimension comprises the following two items, arranged in order of their theoretical importance:

- Violates/does not violate an unwritten contract
- Violates/does not violate an unspoken promise

These items are derived from the philosophy of "deontology". Deontologists argue that individuals have a duty to satisfy the legitimate claims or needs of others as determined by applying logic to an ethical rule. The most prominent ethical rule is based on Immanuel Kant's criteria, "I ought never to act except in such a way that I can also will that my maxim should become a universal law" (Kant, 1964 translation, p. 9).

John Rawls, a contemporary American philosopher, adapted Kantian Deontology to develop an approach called Contractualism:

> The guiding idea behind this account is the social contract in a form similar to that underlying the fifth formulation of Kant's categorical imperative: 'Every rational being must act as if he, by his maxims, were at all times a legislative member in the universal realm of ends.' In this formula Kant uses the concept of the social contract found in Jean-Jacques Rousseau (1712–1778), although he interprets it in his own distinctive way (in Bayles & Henley, 1983, pp. 59–60).

The Contractualism dimension is particularly relevant to business and society because:

> Most business exchanges incorporate either implicit or explicit promises or contracts. Business exchanges involve a *quid pro quo* wherein one party is obligated to provide a product, service, employment, or perform some action in return for something of value. Individuals appear to take this idea of exchange one step further to include an ethics of exchange. This broadened view of exchange includes obligations which may go beyond a purely economic nature and include notions of fair play, truth telling, duty, and rights. Violation of these implicit ideas would result in the condemnation of the exchange process or at least part of the process as unethical (Reidenbach & Robin, 1990, p. 647).

To conclude, Reidenbach and Robin (1988, 1990) provide evidence that the Moral Equity, Relativism and Contractualism dimensions provide an understanding of why a particular business activity is judged to be ethical or unethical. In particular, it is shown that individuals, in varying degrees and extent, rely, either knowingly or unknowingly, on these three philosophical dimensions for evaluating ethical content. The selection of these philosophies is justified because "These encompass most of the 'great' ideas for social survival, not just from the area of moral philosophy, but also from religion. Ideas of fairness, justice, contract, duty, consequence, greatest good and many others that come from these philosophies can be found in the Bible, the Koran, the writings of Buddha, and in other religions" (Reidenbach & Robin, 1990, p. 640).

MULTIDIMENSIONAL ETHICS MEASURE IN ACCOUNTING

Although, as noted earlier, much cross-cultural ethics accounting research has relied on a uni-dimensional rather than Multidimensional Ethics Measure, the Multidimensional Ethics Measure has been used in prior business research generally. For example, the Multidimensional Ethics Measure to examine how African American and white US university students differ in their evaluation of business ethics. In a subsequent study, Tsalikis and Nwachukwu (1991), used the Multidimensional Ethics Measure to study how American and Nigerian business students reacted to various scenarios dealing with bribery and extortion. These studies have shown the usefulness of the Multidimensional Ethics Measure, as compared to a uni-dimensional measure, in examining cross-cultural ethical judgements.

With respect to ethics research in accounting, Flory et al. (1992) were the first accounting researchers to use the Multidimensional Ethics Measure to study how and why accountants make certain ethical judgements. They provided evidence to show that the Moral Equity, Relativism and Contractualism dimensions were being implicitly drawn on by accountants in evaluating ethical issues in accounting. More importantly, they found that the scales for each dimension on each of the four scenarios used in their research, had high reliability coefficients (coefficient alpha ranged from 0.75 to 0.94, with an average of 0.86), that the content validity of the three-dimensional measure was high (R^2 ranged from 0.59 to 0.76), and that predictive validity ranged from 0.45 to 0.76. In addition, in each of the four scenarios used in the research, the Multidimensional Ethics Measure accounted for more "explained variance than univariate measures by 7 to 12 percentage points" (Flory et al., 1992, p. 296). Consequently, Flory et al. (1992) recommended the use of the Multidimensional Ethics Measure for future research on ethical judgements in accounting.

Cohen et al. (1993b) replicated and extended Reidenbach and Robin's (1988, 1990) marketing studies by examining the generalisability of the Multidimensional Ethics Measure from marketing to accounting. The respondents included local and international accounting students, and accounting academics in the US. Support was found for the use of the

Multidimensional Ethics Measure in accounting. In a subsequent study, Cohen et al. (1996a) examined a sample of 127 accountants from big-six firms in Canada to evaluate the usefulness and generalisability of the Multidimensional Ethics Measure within behavioural models of ethical decision-making. They found that Flory et al.'s (1992) factor structure of the three dimensions was robust to a change in sample characteristics (Canadian versus American, and Chartered Accountants versus Institute of Management Accountants) and scenarios. In terms of moral awareness, Canadian accountants were generally most sensitive to the Moral Equity and Relativisim dimensions, but in terms of ethical orientation, placed more importance on the Moral Equity and Contractualism dimensions.

CONTROLLING ERRORS IN MEASUREMENT: SOCIAL DESIRABILITY RESPONSE BIAS

In cross-cultural research, as in all research, systematic errors pose a serious threat. These are the errors that are introduced into the measurement by some factor which has persistent directional effects on the characteristic being measured, or the process of "measurement". SDRB is perhaps the most important systematic error that needs to be controlled in cross-cultural studies. The bias refers to the desire, at either a conscious or an unconscious level, to give a particular picture of oneself by the way one responds to questionnaire items (Watkins & Cheung, 1995, p. 490). SDRB is also described as maintaining a "holier than thou" ethical perception (Tyson, 1990, p. 715), and is a pervasive problem in behavioural ethics research (Rossi et al., 1983; Tyson, 1992).

SDRB has been found in studies of American managers (Baumhart, 1961), Hong Kong managers (McDonald & Zepp, 1988), South African managers (Pitt & Abratt, 1986), American marketing managers (Ferrel & Weaver, 1978), Harvard Business Review readers (Brenner & Molander, 1977), undergraduate American students (Tyson, 1990), auditors in the US, Japan and selected Latin American countries (Cohen et al., 1995) and among Canadian auditors (Cohen et al., 1996a). Evidence shows that individuals see themselves acting more ethically than "comparable others" when confronted with ethically uncertain work-related behaviours. SDRB stems from an individual's need to be seen to be conforming to societal norms. This conveys the notion that an individual's behaviour is more society oriented and less self-centred than is actually the case. This in turn, leads individuals to perceive peers as less ethical than themselves.

In an accounting context, the seriousness of this problem was shown in a study by Cohen et al. (1995), which examined ethical differences among auditors from selected Latin American countries, Japan and the US. On average, the study found that the American auditors demonstrated the highest bias, followed respectively by Latin American and Japanese auditors. However, the results were not consistent in the eight scenarios that included various ethical accounting issues. Thus the results of cultural influences on SDRB are inconclusive.

In another study, Cohen et al. (1996a) found the existence of SDRB among Canadian auditors in each of their eight scenarios relating to general business ethics. In addition, they found that those cases which were believed to be least ethical showed the highest bias. The study made some attempts to discuss the influence on SDRB. However, since the study was intra-country, the results were criticised because any reference to cultural differences can be misleading (Tsui, 1996).

One approach recommended to minimise the potential for self-reporting biases in business ethics research using scenarios is to use third-person rather than first-person reporting in the scenario (Ponemon & Gabhart, 1990; Arnold & Ponemon, 1991). The formulation of the scenario in the third-person is designed to free the individual respondent from the need to state his or her personal response or action in the scenario context, and, thereby, to free the person from the felt pressure to provide a socially desirable response.

This study uses the third-person approach in that each scenario poses the ethical situation for a third person and posits a decision or action taken by that person. The respondent is then asked to evaluate that person's decision or action on both the uni-dimensional and Multidimensional Ethics Measures. However, the study also goes further and seeks to measure the SDRB through asking two additional questions of respondents. The questions are: "If you were responsible for making the decision in the case (scenario), what is the probability that you would make the same decision", and "If your colleagues were responsible for making the decision in the case, what is the probability that they would make the same decision?" Responses were captured on a seven point Likert scale ranging from "highly probable" to "highly improbable". The differences in responses between these two questions are a measure of the SDRB (Tyson, 1992; Cohen et al., 1995, 1996a). Consequently, not only is an attempt made to measure SDRB in this study, but the use of the questions to measure it seeks to provide some insight into the possible relationship between SDRB and culture.

DISTRIBUTION AND COLLECTION OF QUESTIONNAIRES

Contact was made with senior partners from the big-five firms in Australia, India and Malaysia either directly by mail or through a colleague. Four of the big-five firms in Malaysia and three firms each in India and Australia participated in the study. Senior partners of the firms that participated were personally approached to explain the objectives and the relevant details of the survey questionnaires and the follow-up interviews. In all cases, the partners provided all necessary support and provided assurance that they would encourage their senior staff to complete the survey questionnaires as soon as possible. Survey questionnaires were randomly distributed by partners to respondents who were of the rank of supervisors or higher. This allowed for standardised distribution of the survey questionnaires.

It was important to ensure that all respondents received the same instruction and background information, and in the same format. To this end, a covering letter accompanied the questionnaire. The covering letter explained the purpose of the study and assured respondents that the questionnaire was anonymous and the information obtained would be kept confidential. It also instructed respondents that in a real work situation they would normally require more information than was available in the three scenarios, but for the purposes of the study, they were requested to make their decisions based on the limited information provided.

After completing the questionnaire, respondents were required to put it in the self-addressed envelope provided, to seal it, and leave it with their receptionist. These were then personally collected by the researcher or his colleagues. Partners of two firms in Australia wanted their staff to send the completed questionnaires directly to the researcher. Accordingly, respondents from those firms were directed to send their completed responses in the pre-paid, self-addressed envelopes. To allow differentiation between responses from these two firms, different distinguishing marks were made on the questionnaires distributed to each firm.[11] Importantly, both the methods of collection of completed questionnaire in the study assured respondents of the guarantee of anonymity and confidentiality.

PILOT STUDY

This section reports the results of the pilot study of the survey questionnaire. The pilot study was conducted in five stages. The first stage involved testing the questionnaire among academic accountants with expertise in the area of the study at a university in Australia. After incorporating their suggestions, the next stage was the administration of the revised questionnaire among four accounting academics who had extensive experience in professional accounting firms. After these two preliminary tests, the third stage was the pilot testing among 18 senior professional accountants working for two medium-sized firms in Sydney.[12] The fourth stage was the pilot testing among five professional accountants from India who were then working in Sydney, and among two accounting academics in Malaysia who had expertise in the area of the study. The fifth and final stage was obtaining feedback on the revised version of the questionnaire from two senior academic colleagues. The details of the pilot testing follow.

Stage One

Six accounting academics with expertise in the area of the study at a university in Australia were the subjects in the first stage of pilot testing. They were specifically asked to evaluate the accountants' decision-making questionnaire with the objective of improving its understandability and to comment on the realism of the three cases. They were also asked to complete the written questionnaire. Each academic was interviewed to gain further insight into their responses.

Several minor editorial changes were made as a result of the comments that were received. Additionally, two of the academics suggested that the use of polar reversal as a means of controlling a response set effect was confusing and that in the actual study subjects may find this irritating. Random errors of response effect, or response set, are caused by inattentiveness or disinterest on the part of respondents in the subject matter, or once gaining insight into the overall objective of an instrument, systematically giving the same response for the various items (Brownell, 1995, p. 49). Initially, to minimise this error, the polarity of the scales on the two questions related to the Contractualism dimension were reversed. Given the feedback from the two academics and taking into account that subjects for the main study will be senior professional accountants voluntarily participating in the study, it was decided not to use polar reversal to detect response set in the final version of the questionnaire.

The academics also stated that the ethical dilemmas facing the auditor-in-charge/internal auditors in the cases were realistic examples of practices that had been highlighted by the financial media. Overall, the academics believed that the questionnaire scored high on understandability.

More importantly, follow-up interviews revealed the usefulness of the Multidimensional Ethics Measures compared to asking a uni-dimensional question. Recall that the major reason for using the Multidimensional Ethics Measures was to understand the various ethical perspective(s) that is (are) invoked in making evaluations. The interviews revealed the importance of using this approach. That is, respondents believed that the Multidimensional Ethics Measures enabled them to examine the ethical issues from various perspectives. Hence, the Multidimensional Ethics Measures was seen to provide insight into why the respondents made certain judgements.

Stage Two

After making changes to the questionnaire from the feedback from stage one, in the second stage the questionnaire was pilot tested on four academics who had extensive experience in professional accounting firms. They were specifically asked to comment on the realism of the ethical dilemmas and to suggest ways of improving the understandability of the questionnaire.

Two of the respondents did not clearly understand the import of the instruction "Please evaluate (the action of the hypothetical actor)" which was used in each of the cases, being unsure of whose perspective they should be adopting in their evaluation. Therefore, the wording was changed to "How would you evaluate the action", and "Please indicate your evaluation", to emphasise the perspective required. Another suggestion was to improve the clarity of the question " ...what is the probability that you (the respondent) would make the same decision", to ensure that respondents were quite clear as to the meaning of "the same decision". To this end, the wording of the latter half of the question was modified so that it read "make the same decision as the subjects in the case".

Furthermore, and corroborating the opinion of the academics in stage one of the pilot, these respondents believed that the ethical dilemmas presented in the questionnaire were typical of ethical cases they were familiar with.

Stage Three: Descriptive Statistics

After the above preliminary pilot tests, the third stage involved an analysis of the results obtained from 18 senior professional accountants working for two medium-sized firms in Sydney. The descriptive statistics measured on a 7-point Likert scale are provided in Table 4.1. Table 4.1 shows the mean and standard deviation for all 11 items (dependent variables), for the single item

Table 4.1. Descriptive Statistics of the Pilot Test.

	Case One		Case Two		Case Three	
	Mean	SD	Mean	SD	Mean	SD
For all 11 items	5.31	1.23	4.91	1.11	5.40	1.32
Ethical (single item)	5.92	0.97	5.53	1.36	6.17	1.04
Multidimensional Ethics Measures (8 items)	5.28	1.26	4.83	1.38	5.39	1.32
Moral Equity Dimension	**5.54**	**1.18**	**5.32**	**1.16**	**5.71**	**1.26**
Fair	5.36	1.26	5.19	1.18	5.39	1.29
Just	5.41	1.22	5.03	1.27	5.83	1.09
Morally right	5.86	0.99	5.64	1.30	6.06	1.11
Acceptable to my family	5.53	1.27	5.42	1.24	5.55	1.54
Relativism Dimension	**4.61**	**1.33**	**4.17**	**1.45**	**4.83**	**1.41**
Culturally accept.	4.53	1.42	4.14	1.47	4.83	1.47
Traditionally accept.	4.69	1.27	4.19	1.55	4.83	1.43
Contractualism Dimension	**5.44**	**1.02**	**4.50**	**1.49**	**5.33**	**1.31**
Unwritten contract	5.42	1.03	4.53	1.44	5.33	1.19
Unspoken contract	5.47	1.03	4.47	1.56	5.33	1.56
You would make the same decision (single item)	5.52	0.98	5.14	1.45	5.33	1.49
Your colleagues would make the same decision (single item)	4.69	1.53	4.81	1.63	4.72	1.53

Note: Response scale ranged from 1 to 7 (where 1 refers to ethical/fair/just/highly probable etc. and 7 to unethical, unjust, highly improbable etc.).

"ethical" question, for the eight item Multidimensional Ethics Measure, and also for the total and the individual scores for each of the three dimensions of Moral Equity, Relativism and Contractualism. Recall that the Multidimensional Ethics Measure consists of eight bipolar scales divided into three dimensions. These are the Moral Equity dimension, which comprises four items, and Relativism and Contractualism dimensions, each comprising two items.

Table 4.1 also provides the scores on each of the single questions which measure the likelihood that respondents would make the same decision, and that their colleagues would make the same decision, as the actors in each of the three cases. The 7-point Likert scales for the ethical questions are anchored by one (ethical/fair/just/highly probable, etc.) and seven (unethical, unjust, highly improbable, etc.). Mean responses to "all items", the single-item "ethical" question, and to the total and individual components of each of the three dimensions are uniformly greater than the (3.5) mid-point on the scale. These results show that respondents have evaluated the actions of the actors as unethical, unfair, unjust, etc., in each of the three cases.

Table 4.2. Reliability Coefficients (Cronbach's alpha) for Each Dimension of the Multidimensional Ethics Measures on Each Case.

Dimension	Case Number		
	1	2	3
Moral Equity (4 items)	0.87	0.75	0.79
Relativism (2 items)	0.95	0.95	0.89
Contractualism (2 items)	1.00	0.99	1.00
All 8 items	0.88	0.89	0.89

Internal Consistency of Accountants' Decision-Making Questionnaire

The reliability of the Multidimensional Ethics Measures in the pilot test for accountants in Australia was obtained by using Cronbach's (1951) alpha which is derived from the average correlations, or covariances, between items within the scale. Alpha is "the mean of all possible split-half coefficients" (Cronbach, 1951, p. 331).

The results are presented in Table 4.2. Cronbach's alpha for eight dependent variables taken together to comprise the Multidimensional Ethics Measures for cases one, two and three are 0.88, 0.89 and 0.89 respectively. These coefficients, plus those for each of the three dimensions (also shown in Table 4.2) are well above the 0.7 level of acceptability for construct measurement as defined by Nunnally (1978, p. 245). The coefficients for each of the two-item Relativism and Contractualism dimensions are particularly high, given that a smaller number of scale items produce lower alpha coefficients (Nunnally, 1967; de Vaus, 1991).

These results also compare favourably with those of two other studies that have examined ethical issues in accounting using Multidimensional Ethics Measures. Flory et al. (1992, p. 294) reported alphas ranging from 0.75 for the Contractualism dimension to 0.94 for the Moral Equity dimension. Cohen et al. (1996a, p. 105) reported that reliability tests of the item scores in each factor indicated satisfactory (>0.6) Cronbach's alpha scores for all factors.

Stage Four: Pilot Testing Among Indian and Malaysian Accountants

After incorporating a few minor editorial changes suggested in the previous stage, the next step was pilot testing the questionnaire with five professional accountants from India currently working in Sydney and who had worked in Australia for less than three years, and with two accounting academics from a university in Malaysia with expertise in the area of the study.

Preliminary support for the directional expectations in the hypotheses was provided by a comparison of the results from the 18 Australian professional accountants in Sydney with those from the five professional accountants from India. The overall mean scores (and standard deviations) for the Indian accountants for all items were; case one 3.94 (1.11), case two 4.18 (1.30) and case three 4.53 (0.89), compared with 5.31 (1.23), 4.91 (1.11) and 5.40 (1.32) respectively for the Australian pilot sample. While no statistical testing is possible with these small pilot samples, nonetheless the surface differences and direction of differences between the two pilot samples lent support to the progression of the hypotheses in the main study.

The respondents from India and Malaysia in this stage of the pilot agreed with the proposition that the names of the companies and the actors in the cases should be changed to reflect what would be considered typically indigenous names in India and Malaysia. This is necessary because the purpose of this study is a comparative examination of indigenous culture's influence on judgements of professional accountants in each of the three countries. The failure to make this change is likely to introduce additional confounding variables in the study. That is, how a professional accountant in India or Malaysia evaluates the behaviour of an indigenous accountant may differ from his or her evaluation of an accountant from another culture. The origin of this difference may be traced to the process of colonisation of India and Malaysia by the British (Ross, 1961; Tripathi, 1990). Spitzer (1979, pp. 67–70) notes that the entire history of colonisation is based on the assumption of superiority of one culture over another and this has affected the way the indigenous people view westerners.[13] Consequently, in consultation with these respondents, the following changes were made to the company and actor names shown in the scenarios in the appendix. The scenarios in the appendix of this chapter refer to the Australian accountants' questionnaire.

In case one, Jackson Manufacturing was changed to Mumbai Manufacturing Ltd, and to Kuala Lumpur Manufacturing Ltd, respectively in India and Malaysia. In case two, Steve English is changed to Ramesh Arora in India, and to Hai Yap in Malaysia. Bossix Ltd is changed to Taj Ltd in India and to Star Ltd in Malaysia. Henry Grant is changed to Shashi Singh in India and to Chew Sun in Malaysia. R.J. Whitman is changed to R.J. Sinha, and R.J. Teoh in India and Malaysia respectively. In case three, Tim is changed to Mahendra and Chi Liang, and ABC plant changed to Jaipur plant and Jahore plant respectively in India and Malaysia.

The Indian and Malaysian respondents also stated that the cases were realistic depictions of some of the ethical problems facing accountants in their respective countries. They further believed that the questionnaire rated high on understandability.

Stage Five

After making the above changes in the names, the fifth and the final stage was obtaining feedback from the two senior academic colleagues. A few editorial changes were suggested by the colleagues and these were incorporated in the research instrument.

INTERVIEWS WITH ACADEMICS

It was shown in Chapter 2 that cross-cultural accounting research has been largely based on the five-dimensional cultural model, and that there is a need to enhance the quality of research by providing greater insight into the depth, richness and complexity of cultural similarities and differences. Chapter 3 provided additional insight into the Australian, Indian and Chinese Malaysian cultures by complementing the five-dimensional cultural model with relevant historical, sociological and psychological literatures.

To provide additional understanding of the influence of culture on professional judgements, this study was extended to include interviews with academics with a research interest in culture, in each of the three countries.[14] University academics were selected because they were considered to possess expert knowledge about their cultures. The university academics chosen for interviews were either known to the researcher or were recommended by the researcher's colleagues or acquaintances. Most of the questions were aimed at identifying the core cultural values in Australia, India and Malaysia, as well as their likely impact on making decisions about what is considered ethical or unethical in those nations. Indian and Malaysian academics did not want their interviews to be recorded on a cassette, while Australian academics were happy to be tape-recorded. The structured interview questions were provided to academics prior to the interviews to enable them to think about the issues and for them to make notes in the space provided next to the questions. During the interviews, clarification and further elaboration was sought and relevant notes were taken. This approach was used for data collection from university academics from all three nations.

Six questions were asked. These are presented below followed by a discussion of the reasons for asking each question.

1. What attributes of your organisational culture are important and valued by you? That is, aspects of your organisational culture that are viewed positively by you, and that facilitate both your work and your motivation to work harder?
2. What attributes of your organisational culture are *not* important and *not* valued by you? That is, aspects of your organisational culture that are viewed negatively by you, and that hinder your work and do not motivate you to work harder?
3. What attributes of Australian (Indian, Chinese Malaysian) culture do you value and consider important in your work and also in your personal life?
4. What attributes of Australian (Indian, Chinese Malaysian) culture do you consider to have a negative influence in your work and also in your personal life?
5. In making a decision about what is ethical/unethical, just/unjust, right/wrong, what importance do you think your colleagues generally place on the influence of: their own judgement, their family, their close relatives, their distant relatives, their superior officers, their subordinates and their friends?[15]
6. What are some of the factors that would make your colleagues compromise their judgements of what is ethical or unethical?

Since 14 of the 20 questions in Hofstede's Values Survey Module are on aspects related to organisational culture, it was considered appropriate that further information on these issues be obtained. Questions one and two in the interview questions were included to complement the cultural measures obtained from Hofstede's Values Survey Module (1994).

The objectives of questions three and four were to provide insight into aspects of Australian, Indian and Chinese Malaysian cultures, which were either considered important and valued, or were viewed negatively. These questions were designed to complement Hofstede's dimensions and the cross-cultural literature generally.

The objective of question five was to establish the extent to which individuals in India, Malaysia and Australia are influenced by other people in making an ethical judgement (the relevance of this issue was discussed earlier). The purpose of question six was to compare perceived national differences on the various factors that would make individuals compromise their ethical judgements. In order to minimise any SDRB, questions five and six required university academics to evaluate their colleagues' action rather than their own. Note that interviews with university academics are not part of the hypothesis testing, but has the purpose of supporting the theoretical arguments and expectations.

CHAPTER SUMMARY

This chapter described the research method used in the study. Important features of the research design are summarised in Fig. 4.1.

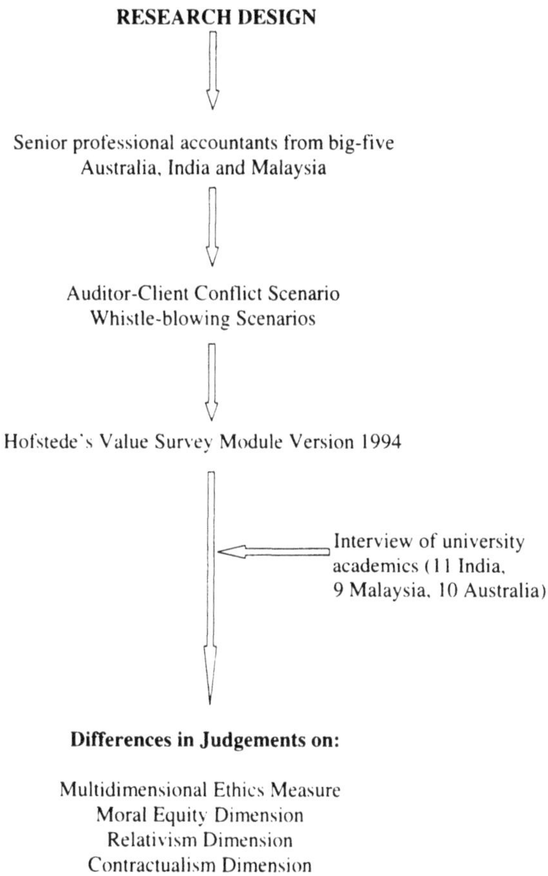

Fig. 4.1. Measurement of Social Desirability Response Bias.

APPENDIX I

Jackson Manufacturing Ltd is a large publicly owned producer of electronic equipment used in hospitals and medical laboratories.

In the current year's audit, a dispute has arisen between the auditor-in-charge and the management of Jackson over the materiality of certain unrecorded liabilities discovered during the audit. Jackson's Chief Financial Officer argues that the total amount of unrecorded liabilities is immaterial and therefore it is unnecessary to make adjusting entries in the financial statements. Jackson's management believes that it should know as well as anyone what financial statement readers would or would not deem to be material. The auditor-in-charge feels that the amount is material and that the financial statements should be adjusted accordingly.

But the auditor-in-charge also has to consider the fact that Jackson Manufacturing is an important client contributing significantly to the total audit revenue of the firm. Furthermore, the current audit market is characterised by a large number of auditing firms that are aggressively pursuing expansion programmes.

After lengthy discussion with Jackson's management, the auditor-n-charge decides that the unrecorded liabilities will be ignored for purposes of the financial statements as well as the auditor's report.

How would you evaluate the decision made by the auditor-in-charge of Jackson Manufacturing Ltd? Please indicate your evaluation by marking a **[X]** on a specific point on each of the following scales:

(Q1)	ETHICAL	___:___:___:___:___	UNETHICAL
(Q2)	FAIR	___:___:___:___:___	UNFAIR
(Q3)	JUST	___:___:___:___:___	UNJUST
(Q4)	MORALLY RIGHT	___:___:___:___:___	NOT MORALLY RIGHT
(Q5)	ACCEPTABLE TO MY FAMILY	___:___:___:___:___	UNACCEPTABLE TO MY FAMILY
(Q6)	CULTURALLY ACCEPTABLE	___:___:___:___:___	CULTURALLY UNACCEPTABLE
(Q7)	TRADITIONALLY ACCEPTABLE	___:___:___:___:___	TRADITIONALLY UNACCEPTABLE
(Q8)	DOES NOT VIOLATE AN UNWRITTEN SOCIAL CONTRACT	___:___:___:___:___	VIOLATES AN UNWRITTEN SOCIAL CONTRACT
(Q9)	DOES NOT VIOLATE AN UNSPOKEN SOCIAL CONTRACT	___:___:___:___:___	VIOLATES AN UNSPOKEN SOCIAL CONTRACT

(Q10) If you were responsible for making the decision in the above case, what is the probability that you would make the same decision as Steve?

HIGHLY PROBABLE ___:___:___:___:___ HIGHLY IMPROBABLE

(Q11) If your colleagues were responsible for making the decision in the above case, what is the probability that they would make the same decision as Steve?

HIGHLY PROBABLE ___:___:___:___:___ HIGHLY IMPROBABLE

Scenario Two

Steve English is an internal audit supervisor in BOSSIX Ltd., a large chemical company in Sydney. One routine part of Steve's job is reviewing expense accounts. When Henry Grant's expense reimbursement came to the top of the pile, Steve was intrigued as he knew that as manager of marketing, Grant has quite a reputation as a big spender. His interest quickly turned to consternation as he found reimbursement requests for items such as a moderately expensive necklace, and a bill for Mrs Grant's personal secretary, with no real justification. He knew these items were not reimbursable according to company policy.

He decided to ask Grant about them. Grant was clearly upset about the inquiry and responded, "See R.J. Whitman's signature on those requests. What other document do you need? He knows I'm responsible for the success we have had in developing the Australian market".

On his way back to his office, Steve realised that the general manager, R.J. Whitman, was Grant's close friend and that Steve's promotion chances could be greatly reduced if he questioned the general manager's authority. Should Steve report the questionable activity to the next higher level of management, the chairperson of the board of directors of the company?

After thinking about the issue for a few days, Steve decided not to report the matter to the chairperson of the board.

How would you evaluate Steve's decision? Please indicate your evaluation of Steve's decision by marking a cross **[X]** on a specific point on each of the following scales:

(Q1)	ETHICAL	____:____:____:____:____	UNETHICAL
(Q2)	FAIR	____:____:____:____:____	UNFAIR
(Q3)	JUST	____:____:____:____:____	UNJUST
(Q4)	MORALLY RIGHT	____:____:____:____:____	NOT MORALLY RIGHT
(Q5)	ACCEPTABLE TO MY FAMILY	____:____:____:____:____	UNACCEPTABLE TO MY FAMILY
(Q6)	CULTURALLY ACCEPTABLE	____:____:____:____:____	CULTURALLY UNACCEPTABLE
(Q7)	TRADITIONALLY ACCEPTABLE	____:____:____:____:____	TRADITIONALLY UNACCEPTABLE
(Q8)	DOES NOT VIOLATE AN UNWRITTEN SOCIAL CONTRACT	____:____:____:____:____	VIOLATES AN UNWRITTEN SOCIAL CONTRACT
(Q9)	DOES NOT VIOLATE AN UNSPOKEN SOCIAL CONTRACT	____:____:____:____:____	VIOLATES AN UNSPOKEN SOCIAL CONTRACT

(Q10) If you were responsible for making the decision in the above case, what is the probability that you would make the same decision as Steve?
HIGHLY PROBABLE ____:____:____:____:____ HIGHLY IMPROBABLE

(Q11) If your colleagues were responsible for making the decision in the above case, what is the probability that they would make the same decision as Steve?
HIGHLY PROBABLE ____:____:____:____:____ HIGHLY IMPROBABLE

Scenario Three

Tim has been an internal auditor for 7 years with an organisation that is a primary contractor for the Australian Government. Tim recently completed an audit of a subsidiary business unit (ABC plant), which is completing large contracts for various government agencies. The billings of the subsidiary have been audited previously and no major problems were detected. During the present audit, Tim discovered, within the subsidiary's billing system, a series of bogus (inflated or falsified) invoices to customers that had already been paid. Tim reported this finding to the director of internal audit. The director said that he would report it to authorities within the company. After a few days, the director told Tim, "Forget about it". Tim argued that further action should be taken but the director shouted, "If you pursue this, you will be fired".

Tim is aware that, with his qualifications, he is not likely to find another such well-paid position in the current economic climate. After thinking about this for a few days, Tim decided not to report the matter to the next higher level of management.

How would you evaluate Tim's decision? Please indicate your evaluation of Tim's decision by marking a cross **[X]** on a specific point on each of the following scales:

(Q1)	ETHICAL	____:____:____:____:____	UNETHICAL
(Q2)	FAIR	____:____:____:____:____	UNFAIR
(Q3)	JUST	____:____:____:____:____	UNJUST
(Q4)	MORALLY RIGHT	____:____:____:____:____	NOT MORALLY RIGHT
(Q5)	ACCEPTABLE TO MY FAMILY	____:____:____:____:____	UNACCEPTABLE TO MY FAMILY
(Q6)	CULTURALLY ACCEPTABLE	____:____:____:____:____	CULTURALLY UNACCEPTABLE
(Q7)	TRADITIONALLY ACCEPTABLE	____:____:____:____:____	TRADITIONALLY UNACCEPTABLE
(Q8)	DOES NOT VIOLATE AN UNWRITTEN SOCIAL CONTRACT	____:____:____:____:____	VIOLATES AN UNWRITTEN SOCIAL CONTRACT

(Q9) DOES NOT VIOLATE AN UNSPOKEN SOCIAL CONTRACT ____:____:____:____:____ VIOLATES AN UNSPOKEN SOCIAL CONTRACT

(Q10) If you were responsible for making the decision in the above case, what is the probability that you would make the same decision as Tim?

HIGHLY PROBABLE ____:____:____:____:____ HIGHLY IMPROBABLE

(Q11) If your colleagues were responsible for making the decision in the above case, what is the probability that they would make the same decision as Tim?

HIGHLY PROBABLE ____:____:____:____:____ HIGHLY IMPROBABLE

CHAPTER 5
RESULTS: CULTURAL VALUES

To gain insight into the cultural values of senior professional accountants from Australia, India and Malaysia and to ensure that the respondent samples matched the cultural characteristics underlying theory development in Chapter 2, this study used the updated version of Hofstede's Values Survey Module (1994) to calculate the cultural dimensions of Power Distance, Individualism and Long-term Orientation for the sample of 72, 84 and 92 respondents from Australia, India and Malaysia, respectively. Recall that Chapter 3 discussed the location of Australia, India and Malaysia on each of Hofstede's cultural dimensions of Power Distance, Individualism and Long-term Orientation, and classified Indians and Chinese Malaysians in one cluster (comprising large Power Distance, low Individualism and Long-term Orientation), and Australians in another cluster (comprising small Power Distance, high Individualism and Short-term Orientation). Additionally, interviews were conducted with 11 university academics in India, 9 in Malaysia and 10 in Australia, with an interest in culture. These latter interviews were designed to supplement relevant psychological, sociological and historical literatures for the three countries, and thereby provide a more holistic and richer understanding of the cultural values in each of the three countries under examination.

This chapter is organised into two sections. The first section discusses the results with respect to the calculation of the cultural indices of Power Distance, Individualism and Long-term Orientation of the three countries based on senior professional accountants' responses to Hofstede's Values Survey Module (1994). The next section summarises the results of the interviews with university academics with an interest in culture in each of the three countries. This section then goes on to show that the major findings from the structured interviews with academics in each of the three countries are generally consistent with the cultural differences between Australians in one cluster, and Indians and Chinese Malaysians in another cluster, presented in the earlier chapters.

CULTURAL DIMENSION OF POWER DISTANCE

The calculation of the Power Distance index for each of the three countries under examination is based on the responses to Questions 3, 6, 14 and 17 of the survey questionnaire. The Power Distance index calculation is based on the following formula (Values Survey Module Manual, 1994, p. 3):

$$\text{Power Distance Index} = -35\,M(Q3) + 35\,M(Q6) + 25\,M(Q14) - 20\,M(Q17) - 20$$

M(Q3) in the above formula is the mean score for Question 3, M(Q6) the mean for Question 6, and so on. The details of the specific questions are as follows.

The first two questions in this formula required respondents to choose an ideal job and then to evaluate how important it would be to them to "have a good working relationship with your direct supervisor" (question 3), and "be consulted by your direct superior in his/her decisions" (question 6). These two questions were anchored by 1 (of utmost importance) and 5 (of very little or no importance). Question 14 asked respondents, "How frequently, in your experience, are subordinates afraid to express disagreement with their superiors?" This question was anchored by 1 (very seldom) and 5 (very frequently). Question 17 asked respondents whether they agreed or disagreed with the statement that "An organisation structure in which certain subordinates have two bosses should be avoided at all cost". This question was anchored by 1 (strongly agree) and 5 (strongly disagree).

The Power Distance indices calculated from the present samples for Australia, India and Malaysia are shown in Table 5.1. This table also compares the indices obtained in this study with those calculated by Hofstede (1980). A lower index suggests a smaller Power Distance society. Note that the index for Australia in this study is a negative 23. Also note that the formulae for calculating the cultural dimensions based on Hofstede's Values Survey Module (1994) are different to that used by Hofstede (1980) and that there are considerable differences between the questions used in the two formulae. Hofstede (1994b, p. 7) clarified that "Indexes calculated with the old and

Table 5.1. Power Distance Indices.

Country	Present Sample	Hofstede's (1980, 1983a)
Australia	−23	36
India	24	77
Malaysia	52	104

new formulas are not necessarily the same! However, they should produce approximately the same score differences between countries". The Power Distance indices calculated from the present sample are in the same direction as those of Hofstede (1980), and the absolute differences between them are approximately the same as the differences in Hofstede (1980).[1]

To test for significant differences between the three pairs of countries with respect to the indices obtained in this study, one-way analysis of variance (ANOVA) was used. The results suggested that there were significant differences ($p = 0.0000$) among respondents from Australia, India and Malaysia with respect to their Power Distance indices. To follow-up differences between each of the three pairs of countries, Tukey's HSD and Scheffe's tests were used. The results from these tests showed significant differences between each of the three pairs of countries under examination. Additionally, nonparametric Kruskal–Wallis one-way ANOVA also confirmed differences between the countries ($p = 0.0000$), and follow-up Mann–Whitney U tests showed results consistent with those from Tukey's HSD and Scheffe's tests (Australia and India, $z = -4.6512$, 2-tailed $p = 0.0000$; Australia and Malaysia, $z = -7.2595$, 2-tailed $p = 0.0000$; India and Malaysia, $z = -3.9966$, 2-tailed $p = 0.0001$).

The results from this study support that there are significant differences in the Power Distance indices between Australian professional accountants on the one hand, and Chinese Malaysians and Indians, on the other. Taking the results from this study and their differences in conjunction with Hofstede's (1980) clustering of 50 countries, there is support for Australia being seen to lie in the small Power Distance, and India and Malaysia in the large Power Distance clusters of countries generally. Specifically, the results suggest that Chinese Malaysian and Indian respondents are drawn from the cluster comprising large Power Distance societies, and Australians from the cluster comprising small Power Distance societies.

CULTURAL DIMENSION OF INDIVIDUALISM

The calculation of the Individualism index for each country is based on the responses to Questions 1, 2, 4 and 8 of the survey questionnaire. The calculation is based on the following formula (Values Survey Module Manual, 1994, p. 3):

$$\text{Individualism index} = -50\,M(Q1) + 30\,M(Q2) + 20\,M(Q4) - 25\,M(Q8) + 130$$

M(Q1) in the above formula is the mean score for Question 3, and so on. The details of the specific questions are as follows.

The four questions in this formula require respondents to choose an ideal job and then to evaluate how important it would be to them to "have sufficient time left for your personal or family life" (question 1); "have good physical working conditions (good ventilation and lighting, adequate work space, etc.)" (question 2); "have security of employment" (question 4); and "have an element of variety and adventure in the job" (question 8). These four questions were anchored by 1 (of utmost importance) and 5 (of very little or no importance).

The Individualism indices calculated from the present samples for Australia, India and Malaysia are shown in Table 5.2. This table also compares the indices obtained in the current study with the indices calculated by Hofstede (1980). A larger index suggests a higher Individualism society. Again, note that the indices in this study are not directly comparable with Hofstede's (1980) indices given differences between the formulae, including differences in the questions on which the formulae are based.

The Individualism indices calculated from the present sample are in the same direction as those of Hofstede (1980). Additionally, the absolute difference in indices between Australia and India are approximately the same for both the current study and those calculated by Hofstede (42 in this study and 47 in Hofstede's study). However, the absolute difference between Australia and Malaysia and between India and Malaysia was higher in Hofstede's (1980) study (45 between Australia and Malaysia and 3 between India and Malaysia in this study, compared with 64 and 17, respectively, in Hofstede's study).[2]

To test for significant differences between the three pairs of countries with respect to the indices obtained in the current study, one-way ANOVA was used. The results suggested that there were significant differences ($p = 0.0000$) among respondents from Australia, India and Malaysia with respect to the Individualism indices. To follow-up differences between each of the three pairs of countries, Tukey's HSD and Scheffe's tests were used. The results from these follow-up tests showed that there was a significant

Table 5.2. Individualism Indices.

Country	Present Sample	Hofstede (1980, 1983a)
Australia	125	90
India	83	43
Malaysia	80	26

difference between Australia and India, and between Australia and Malaysia, but not between India and Malaysia. Nonparametric Kruskal–Wallis one-way ANOVA also confirmed differences between the countries ($p = 0.0000$), and follow-up Mann–Whitney U tests showed results consistent with those from Tukey's HSD and Scheffe's tests (Australia and India, $z = -4.7583$, 2-tailed $p = 0.0000$; Australia and Malaysia, $z = -5.0439$, 2-tailed $p = 0.0000$).

The results from this study with respect to the Individualism indices may be viewed as broadly consistent with those from Hofstede (1980). These results support that there are significant differences in the Individualism indices between Australian professional accountants on the one hand, and Chinese Malaysians and Indians, on the other. Specifically, the results support that Malaysian and Indian respondents are drawn from the cluster comprising low Individualism societies, and Australians from the cluster comprising high Individualism societies.[3]

CULTURAL DIMENSION OF LONG-TERM ORIENTATION

The calculation of the Long-term Orientation index for each country was based on the responses to Questions 9, 10, 11 and 12 of the survey questionnaire. The calculation is based on the following formula (Values Survey Module Manual, 1994, p. 4):

$$\text{Long-term Orientation index} = +45\,\text{M(Q9)} - 30\,\text{M(Q10)} - 35\,\text{M(Q11)} + 15\,\text{M(Q12)} + 67$$

M(Q9) in the above formula is the mean score for Question 9, and so on. The details of the specific questions are as follows.

The four questions in this formula asked respondents, "In your private life, how important is each of the following to you?": "personal steadiness and stability" (question 9); "thrift" (question 10); "persistence" (question 11) and "respect for tradition" (question 12). These four questions were anchored by 1 (of utmost importance) and 5 (of very little or no importance).

The Long-term Orientation indices calculated from the present samples are Australia (43), India (46) and Malaysia (39).[4] Hofstede (1994b, p. 5) further explained that "The index will normally have a value between 0 (very short-term oriented) and 100 (very long-term oriented)".

Results from one-way ANOVA and Kruskal–Wallis one-way ANOVA showed that there were no differences between any of the three pairs of countries under examination. That is, results from this study suggest that Hofstede's Values Survey Module (1994) failed to differentiate between professional accountants from Australia, India and Malaysia on the cultural dimension of Long-term Orientation.

Moreover, another study (Lee, 1997), which examined cross-cultural differences with respect to various issues related to managerial performance among middle level managers in manufacturing organisations in Australia and Singapore, also failed to find the predicted results.[5] Lee (1997, p. 22) obtained an index of 32 for Singaporean respondents and 44 for Australian respondents. Lee's (1997) findings are consistent with the results from this study (and contrary to the theoretically predicted results), which show that Australian respondents scored slightly higher on Long-term Orientation index (43) compared to Chinese Malaysians (39).[6]

Based on the above findings, it is suggested that additional research needs to be done to validate Hofstede's Values Survey Module (1994) with respect to calculation of the Long-term Orientation index. Although the Value Survey Module (1994) did not show differences between the three countries on the Long-term Orientation index, the psychological, sociological and historical literatures (these were discussed in Chapter 3), and the interviews with university academics discussed in the next section, suggest that differences do exist.

ADDITIONAL INSIGHT INTO CULTURE: INTERVIEWS WITH ACADEMICS

This study adopted three approaches to provide greater insight into the depth, richness and complexity of cultural similarities and differences among the three countries under examination.

First, recall that Chapter 3 provided reasons for selecting Hofstede's cultural dimensions of Power Distance, Individualism and Long-term Orientation, and for the exclusion of the Uncertainty Avoidance and Masculinity dimensions in the theory development and hypotheses formulation. The results of this study based on Hofstede's Values Survey Module (1994) confirmed the location of the three countries with respect to Power Distance and Individualism dimensions, however, the results failed to distinguish the three countries under examination on the Long-term Orientation dimension.

Second, rather than solely relying on Hofstede's cultural dimensions in theory development and hypotheses formulation, recall that the approach adopted in this study provided insight into the specific nature of cultural dimensions that are applicable to Chinese Malaysians and Indians by drawing on the relevant features of Confucianism and Hinduism, respectively. Additionally, relevant historical and sociological literatures were summarised to provide insight into those aspects of Australian culture that are particularly applicable to the issues examined in the current study. Based on this more holistic and richer insight, the study drew out the various features of cultural differences between Indians and Chinese Malaysians in one cluster and Australians in another cluster, to formulate hypotheses on auditor–client conflict resolution, and whistle-blowing as an internal control mechanism.

The final approach to providing insight into the influence of culture on judgements of professional accountants in the three countries was the inclusion of structured interviews with university academics who had an interest in culture. Interviews were conducted with 11 university academics in India, 9 in Malaysia and 10 in Australia. Recall from Chapter 4 that the structured interview questions were provided to academics prior to the interviews to enable them to think about the issues and for them to make notes in the space provided next to the questions. During the interviews, clarification and further elaboration was sought and relevant notes were taken.

The coding system used in the study to analyse the data collected from the interviews with university academics was based on finding the total frequency distribution of respondents who had suggested a particular issue or concept recorded in the interview notes. For example, if five of the 11 academics from India suggested the importance of "Good working relationship with superior officers", then this aspect of their organisational culture would have a frequency of five. In cases where classifying issues or concepts from the interview notes were not clear, another academic's opinion was sought to verify the accuracy of the classification.[7]

The objective of using this approach for analysing the interview data was to enable the findings from the interviews to be arranged hierarchically in order of their importance as proxied by their frequency of appearance in the interviews. Lachman, Nedd, and Hinings (1995, p. 168) provide theoretical support for this approach in determining relative importance of values in a society or an organisation, "Within a culture, values are organised in a hierarchy or relative order of priority. Values higher in the hierarchy are more important, more enduring or resistant to change, are highly accepted and agreed upon, and hence are more involved in social control than those lower on the hierarchy".

This ordering of interview findings in terms of their relative importance is expected to complement the psychological, sociological and historical literature for each of the three countries. This literature was presented in Chapter 3 and is relied on in this study.

Summaries of the major findings from the interviews with academics in each of the three countries are discussed in turn. The discussion first identifies aspects of organisational culture that the interviewees saw as positive, and then those aspects seen as negative. Following that, positive and negative aspects of national culture are discussed.[8]

ASPECTS OF ORGANISATIONAL CULTURE VIEWED POSITIVELY

Recall from Chapter 4 that this study pursued the issue of culture at two levels, one the national level as the interviewees observed it, and two, the organisational level as it impacted on the interviewees.

The first question asked the academics, "What attributes of your organisation culture are important and valued by you? That is, aspects of your organisational culture that are viewed positively by you, and that facilitate both your work and your motivation to work harder?"

In order of their relative importance, Indian, Malaysian and Australian academics, respectively, suggested that the following aspects of their organisational culture were important and valued by them. The numbers shown in brackets refer to the frequency distribution of respondents who had suggested that particular issue.

India (11 Interviewees)

The existence of good working relationships with their superior officers (6); having superiors who were interested in their welfare (5);[9] the profession is valued by the society and has high status (4); good physical working conditions (3); flexibility of working hours and the freedom to work in an area of one's interest (3); harmonious relationships within the organisation (3); organisational goals and expectations are clearly defined (2); satisfaction of making a positive contribution to society (2) and organisation has a positive attitude towards innovation (2).

Malaysia (9 Interviewees)

Recall that Chapter 3 of this study discussed the long tradition in Malaysia of anti-Chinese legal discrimination. It was also suggested that the Chinese community in Malaysia remain concerned about their future in the country and see themselves as a besieged minority, surviving by their wits and especially by their hard work. Therefore, it was not surprising that most of the Chinese academics approached were reluctant to be interviewed.[10] Six of the nine academics interviewed in Malaysia were of Chinese background, two of Indian background and one a Malay.[11]

Six of the nine academics in Malaysia initially suggested that they found it rather difficult to identify positive aspects of their organisational culture because of the widespread discrimination against non-Malay staff. However, when pressed further, the following aspects of their organisational culture were considered important and valued by them: flexibility of working hours and the freedom to work in an area of one's interest (4); allows time to attend to personal and family matters (2) and enables them to complete their PhD (2).

Australia (10 Interviewees)

Flexibility of working hours and the freedom to work in an area of one's interest (8); absence of strict hierarchy (6); openness in decision making (workplace democracy) (5); sense of collegiality based on participation and individual responsibility (5) and reward for excellence linked to individual initiative and responsibility (2).

ASPECTS OF ORGANISATIONAL CULTURE VIEWED NEGATIVELY

The second question asked academics, "What attributes of your organisation culture are not important, and not valued by you? That is, aspects of your organisational culture that are viewed negatively by you, and that hinder your work and do not motivate you to work harder?"

In order of their relative importance measured by frequency of mention in the interviews, Indian, Malaysian and Australian academics, respectively, suggested that the following aspects of their organisational culture were not valued and were viewed negatively by them. The numbers shown in brackets refer to the frequency distribution of respondents who had suggested that particular issue.

India

Abuse of power and authority by superiors was identified as the most serious problem facing Indian academics. The various subsets of this problem include nepotism and cronyism (8), and use of caste as a means to provide special favours and promotions (3). Another negative aspect of their organisation cultures related to the first was employees "who would bend over backwards" to please their superiors (5). Other problems included their inability to question superiors' actions and decisions (4); communication systems were not adequate and important information was not disclosed to all those affected (4); appraisal system was inadequate and unfair (3); "orthodox mentality" of decision makers (2); excessive conflict (2); organisational objectives were not clear (2); no motivation to work harder (2); political interference (2) and superiors taking credit for respondents' contributions (2).

Malaysia

Because of racial discrimination, respondents' contributions were often not recognised, promotions were based on ethnicity, and "meritocracy" applied only to non-Malays (8); autocratic management decisions (7); greater focus and forced promotion of indigenous language (Bahasa Malaysia and not English) for all ethnic groups (4);[12] excessive administration (4) and indirect pressure to pass Malay students in examinations even when they do not meet the standard criteria (2).

Australia

Rules of accountability differ for "top management and workers" (5); lack of communication by management and secrecy in decision making (3); abuse of privileges by management (2); patriarchal structure (1); excessive administration (1); central bureaucracy and its influence in academic work (1); discriminatory attitude towards people of non-Anglo Saxon background (1) and "invisible and masked centres of power" (1).[13]

ASPECTS OF NATIONAL CULTURE VIEWED POSITIVELY

The next question asked academics, "What attributes of Australian (Indian or Chinese) (national) culture do you value and consider important in your work (organisational culture) and also in your personal life?"[14]

The following aspects of their (national) culture were considered important and valued by respondents in each of the three nations. The numbers shown in brackets refer to the frequency distribution of respondents who had suggested that particular issue.

India

Commitment to work and fulfilling ones "duty" to his or her organisation (7); high regard for senior citizens and "elders"[15] and affection for the younger generation (5); respect for seniors in organisations (5); importance placed on the family and the extended family (4);[16] greater focus on maintaining good interpersonal relationships and team work (4); not as materialistic as the West (3); Hinduism is the greatest asset in India (3); academic excellence is valued and children pushed to work harder (2) and belief in reincarnation is important because it provides "encouragement for doing good things with the hope of getting prizes in next birth" (2).

Malaysia

In order of their relative importance, Malaysian academics suggested that they valued the following aspects of Chinese culture:

Importance placed on the family, the extended family and the social network (8); importance placed on academic excellence and education (8); sincerity and dedication to work and the vision to achieve (7); respect for elders, authority and superiors (7); mutual support within the family and the extended family (6);[17] unlike Islam, religious values are not dogmatic and fundamentalist (5); importance placed on harmony within the family (3).

Australia

In order of their relative importance, Australian academics suggested that they valued the following aspects of the Australian culture:

Multiculturalism and generally tolerant attitude (6); sense of "fair go for all" (5); egalitarianism and collegiality (5); freedom and democracy – "the ability to do and be what you want" (4);[18] "down to earth, relaxed attitude" (2); less emphasis on formality (2) and the importance of leisure time (2).

ASPECTS OF NATIONAL CULTURE VIEWED NEGATIVELY

The next question asked academics, "What attributes of Australian (Indian or Chinese) culture do you consider to have a negative influence in your work and also in your personal life?"

The following aspects of culture were raised in this context. The numbers shown in brackets refer to the frequency distribution of respondents who had suggested that particular issue.

India

Traditional beliefs (such as blaming ones "destiny or Karma") which hinder progress and innovations (7); problems arising from Hinduism's focus on caste (5); "fanaticism in following wrong principles under the name of religion" (3); discrimination based on gender (3);[19] lack of focus on efficiency and effectiveness (3); problems with effective management of time (3) and excessive respect for owners and seniors in enterprises (2).

Malaysia

In order of their relative importance, Malaysian academics suggested that they did not value the following aspects of Chinese culture:

Too much emphasis is placed on materialism and success (6); focus and concern for hard work and education has worked against the Chinese (4); Chinese in Malaysia have been too submissive and this has resulted in greater discrimination against them (4); excessive family obligations (3) and Chinese distrust other ethnic groups and tend to confine their socialising only within themselves (2).

Australia

In order of their relative importance, Australian academics suggested that they did not value the following aspects of Australian culture:

Education is not highly valued (compared with the Chinese culture) (4); "Tall poppy syndrome" applies if one is too successful[20] (3); Still too insular in thinking, "not yet the total commitment to think globally" (3); lessening of tolerance of diversity and dissent (3); more recently, the "work is everything mentality, and associated economic rationality, cost-cutting, dollar-centredness of all things" (2); too much of "she'll be right" mentality (2) and "discriminatory attitude of the many white Australians towards people of non-white backgrounds" (2).

SUMMARY OF THE MAJOR FINDINGS BASED ON INTERVIEWS WITH ACADEMICS

The major findings from the structured interviews with academics in each of the three countries are generally consistent with the cultural differences between Australians in one cluster, and Indians and Chinese Malaysians in another cluster, presented in the earlier chapters. A brief discussion to show this consistency follows.

With respect to both the positive and negative aspects of Indian national and organisational cultures, the findings based on interviews suggest the importance placed in that culture on having good working relationship with superiors who were interested in their welfare ("management by affectionate domination"). Additionally, the interviews revealed the higher value placed on one's family, the extended family, the caste system, and societal and superiors' expectation. Moreover, "duty" to one's organisation and respect for seniors in organisations and "elders" in the society, featured prominently in the interviews. Overall, the interview findings suggest that having hierarchical, harmonious relationships within organisations and society is one of the core cultural values in Indian culture.

These findings are consistent with the discussion on Indian culture presented in Chapter 3, which suggested that the traditional view of work in India is of a "duty", which should be performed either in the family or at one's workplace. Additionally, the interview findings are also consistent with the earlier explanation that Indians prefer personalised relationships based on strict rules, which govern superior and subordinate relationships. The findings from interviews with Indian academics are also compatible with the earlier suggestion that the avoidance of conflict and maintenance of hierarchical equilibrium are the cardinal rules in Indian society.

With respect to the findings from interviews with Malaysian academics, the important aspects of Malaysian Chinese culture identified were: the emphasis placed on the family, the extended family and the social network. Additionally, sincerity and dedication to work, and respect for elders, authority and superiors also featured prominently. Again, these values are compatible with the earlier discussion on theory development and hypotheses formulation which suggested the importance placed in Confucianism on an authoritarian family, one's superiors and the "cultural concern for harmony-within-hierarchy" (Bond & Hwang, 1986, p. 213).[21]

With respect to the findings from interviews with Australian academics, the important aspects of their culture identified in this chapter are also consistent with the earlier discussion presented in Chapter 3. In particular, two core

Australian cultural values emerge from the interview findings: first, the importance placed in Australia on the development of a individualistic "competent self" (a view of oneself as being effective, able to control one's own life and make one's own way in it); and second, the importance placed on striving for power equalisation and the associated "Tall poppy syndrome".

The next section summarises the results of the question that sought to find out the importance placed in each of the three countries on the influence of other people (such as their family, their close relatives, their distant relatives, their superior officers, their subordinates and their friends) on individuals' judgements with respect to ethical issues. Another related question sought to find out the various factors that could lead individuals in each of three countries to compromise their judgements with respect to ethical issues. The objective of this section is to lend further support to the theoretical expectations developed in Chapter 3.

FACTORS INFLUENCING DECISIONS WITH RESPECT TO ETHICAL ISSUES

University academics in each of the three countries were asked, "In making decisions about what is ethical/unethical, just/unjust, right/wrong; what importance do you think your colleagues generally place on the influence of: their own judgement;[22] their family; their close relatives; their distant relatives; their superior officers; their subordinates; their friends". Respondents were asked to rate these seven factors on a scale anchored by 1 (least important) and 5 (most important). The mean scores and the standard deviations for each of the three nations are presented in Table 5.3.

Table 5.3 shows that compared with Indian and Malaysian respondents, Australians placed slightly greater emphasis on the influence of their own judgement (but the results are not significant as shown in the next paragraph). Other people (such as their family, their close relatives, their distant relatives, their superior officers, their subordinates and their friends) were seen to have less influence on Australian academics compared with Indians and Malaysians.

Results from one-way ANOVA (and where relevant, nonparametric Kruskal–Wallis one-way ANOVA) showed no difference between the three pairs of countries under examination with respect to the questions on "their own judgement", and "their friends". However, with respect to the questions on the influence of "their family; their close relatives; their distant relatives, and their superior officers", results from one-way ANOVA and the follow-up Tukey's HSD and Scheffe's tests showed that there were significant differences

Table 5.3. Factors Influencing judgements with Respect to Ethical Issues.

Factors	Frequency Distribution					
	Australia		India		Malaysia	
	Mean	SD	Mean	SD	Mean	SD
Their own judgement	4.90	0.32	4.46	0.69	4.67	0.50
Their family	2.70	0.68	3.91	0.54	4.11	0.78
Their close relatives	1.50	0.71	2.81	1.25	2.77	1.09
Their distant relatives	1.00	0.00	1.82	0.76	1.88	1.05
Their superior officers	2.20	0.43	3.82	0.76	4.11	0.60
Their subordinates	1.40	0.52	2.18	0.87	2.00	0.50
Their friends	2.70	1.25	3.35	1.03	3.11	0.60

between Australians and Indians and between Australians and Malaysians.[23] With respect to the question on the influence of "their subordinates", results showed that there was a difference between Australian and Indian academics, but no difference was found between Australians and Malaysians.

These findings are consistent with the literature presented in Chapter 3, which suggested that compared with the Indian and Chinese cultures, Australians place greater importance on individualism and independence. The results of the interviews suggest that, compared to India and Malaysia, in Australia "other people" have comparatively less influence on an individual's decision with respect to ethical issues. In contrast, greater emphasis on the influence of "other people" on judgements of Indian and Malaysian respondents is consistent with the greater importance placed on the family, the extended family and one's superiors in Hinduism and Confucianism. The findings in this section are also consistent with the theory development in the current study, which suggested that in Indian and Chinese cultures, judgements related to what is considered ethical or unethical is not an individual choice but is contextual, depending on the status and relationships among the people involved.

FACTORS LEADING TO COMPROMISE OF JUDGEMENTS WITH RESPECT TO ETHICAL ISSUES

The final question asked academics, "What are some of the factors that would make your colleagues compromise their judgement of what is ethical or unethical?"[24]

With respect to the above question, the following factors were identified by academics in each of the three nations. Again, the numbers shown in brackets refer to the frequency distribution of respondents who had suggested that particular issue.

India

Prevalence of unethical practices (accepted part of organisational culture) (6); pressure to do favours for the family, extended family and friends (6); fear of superiors (whistle-blowing is not an option) (5); internal control systems are generally designed by top management to further their own interest and one is forced to fit into that system (4) and personal ambition (4).

Malaysia

Prevalence of unethical practices (accepted part of organisational culture) (6); "self-preservation, go-ahead mentality and as long as it is legal, ethics is not too important" (6); being pragmatic about the "contextual" aspects of ethical issues (6); support from superiors is important (3); personal ambition (2) and chances of being caught (2).

Australia

Personal ambition and to enhance promotion chances (7); "what will wash with the boss is, too often, what counts" (2); job security (2) and lack of critical thought (1). Two academics suggested that they were "unaware of any such compromises having taken place and on such an issue, I would not wish to speculate".

SUMMARY

Most of the differences between Indian and Chinese Malaysian cultures on the one hand, and Australian, on the other, identified in the interviews with academics, supplement the psychological, sociological and historical literature for each of the three countries presented in Chapter 3. The cultural differences between these two clusters largely relate to the following essential aspects of Confucianism and Hinduism in constructing Chinese and Indian cultures, respectively: an individual exists through, and is defined by his or her relationship to others; these relationships are structured hierarchically; and social harmony is ensured through each individual honouring the requirements in the role relationships. As such, with respect to judgements related to ethical issues, Indians and Chinese Malaysians also consider the influence of "other people" such as their family, their close relatives and their superior officers. Thus, judgements related to what is considered ethical or unethical are not an individual choice but are contextual, depending on the prevalence of unethical practices, and the status and the relationships among the people involved.

In contrast, Australians are likely to be motivated by their own needs, rights and preferences, giving priority to personal rather than group, organisational, or societal goals. Furthermore, the importance of equalitarianism and egalitarianism in Australian culture suggests that value standards should apply to all irrespective of their positions. These core Australian cultural values in turn emphasise the development of unique and internalised moral judgements, rather than relying on external incentives such as maintaining organisational hierarchy and harmony, or the prevalence of unethical practices in one's organisation.

While the findings based on interviews with university academics provide useful information, these should be interpreted with caution because respondents were not selected on a random basis. Rather, recall that academics with an interest in culture were selected because they were known or were recommended by this researcher's colleagues or acquaintances in the three nations under examination. Moreover, the small sample size of respondents (10 in Australia, 9 in Malaysia and 11 in India) further limits the external validity of the interview findings.

CHAPTER 6
RESULTS: HYPOTHESES TESTS

In Chapter 4 it was explained that data to test the two hypotheses formulated in this study were collected using a survey questionnaire administered to a sample of senior professional accountants from "big-five" accounting firms in India, Malaysia and Australia.

This chapter presents the results of the hypotheses tests and is organised as follows. The first section summarises the various methods used for the distribution and collection of the survey questionnaires and then goes on to describe the response rates for each of the three countries. The second section tabulates the descriptive statistics for the dependent variables measured using the survey questionnaire and also assesses the reliability of the Multidimensional Ethics Measure. The third section summaries the demographic data, while the fourth section presents and discusses the results of the hypotheses tests. This is followed by a discussion of the SDRB found in this study. The fifth section provides evidence on the usefulness of the Multidimensional Ethics Measure compared to the univariate measure. The final section presents overall conclusions in relation to the results.

DISTRIBUTION AND COLLECTION OF QUESTIONNAIRES

As discussed in the previous chapter, four of the big-five accounting firms in Malaysia and three firms each in India and Australia participated in the study. Senior partners of the firms that participated were personally met to explain the objectives and relevant details of the survey questionnaires. In all cases, the partners provided the necessary support and assured the researcher that they would encourage their senior staff to complete the survey questionnaires as soon as possible. The number of survey questionnaires given to the partners was based on the number of respondents each partner was prepared to ask to complete the questionnaire. The partners were asked to randomly distribute the survey questionnaires to respondents who were of the rank of supervisors or higher. After completing the questionnaires, respondents were required to put it in the self-addressed envelope provided, to seal it and leave it with their receptionist or at a central collection point in each organisation. These were then personally collected or were collected by a colleague.

RESPONSE RATE – MALAYSIA

Four of the big-five accounting firms located in Kuala Lumpur participated in the study. The number of survey questionnaires distributed to each of the four firms was 50, 25, 35 and 25. Completed responses from each of the firms were 36, 19, 22 and 15, respectively, totalling 92 and representing a response rate of 68%.[1]

Recall that the purpose of this study is to draw respondents of Chinese Malaysian origin. It was explained in the previous chapter that since the topic of ethnicity in Malaysia was raised by two of the four partners and they were comfortable in discussing this issue, the partners were requested to select only Chinese Malaysian respondents in their firms. In the case of the other two partners, no such request was made because of the sensitivity of the ethnicity issue. Statistical tests to confirm that there was no difference in responses between the two firms where the respondents were Chinese Malaysian, and the two firms where the ethnic background of respondents was not known, are discussed later in the chapter under the section entitled, Aggregation of Data.

RESPONSE RATE – INDIA

Three of the big-five accounting firms in India participated in the study. Of these, two had branches both in Mumbai (previously Bombay) and New Delhi, and one was located only in Mumbai. The number of survey questionnaires distributed to each of the three firms, respectively, was 45 (25 in Mumbai and 20 in New Delhi), 50 (30 in Mumbai and 20 in New Delhi) and 35 (in Mumbai only). Completed responses from each of the three firms were 30 (16 in Mumbai and 14 in New Delhi), 31 (19 in Mumbai and 12 in New Delhi) and 23 (in Mumbai only), respectively. The overall response rate was 65% (84 responses received from 130 distributed). The response rate from Mumbai was 64% (58 responses from 90 distributed), and from New Delhi was 65% (26 responses from 40 distributed).[2]

RESPONSE RATE – AUSTRALIA

Three of the big-five accounting firms in Australia participated in the study. Of these, three firms are from Sydney and one has branches both in Sydney and Newcastle. Partners of two of the firms in Sydney wanted their staff to send the completed questionnaires directly to the researcher. Accordingly, respondents from those firms were directed to send their completed responses in the pre-paid, self-addressed envelopes provided directly to the researcher at his work address. To allow differentiation between responses from these two firms, different distinguishing marks were made on the questionnaires distributed to each firm. It was necessary to do this to check that there were no differences between completed responses that were collected personally and those that were sent in prepaid, self-addressed envelopes.

The number of survey questionnaires distributed to each of the three firms was 25, 50 and 45 (comprising 25 in Sydney and 20 in Newcastle). Completed responses from each of the three firms, respectively, were 14, 26 and 32 (comprising 20 from Sydney and 12 from Newcastle). The overall response rate was 60% (72 responses received from 120 distributed).[3] The response rate from Sydney was 60% (60 responses from 100 distributed) and from Newcastle was also 60% (12 from 20 distributed).

The completed questionnaires from one firm (Sydney and Newcastle Branches) were personally collected by the researcher from a central collection point in the firm. The response rate for this mode of collection was 71% (32 responses received from 45 distributed).

Given that two modes of collection of the survey questionnaires were used in Australia, data were categorised into two groups classified by mode of collection. If the two groups had different perceptions of the confidentiality of their responses, then it is the dependent variables that are likely to be affected. Statistical tests were conducted to find out if there was any difference between the two methods of collecting responses in Australia.

Additionally, with respect to the two firms where respondents had sent their completed questionnaires in prepaid, self-addressed envelopes directly to the researcher's work address, tests were run to confirm that there was no difference between early respondents (27 completed responses were received within the first five weeks after the questionnaires were given to the partners) and late respondents (13 completed responses were received after five weeks). Since the partners had assured their complete support for this research project, reminder letters were not sent to them. However, after four weeks of receiving the questionnaires, partners were contacted by telephone to thank them for the large number of completed responses received from their firms. This served as a form of reminder.

Statistical tests were also conducted to establish that there was no city-effect difference on the dependent variables among respondents within Australia (between responses from Newcastle and Sydney), and among respondents within India (between responses from Mumbai and New Delhi). In addition, it was necessary to show that there was no difference on the dependent variables among the firms in each of the three nations (firm effect). It was also necessary to establish that there was no "city" or "firm" effect within the countries to enable the data sets within each of the three nations to be aggregated for the purpose of hypotheses testing. Details of the specific statistical tests are discussed later in the chapter under the section, Aggregation of the Data.

DESCRIPTIVE STATISTICS AND SCALE RELIABILITY MEASURES

This section provides a brief description of the dependent variables and then tabulates the descriptive statistics for all dependent variables. To assess reliability of the Multidimensional Ethics Measure, Cronbach's (1951) alphas are computed.

Recall that the dependent variables for each of the three cases used in the study consist of 11 items. These are the eight items comprising the Multidimensional Ethics Measure,[4] one single-item "ethical" question, and two single-items which measure the likelihood that respondents would make the same decision, and that their colleagues would make the same decision, as the actors in each of the three cases. Each of the 11 dependent variables is measured on a 7-point Likert scale anchored by 1 (ethical/fair/just/highly probable, etc.) and 7 (unethical, unjust, highly improbable, etc.).

The descriptive statistics for the dependent variables for each of the three cases are provided in Table 6.1A (Case One relating to auditor–client conflict resolution) and Tables 6.1B and C (Cases Two and Three, respectively, relating to whistle-blowing as an internal control mechanism). The three tables show the mean and standard deviation for all 11 items, for the single-item "ethical" question, for the eight-item Multidimensional Ethics Measure, and also for the total and the individual scores for each of the three dimensions of Moral Equity, Relativism and Contractualism. The three tables also provide the scores on each of the single questions that measure the likelihood that respondents would make the same decision, and that

Table 6.1A. Descriptive Statistics for Case One: Auditor–Client Conflict.

	Malaysia		India		Australia	
	Mean	SD	Mean	SD	Mean	SD
For all 11 items	3.90	1.72	4.30	1.01	5.11	1.20
Ethical (single item)	4.33	1.75	5.00	1.60	5.61	1.23
Multidimensional Ethics Measures (8 items)	3.59	1.33	4.24	1.03	5.11	1.22
Moral Equity Dimension	**4.04**	**1.67**	**4.48**	**1.11**	**5.31**	**1.20**
Fair	4.05	1.75	4.28	1.39	5.18	1.36
Just	4.06	1.73	4.20	1.31	5.25	1.31
Morally right	4.15	1.86	5.30	1.54	5.56	1.27
Acceptable to my family	3.92	1.75	4.17	1.63	5.26	1.40
Relativism Dimension	**3.26**	**1.42**	**3.93**	**1.65**	**4.84**	**1.39**
Culturally acceptable	3.21	1.44	3.43	1.52	4.93	1.39
Traditionally acceptable	3.30	1.55	3.60	1.71	4.75	1.61
Contractualism Dimension	**3.63**	**1.66**	**4.49**	**1.81**	**4.96**	**1.55**
Unwritten contract	3.60	1.67	4.54	1.89	4.97	1.55
Unspoken contract	3.65	1.69	4.45	1.88	4.85	1.61
You would make the same decision (single item)	3.79	1.67	4.51	1.72	5.18	1.71
Your colleagues would make the same decision (single item)	3.22	1.74	3.80	1.73	4.53	1.64

Note: Response scale ranged from 1 to 7 (where 1 refers to ethical/fair/just/highly probable, etc., and 7 to unethical, unjust, highly improbable, etc.).

their colleagues would make the same decision, as the actors in each of the three cases. The tables show that for each of the 11 dependent variables, the mean scores of Australian professional accountants are greater than those of Chinese Malaysian and Indian professional accountants. These mean scores are in the direction predicted in the hypotheses. Furthermore, the tables show that the mean scores of Indians on each of the 11 dependent variables are between those of Australians and Chinese Malaysians. The details regarding these issues are discussed later in this chapter.

INTERNAL CONSISTENCY OF ACCOUNTANTS' DECISION-MAKING QUESTIONNAIRE

The reliability of the Multidimensional Ethics Measure was tested using Cronbach's (1951) alpha, which is computed from the average correlations,

Table 6.1B. Descriptive Statistics for Case Two: Whistle-Blowing.

	Malaysia		India		Australia	
	Mean	SD	Mean	SD	Mean	SD
For all 11 items	4.06	1.67	4.79	1.25	5.44	0.99
Ethical (single item)	4.65	1.94	5.56	1.51	5.85	1.13
Multidimensional Ethics Measures (8 items)	4.01	1.71	4.72	1.31	5.41	1.07
Moral Equity Dimension	**4.39**	**1.88**	**5.12**	**1.37**	**5.74**	**0.92**
Fair	4.35	1.91	5.06	1.62	5.51	1.14
Just	4.38	1.95	4.92	1.64	5.71	1.09
Morally right	4.54	2.03	5.60	1.45	6.03	0.96
Acceptable to my family	4.30	2.03	4.92	1.70	5.71	1.04
Relativism Dimension	**3.49**	**1.74**	**4.07**	**1.72**	**5.03**	**1.35**
Culturally acceptable	3.48	1.79	4.13	1.78	4.96	1.48
Traditionally acceptable	3.50	1.78	4.01	1.85	5.11	1.41
Contractualism Dimension	**3.80**	**1.89**	**4.55**	**1.81**	**5.12**	**1.60**
Unwritten contract	3.77	1.90	4.54	1.81	5.11	1.64
Unspoken contract	3.84	1.90	4.55	1.83	5.13	1.60
You would make the same decision (single item)	4.37	1.81	5.17	1.72	5.65	1.36
Your colleagues would make the same decision (single item)	3.50	1.86	4.29	1.63	5.11	1.34

Note: Response scale ranged from 1 to 7 (where 1 refers to ethical/fair/just/highly probable, etc., and 7 to unethical, unjust, highly improbable, etc.).

or covariances, between items within the scale. The results are presented in Table 6.2, Panels A–C, which show Cronbach's alpha for the eight dependent variables comprising the Multidimensional Ethics Measure taken together, plus those for each of the three dimensions in the measure, for each of the three cases used in the study. These coefficients are well above the 0.7 level of acceptability for construct measurement as defined by Nunnally (1978, p. 245). The coefficients for each of the two-item Relativism and Contractualism dimensions are particularly high, given that a smaller number of scale items produce lower alpha coefficients (Nunnally, 1967, p. 233; de Vaus, 1991, p. 55).

These results compare favourably with those of two other studies that have examined ethical issues in accounting using the Multidimensional Ethics Measure. Flory et al. (1992, p. 294) reported alphas ranging from 0.75 to 0.94, while Cohen et al. (1996a, p. 105) reported alpha as low as 0.45 for the Relativism Dimension (the range of alphas was not provided).

Table 6.1C. Descriptive Statistics for Case Three: Whistle-Blowing.

	Malaysia		India		Australia	
	Mean	SD	Mean	SD	Mean	SD
For all 11 items	4.06	1.78	4.70	1.27	5.39	1.05
Ethical (single item)	4.71	2.15	5.63	1.59	5.88	1.24
Multidimensional Ethics Measures (8 items)	4.06	1.85	4.64	1.28	5.40	1.11
Moral Equity Dimension	**4.30**	**2.04**	**5.00**	**1.33**	**5.68**	**0.99**
Fair	4.31	2.15	4.82	1.68	5.58	1.21
Just	4.24	2.18	4.78	1.58	5.71	1.12
Morally right	4.50	2.21	5.71	1.41	5.99	0.88
Acceptable to my family	4.17	2.04	4.69	1.73	5.55	1.38
Relativism Dimension	**3.70**	**1.79**	**3.99**	**1.63**	**4.94**	**1.48**
Culturally acceptable	3.74	1.83	3.96	1.69	4.90	1.52
Traditionally acceptable	3.66	1.84	4.02	1.79	4.99	1.52
Contractualism Dimension	**3.93**	**2.00**	**4.59**	**1.75**	**5.30**	**1.51**
Unwritten contract	3.91	2.03	4.60	1.75	5.32	1.52
Unspoken contract	3.95	2.01	4.57	1.77	5.29	1.52
You would make the same decision (single item)	4.09	1.83	4.81	1.92	5.44	1.55
Your colleagues would make the same decision (single item)	3.40	1.92	4.05	1.83	4.78	1.48

Note: Response scale ranged from 1 to 7 (where 1 refers to ethical/fair/just/highly probable, etc., and 7 to unethical, unjust, highly improbable, etc.).

DEMOGRAPHIC DATA

Tables 6.3A and B summarise demographic data for the respondents. Panel A of Table 6.3A presents the age categories of respondents, Panel B provides data on gender, and Panel C, the highest academic qualifications of respondents in each of the three countries.

Table 6.3A, Panel A shows that only one Malaysian respondent was in the age category 20–24 years, compared to 15 and 20, respectively, in India and Australia. However, the mode in each country was the category 25–29 years, and over 75% of respondents in each country are less than 35 years. Table 6.3A, Panel B reveals that males were a majority of respondents in each of the three countries. Moreover, there were more male respondents in India and Australia than in Malaysia. Table 6.3A, Panel C shows that approximately 90% of respondents in Australia and Malaysia had a

Table 6.2. Reliability Coefficients (Cronbach's Alpha) for Each Dimension of the Multidimensional Ethics Measure.

Dimensions	Malaysia	India	Australia
Panel A: Case One, Auditor–Client Conflict Resolution			
Moral equity (4 items)	0.96	0.75	0.86
Relativism (2 items)	0.89	0.72	0.94
Contractualism (2 items)	0.97	0.92	0.96
All 8 items	0.96	0.79	0.93
Panel B: Case Two, Whistle-Blowing			
Moral equity (4 items)	0.96	0.88	0.89
Relativism (2 items)	0.95	0.99	0.98
Contractualism (2 items)	0.99	0.92	0.96
All 8 items	0.96	0.90	0.92
Panel C: Case Three, Whistle-Blowing			
Moral equity (4 items)	0.97	0.85	0.86
Relativism (2 items)	0.95	0.86	0.94
Contractualism (2 items)	0.99	0.99	0.99
All 8 items	0.97	0.90	0.93

bachelor's degree. In contrast, a majority of respondents from India (57%) had also qualified for a master's degree.[5]

Panel A of Table 6.3B presents the number of years of professional work experience of respondents. Panel B shows their organisation positions, and Panel C, the percentage of working time spent by respondents in provision of management advisory services or consulting services.[6]

Table 6.3B, Panel A shows that in each of the three countries, at least 81% of respondents had less than 12 years of professional work experience. Table 6.3B, Panel B reveals that in each of the three countries, at least 84% of respondents were below the rank of partners (they were either supervisors, seniors or managers). Table 6.3B, Panel C indicates that a majority of respondents in each of the three countries spent less than 50% of their working time in the provision of management advisory services.

Statistical tests to confirm that the six demographic variables did not significantly affect respondents' scores in each of the three countries on the eight questions comprising the Multidimensional Ethics Measure and on the three single-item questions, are discussed under the heading, Aggregation of Data.

Table 6.3A. Demographic Details.

	Malaysia		India		Australia	
	Frequency	Percentage	Frequency	Percentage	Frequency	Percentage
Panel A: Age of Respondents (years)						
20–24	1	1.1	15	17.9	20	27.7
25–29	58	63.0	45	53.5	28	39.0
30–34	27	29.4	13	15.5	8	11.1
35–39	2	2.2	7	8.3	8	11.1
40–49	4	4.3	3	3.6	2	2.8
50–59	0	0.0	1	1.2	5	6.9
60 or over	0	0.0	0	0.0	1	1.4
Total	92	100	84	100	72	100
Panel B: Gender of Respondents						
Male	47	51.1	64	76.2	50	69.4
Female	45	48.9	20	23.8	22	30.6
Total	92	100	84	100	72	100
Panel C: Highest Academic Qualifications						
Diploma	0	0.0	0	0.0	1	1.4
Bachelor's degree	84	91.3	34	40.5	66	91.7
Master's degree	8	8.7	48	57.1	5	6.9
Ph.D.	0	0.0	2	2.4	0	0.0
Total	92	100	84	100	72	100

STATISTICAL TESTS USED

As discussed in Chapter 4, this study uses both multidimensional and unidimensional measures for the ethics construct to enable the study to provide empirical evidence on the proposition that the explanatory power of the Multidimensional Ethics Measure is greater than that of the univariate (ethical unethical) measure. The Multidimensional Ethics Measure comprises eight items as dependent variables, capturing various aspects of the complex ethics construct. Therefore, MANOVA is the relevant statistical test (Tabachnick & Fidell, 1989, pp. 30–31) to examine whether culture (the independent variable, operationalised as country) influences respondents' judgements on the eight dependent variables (these comprise the Multidimensional Ethics Measure).

Table 6.3B. Demographic Details.

	Malaysia		India		Australia	
	Frequency	Percentage	Frequency	Percentage	Frequency	Percentage
Panel A: Years of Professional Work Experience (years)						
3–5	35	38.0	49	58.3	33	45.8
6–8	35	38.0	20	23.8	14	19.5
9–11	17	18.7	7	8.4	12	16.6
12–14	4	4.2	5	5.9	6	8.4
>14	1	1.1	3	3.6	7	9.7
Total	92	100	84	100	72	100
Panel B: Organisational Position						
Supervisor	5	5.4	9	10.6	10	13.9
Senior	24	26.1	35	41.7	28	38.9
Manager	60	65.2	35	41.7	23	31.9
Partner	3	3.3	5	6.0	11	15.3
Total	92	100	84	100	72	100
Panel C: Percentage of Working Time Spent in Provision of Management Advisory Services						
Nil	12	13.0	17	20.2	16	22.2
Less than 50%	64	69.6	50	59.6	47	65.3
Between 50% and 70%	14	15.2	13	15.4	4	5.6
Greater than 70%	2	2.2	4	4.8	5	6.9
Total	92	100	84	100	72	100

One-way ANOVA tests whether mean differences among the various groups being examined on a single dependent variable are likely to have occurred by chance. In contrast, MANOVA tests whether mean differences among groups on a combination of dependent variables are likely to have occurred by chance. Tabachnick and Fidell (1989, p. 371) further explain that, "In MANOVA, a new dependent variable that maximizes group differences is created from a set of dependent variables. The new dependent variable is a linear combination of measured dependent variables, combined so as to separate the groups, as much as possible. ANOVA is then performed on the newly created dependent variable" (Tabachnick & Fidell, 1989, p. 371).

The following multivariate statistics are available in MANOVA to test the significance of main effects and interactions: Wilks' Lambda, Hotelling's trace criterion, Pillai's criterion and Roy's GCR criterion. Pillai's criterion is selected for use in this study because it is most robust to possible violations of the assumptions necessary for MANOVA (Tabachnick & Fidell, 1989, pp. 379, 399; Bray & Maxwell, 1985, p. 34). However, for comparative purpose, the study also provides the results of Wilks' Lambda and Hotelling's trace criterion.

A significant result from MANOVA indicates that the eight dependent variables taken together (these comprise the Multidimensional Ethics Measure) differ on the independent variable (three national cultural groups). However, the results do not show which of the three countries are significantly different from one another on the four items that comprise the Moral Equity Dimension, and on the two items that comprise each of the Relativism and the Contractualism Dimensions. Because these questions still need to be answered, the Pillai's criterion is viewed as a preliminary test.[7]

After finding significant results from MANOVA, two follow-up tests are recommended by Tabachnick and Fidell (1989, pp. 98–403). These are Univariate *F* tests and Stepdown Analysis. Roy–Bargman's Stepdown *F* test is applied in this study to overcome the problem of using correlated univariate *F* tests with dependent variables (Tabachnick & Fidell, 1989, p. 400).[8] Recall that the Multidimensional Ethics Measure was designed by taking into account the theoretical importance of the various items in each of the Moral Equity, Relativism and Contractualism dimensions, respectively. This hierarchical arrangement in the design of the Multidimensional Ethics Measure suggests that Stepdown Analysis tests on each of the three dimensions are useful in interpreting the results of this study. However, Tabachnick and Fidell (1989, p. 402) suggest that results from univariate *F* tests should be included as supplementary information. Accordingly, as well as reporting the results from Stepdown Analysis, this study also shows the results from univariate *F* tests.

With respect to interpreting the results from Stepdown Analysis, Bray and Maxwell (1985, pp. 48–49) explain, "Stepdown analysis is a form of analysis of covariance in which the criterion variables are entered in a specified order to test the relative contribution of successive measures. The first stepdown *F* and the univariate *F* ratio for that variable are identical. However, successive steps are not equivalent. The second step is the effect on the second criterion with the first criterion covaried out or removed. The third step is the effect with the first two variables' effects removed, and so on.

PRELIMINARY TESTS FOR MANOVA

Huck, Cormier, and Bounds (1974, p. 190) specify that the following two simple rules must be followed to obtain meaningful interpretation from

MANOVA tests. First, there should not be fewer dependent variables than there are groups being compared. This study satisfies this requirement because the three countries are compared on the eight dependent variables that comprise the Multidimensional Ethics Measure. The second rule requires that the total number of respondents be at least twice as large as the number of dependent variables. That is, there should be at least 22 respondents in each country. Since the numbers of respondents were 72 in Australia, 92 in Malaysia and 84 in India, the second requirement is also satisfied.

Since there is no reason to use MANOVA if the dependent variables are not correlated, it is necessary to examine the correlation matrix of the eight dependent variables that comprise the Multidimensional Ethics Measure. If the variables are independent, the observed correlation matrix is expected to have "small off-diagonal elements" (Tabachnick & Fidell, 1989, p. 405; Bray & Maxwell, 1985, pp. 32–33). Bartlett's Test of Sphericity is used to test the hypothesis that the dependent variables are independent (Tabachnick & Fidell, 1989, p. 405). Consistent with the suggested approach (Bray & Maxwell, 1985, p. 34; Tabachnick & Fidell, 1989, p. 405), this study applies this preliminary test before the use of MANOVA.

The second preliminary test in MANOVA is the assumption of "equal dispersion matrices". MANOVA has as many dispersion matrices as there are levels of independent variables. This assumption is analogous to the homogeneity of variance assumption that underlies univariate analysis. Box's *M* test provides a multivariate test for the homogeneity of the matrices. However, Box's *M* is a "notoriously sensitive test of homogeneity" (Tabachnick & Fidell, 1989, p. 379).[9] Therefore, if this assumption is violated, it is suggested that Pillai's criterion should be used to test multivariate significance because of its robustness (Tabachnick & Fidell, 1989, p. 379; and Bray & Maxwell, 1985, p. 34). This study follows this recommendation.

AGGREGATION OF DATA

As discussed earlier, before the responses for each of the three cases used in this study can be aggregated, it is necessary to show that respondents' scores on the 11 dependent variables within each of the three nations were not influenced by any other factors such as "firm" and "city" effects, or the two different methods used for collecting completed responses in Australia. Results from MANOVA on the eight dependent variables taken together (these comprise the Multidimensional Ethics Measure) and from ANOVA (where relevant, Kruskal–Wallis one-way ANOVA tests[10]) on the remaining three single-item questions,[11] are used to test for the presence of within-country differences among respondents. The details of the tests in each of the three nations are as follows.[12]

Results from MANOVA and ANOVA showed that there was no difference among respondents' judgements between the two firms in Malaysia where the respondents were Chinese Malaysian, and the other two firms where the ethnic background of respondents was not known. Additionally, there were no differences among respondents' judgements on the dependent variables among respondents from each of the four firms in Malaysia, and three firms each in India and Australia that participated in the study. That is, there was no "firm" effect on respondents' scores.

Recall that two of the participating firms in India have branches both in Mumbai and New Delhi, and one firm is located only in Mumbai; with respect to Australia, one firm had branches both in Newcastle and Sydney. Results from MANOVA on the eight questions that comprised the Multidimensional Ethics Measure, and results from ANOVA (where relevant, Kruskal–Wallis one-way ANOVA) on the three single-item questions, showed no "city" effect on Indian and Australian respondents' scores.

Statistical tests were also conducted to test for differences between the two methods of collecting responses in Australia; that is, to test if there was any significant difference between completed responses that were collected personally (from one firm) and those that were sent in pre-paid, self-addressed envelopes (two firms). Results from MANOVA and ANOVA (where relevant, Kruskal–Wallis one-way ANOVA) showed no difference among the three firms. With respect to the two firms where completed responses were posted to the researcher directly at his work address, the results confirmed that there was no difference between early and late respondents. The various categories in age, gender, highest academic qualifications, years of professional work experience, organisational position and percentage of working time spent in provision of management advisory services, did not significantly affect respondents' scores in any of the three countries on the eight questions comprising the Multidimensional Ethics Measure (MANOVA tests). Also, results from ANOVA (where relevant, Kruskal–Wallis one-way ANOVA tests) showed that respondents' scores on the three single-item questions did not differ significantly on any of the categories comprising the six demographic variables.

As a result of the above tests, responses of 92 Malaysian professional accountants, 84 Indians, and 72 Australian professional accountants are aggregated for the purpose of hypotheses testing.

RESULTS OF THE HYPOTHESES TESTS

Hypothesis 1: Resolution of Auditor–Client Conflicts

The first hypothesis examines differences between Australian professional accountants, on the one hand, and Indian and Chinese Malaysian, on the other, on both the likelihood and acceptance of resolving audit conflicts by acceding to clients. The hypotheses stated in directional form are as follows:

H1a: Australian professional accountants are *less likely* to resolve audit conflicts by acceding to clients than Indian and Chinese Malaysian professional accountants.

H1b: Australian professional accountants are *less accepting* of resolving audit conflicts by acceding to clients than Indian and Chinese Malaysian professional accountants.

The means and standard deviations of the scores of respondents on the 11 dependent variables were provided earlier in Table 6.1A. Recall that Table 6.1A shows that the scores on all 11 dependent variables are in the direction predicted in the hypotheses. Results of statistical tests in relation to hypotheses H1a and H1b are discussed in turn.

Hypothesis H1a: Likelihood of Resolving Audit Conflicts by Acceding to Clients

Data to examine hypothesis H1a were obtained by asking two single-item questions which measured the likelihood that respondents in each of the three nations would make the same decision ("you" question), and whether their colleagues would make the same decision ("your colleagues" question), as the auditor-in-charge in Case One (see appendix at the end of Chapter 4).[13] Recall that the purpose of asking the question from the respondent's perspective, as well as the respondent's perception of their colleagues' judgement, was to attempt to control any systematic errors resulting from SDRB. Additional details on the results related to the SDRB found in this study are discussed later in this chapter.

Data on both questions satisfied the assumption of homogeneity of variance (Levene's test, 2-tailed $p = 0.71$ and 0.97, respectively, for the two questions). This test was followed by one-way ANOVA tests to establish whether any significant differences existed among respondents from the three nations on each of the two single-item questions. The results are shown in Table 6.4, Panels A and B. Table 6.4 shows that there are significant

Table 6.4. ANOVA Results.

Source	DF	Sum of Squares	Mean Squares	*F* Ratio	*F* Probability
Panel A: ANOVA, Respondents' Judgements ("You" Question) by Country					
Between groups	2	78.38	39.19	13.59	0.00
Within groups	245	706.72	2.88		
Total	247	785.09			
Panel B: ANOVA, Respondents' Judgements of their Colleagues ("Your Colleagues" Question) by Country					
Between groups	2	68.21	34.10	11.68	0.00
Within groups	245	715.71	2.92		
Total	247	783.92			

differences between the respondent groups from Australia, India and Malaysia on their responses to each of the two questions (this study applies statistical significance at the 5% level of significance). Follow-up Tukey's HSD and Scheffe's tests[14] for significant results from Table 6.4, Panel A (scores of respondents' own judgement) showed that there were significant differences between all three pairs of countries (between Australia and Malaysia, Australia and India, and between India and Malaysia[15]).

With respect to the dependent variable that measured respondents' perception of colleagues' judgement, follow-up Tukey's HSD and Scheffe's tests showed significant difference between Australians on the one hand, and Indians and Chinese Malaysians, on the other. However, no difference was found between these latter two groups.

Hence, based on the results presented in Table 6.1A (showing the directional differences among the three countries) and Table 6.4 (showing those differences as significant), the results are supportive of the hypothesis that Australian professional accountants are less likely to resolve audit conflicts by acceding to clients than Indian and Chinese Malaysian professional accountants. Furthermore, these results are consistent for both respondents' reporting of their own judgements, as well as their perception of their colleagues' judgements.

Hypothesis H1b: Acceptance of Resolving Audit Conflicts by Acceding to Clients

Data to examine differences in judgements related to acceptance of resolving audit conflicts by acceding to clients were obtained through measures of the following dependent variables:

- Single-item ethical/unethical question
- Multidimensional Ethics Measure, which comprises the Moral Equity Dimension (four items), the Relativism Dimension (two items) and the Contractualism Dimension (two items).

Each of these dependent variables is discussed in turn.

Single-Item Ethical/Unethical Question. Since the assumption of homogeneity of variance was violated on this question (Levene's test, 2-tailed $p = 0.008$), results for both parametric and nonparametric tests are discussed.[16] Table 6.5 shows the results for ANOVA.

Table 6.5 shows that there are significant differences among professional accountants from Australia, India and Malaysia on their judgements related to how ethical was the behaviour of the auditor-in-charge described in Case One. Follow-up Tukey's HSD and Scheffe's tests indicate that there were significant differences between all three pairs of countries (Australia and Malaysia, Australia and India, and India and Malaysia) on the single-item ethical question.

Nonparametric Kruskal–Wallis one-way ANOVA ($\chi^2 = 16.35$, df = 2, $p = 0.0003$), and follow-up Mann–Whitney U tests[17] (Australia and India, $z = -2.4540$, 2-tailed $p = 0.0141$; Australia and Malaysia, $z = -5.0163$, 2-tailed $p = 0.0000$; Malaysia and India, $z = 2.2418$, 2-tailed $p = 0.0142$), showed results consistent with those from Tukey's HSD and Scheffe's tests.

Hence, based on the results presented in Table 6.1A (showing the directional differences among the three countries) and Table 6.5 (showing those differences as significant), the results in relation to the single-item ethical/unethical question provide support for hypothesis H1b. That is, Australian professional accountants were found to be less accepting of resolving audit conflicts by acceding to clients than Indian and Chinese Malaysian professional accountants. Furthermore, the results also suggest that Indians were less accepting of resolving audit conflicts by acceding to clients than Chinese

Table 6.5. ANOVA: judgements on Single-Item "Ethical" Question by Country.

Source	DF	Sum of Squares	Mean Squares	*F* Ratio	*F* Probability
Between groups	2	66.17	33.08	13.56	0.00
Within groups	245	597.67	2.44		
Total	247	663.83			

Malaysians. As stated earlier, a possible explanation for this difference is provided in the conclusion section of this chapter.

Multidimensional Ethics Measure. It was discussed earlier that a number of criteria must be satisfied before the use of one-way MANOVA. As suggested by Tabachnick and Fidell (1989, p. 405), Bartlett's test of sphericity is used to test the hypothesis that the eight dependent variables are independent of each other. Since the results did not support the hypothesis of independence (that is, the eight dependent variables are correlated) (F maximum criterion = 1.41952 with (8,245) df, $p = 0.000$), MANOVA tests were run to find out if there was any significant difference among the three nations on the eight dependent variables taken together (these comprise the Multidimensional Ethics Measure). The results from MANOVA based on Pillai's criterion reveal significant difference among the three nations (approximate $F = 7.02$, hypothetical df = 16, error df = 478, $p = 0.000$).[18]

As discussed earlier, after finding significant results from MANOVA, two follow-up tests are recommended. However, since the dependent variables are correlated and the Multidimensional Ethics Measure was designed by taking into account the theoretical importance of the various items comprising the Moral Equity, Relativism and Contractualism dimensions, Stepdown Analysis applied to each of these three dimensions provides the most useful insight into interpreting the results of the current study (see Tabachnick & Fidell, 1989, pp. 398–403; Bray & Maxwell, 1985, pp. 48–49 for details).

Roy–Bargman's Stepdown F tests showed that there was significant difference among the three countries on all four items, which comprise the Moral Equity Dimension, and on one item each of the Relativism and Contractualism Dimensions.[19] The details of Roy–Bargman's Stepdown F tests which show significant differences are as follows:

- *Moral Equity Dimension.* Fair/unfair ($p = 0.000$), just/unjust ($p = 0.048$), morally right/not morally right ($p = 0.000$) and acceptable to my family/unacceptable to family ($p = 0.014$).
- *Relativism Dimension.* Culturally acceptable/culturally unacceptable ($p = 0.000$).
- *Contractualism Dimension.* Does not violate an unwritten social contract/violate an unwritten social contract ($p = 0.000$).

The next section provides the results of follow-up parametric, and where relevant, nonparametric tests,[20] to test for differences among the various pairs of the countries under examination.

FOLLOW-UP TESTS

Table 6.6 shows the results of the follow-up tests that were performed after finding significant differences from Roy–Bargman's Stepdown *F* tests. Both parametric and nonparametric tests are reported where the assumption of

Table 6.6. Follow-Up Tests.

	Australia/Malaysia	Australia/India	India/Malaysia
Moral Equity Dimension			
Fair/unfair			
Parametric			
Tukey's HSD	Yes	Yes	No
Scheffe's	Yes	Yes	No
Nonparametric			
Mann–Whitney *U*	Yes ($z = -3.89$)	Yes ($z = -3.77$)	No
Just/unjust			
Parametric			
Tukey's HSD	Yes	Yes	No
Scheffe's	Yes	Yes	No
Nonparametric			
Mann–Whitney *U*	Yes ($z = -3.89$)	Yes ($z = -3.76$)	No
Morally right/not			
Parametric			
Tukey's HSD	Yes	No	Yes
Scheffe's	Yes	No	Yes
Nonparametric			
Mann–Whitney *U*	Yes ($z = -4.94$)	No	Yes ($z = -4.14$)
Acceptable to my family/not			
Parametric			
Tukey's HSD	Yes	Yes	No
Scheffe's	Yes	Yes	No
Relativism Dimension			
Culturally acceptable/not			
Parametric			
Tukey's HSD	Yes	Yes	No
Scheffe's	Yes	Yes	No
Contractualism Dimension			
Unwritten contract			
Parametric			
Tukey's HSD	Yes	No	Yes
Scheffe's			

homogeneity of variance was violated (Levene's test). "Yes" in the table indicates that the results were significant ($p < 0.05$), and "No" indicates that the results were not significant with respect to the follow-up tests shown in the left-hand column of the table. The three pairs of countries are in the right-hand columns of the table.

Summary

Table 6.7 provides a summary of the results related to auditor–client conflict resolution. "Support" indicates that with respect to the relevant dependent variables shown in the left-hand column, the results supported the two hypotheses H1a and H1b. "Partial" indicates partial support for the hypotheses (i.e., these results suggest that there was significant difference between Australian and Chinese Malaysians professional accountants, but no difference was found between Australians and Indians). The word "no" indicates that the results did not support the hypotheses.

The results presented in Table 6.7 are supportive of the hypothesis that Australian professional accountants are less likely to resolve audit conflicts

Table 6.7. Summary of Results Auditor–Client Conflict Resolution Hypotheses.

Dependent Variables	Findings
Single-item Questions	
Ethical unethical	Support
You would make the same decision	Support
Your colleagues would make the same decision	Support
Multidimensional Ethics Measures	
Moral Equity Dimension	
Fair	Support
Just	Support
Morally right	Partial
Acceptable to my family	Support
Relativism Dimension	
Culturally acceptable	Support
Traditionally acceptable	No
Contractualism Dimension	
Unwritten contract	Partial
Unspoken contract	No

by acceding to clients than Indian and Chinese Malaysian professional accountants. Furthermore, these results are consistent for both respondents' own judgements, as well as their perception of their colleagues' judgements.

With respect to the single-item ethical question, the results support the hypothesis that Australian professional accountants are less accepting of resolving audit conflicts by acceding to clients than Indian and Chinese Malaysian professional accountants. The results from judgements measured on the Multidimensional Ethics Measure are also generally supportive of this hypothesis. The details of the results from the Multidimensional Ethics Measure are as follows.

Results from three dependent variables which comprise the Moral Equity Dimension (fair/unfair, just/unjust, acceptable to my family/unacceptable to family), and from one of the two dependent variables comprising the Relativism Dimension (culturally acceptable/culturally unacceptable), also provide support for the hypothesis that Australian professional accountants are less accepting of resolving audit conflicts by acceding to clients than Indian and Chinese Malaysian professional accountants.

However, the results only partially supported the above hypothesis with respect to one item for each of the Moral Equity Dimension (morally right/not morally right), and the Contractualism Dimension (does not violate an unwritten social contract/violates an unwritten social contract). Results from these two items suggest that Australian professional accountants are less accepting of resolving audit conflicts by acceding to clients than Chinese Malaysians. However, there was no difference between judgements of Australians and Indians.

Hypothesis 2: Whistle-Blowing as an Internal Control Mechanism

The second hypothesis examines differences in judgements between Australian professional accountants on the one hand, and Indian and Chinese Malaysian on the other, on both the likelihood, and the acceptance of whistle-blowing as an internal control mechanism. The hypotheses stated in directional form are as follows:

H2a: Australian professional accountants are *more likely* to engage in whistle-blowing as an internal control mechanism than Indian and Chinese Malaysian professional accountants.

H2b: Australian professional accountants are *more accepting* of engaging in whistle-blowing as an internal control mechanism than Indian and Chinese Malaysian professional accountants.

Also, recall that data to test the above hypotheses were collected from two separate cases related to whistle-blowing as an internal control mechanism. Results from each of the two cases are discussed in turn. Appendix at the end of Chapter 4 provides details of these cases (Cases Two and Three).

Case Two: Hypothesis H2a: Likelihood of Engaging in Whistle-Blowing

Consistent with the approach used to collect data to test the first hypothesis H1a, data related to whistle-blowing as an internal control mechanism were also obtained by asking two single-item questions. These questions captured the likelihood that respondents in each of the three nations under examination would make the same decision ("you" question), and that respondents' colleagues would make the same decision ("your colleagues" question), as the actor in Case Two (who decided against whistle-blowing).[21] Note that Table 6.1B, presented earlier, shows that on each of the 11 dependent variables, the mean scores of Australian professional accountants are higher than those of Chinese Malaysian and Indian professional accountants, with a higher score indicating a greater likelihood of engaging in whistle-blowing. This table also shows that the scores on all dependent variables are in the direction predicted in the hypothesis.

One-way ANOVA tests were run to establish if any significant difference existed among respondents from the three nations under examination on each of the two single-item questions. The results are shown in Table 6.8, Panels A and B.

Table 6.8

Source	DF	Sum of Squares	Mean Squares	*F* Ratio	*F* Probability
Panel A: ANOVA, Respondents' judgements ("You" Question) by Country					
Between groups	2	69.54	34.77	12.61	0.0000
Within groups	245	675.42	2.76		
Total	247	744.96			
Panel B: ANOVA, Respondents' judgements of their Colleagues' judgements ("Colleague" Question) by Country					
Between groups	2	105.18	52.59	19.54	0.0000
Within groups	245	659.25	2.69		
Total	247	764.43			

Note: Consequently, results of both parametric and nonparametric are presented.

Table 6.8 suggests that there were significant differences among respondents from Australia, India and Malaysia on their responses to each of the two questions.

Tukey's HSD and Scheffe's tests, used to follow-up significant results from Table 6.8, Panel A (scores of respondents' own judgements), suggest that there was a significant difference between Australians and Chinese Malaysians, and between Indians and Chinese Malaysians),[22] thus suggesting partial support for the hypothesis. However, no difference was found between Australians and Indians on this question. Nonparametric follow-up Mann–Whitney *U* tests showed results consistent with Tukey's HSD and Scheffe's tests (Australia and Malaysia, $z = -4.5642$, 2-tailed $p = 0.0000$; Malaysia and India, $z = -2.9567$, 2-tailed $p = 0.0031$).

With respect to the dependent variable that measured respondents' perceptions of their colleagues' judgement (colleague question), follow-up Tukey's HSD and Scheffe's tests suggested support for the hypothesis (results showed significant difference between Australians on the one hand, and Indian and Chinese Malaysians on the other). Follow-up Mann–Whitney *U* tests showed results consistent with Tukey's HSD and Scheffe's tests (Australia and India, $z = -3.1976$, 2-tailed $p = 0.0014$; Australia and Malaysia, $z = -5.4622$, 2-tailed $p = 0.0000$).

Hypothesis H2b: Acceptance of Engaging in Whistle-Blowing

Consistent with the approach used in collecting data to test the first hypothesis H1b, data to examine differences in judgements related to acceptance of engaging in whistle-blowing as an internal control mechanism, were obtained through measurement of the following dependent variables:

- Single-item ethical/unethical question
- Multidimensional Ethics Measure which comprises the Moral Equity Dimension (four items), the Relativism Dimension (two items) and the Contractualism Dimension (two items).

Results with respect to each of the above scales are discussed in turn.

Single-item Ethical/Unethical Question. Since the assumption of homogeneity of variance was violated on this question (Levene's test, 2-tailed $p = 0.0000$), results from both parametric and nonparametric tests are discussed. Table 6.9 shows the results from ANOVA.

Table 6.9 shows that there are significant differences among professional accountants from Australia, India and Malaysia in their judgements related

Table 6.9. ANOVA: judgements on Single-Item Ethical Question by Country.

Source	DF	Sum of Squares	Mean Squares	*F* Ratio	*F* Probability
Between groups	2	65.81	32.90	12.94	0.0000
Within groups	245	622.89	2.54		
Total	247	688.70			

to how ethical was the behaviour of the actor described in Case Two who decided against whistle-blowing. Follow-up Tukey's HSD and Scheffe's tests indicate that there were significant differences between Australians and Chinese Malaysians, and between and Indians and Chinese Malaysians. However, no difference was found between Australians and Indians. Non-parametric follow-up Mann–Whitney *U* tests, showed results consistent with Tukey's HSD and Scheffe's tests (Australia and Malaysia, $z = -4.0795$, 2-tailed $p = 0.0000$; Malaysia and India, $z = -3.2217$, 2-tailed $p = 0.0013$).

These results suggest that with respect to the single-item ethical/unethical question, hypothesis H2b is partially supported. There was a significant difference between Australians and Chinese Malaysians, and between Indians and Chinese Malaysians, but no difference was found between Australians and Indians.

Multidimensional Ethics Measure. Consistent with the earlier discussion regarding the choice of relevant statistical techniques for the current study, results from Bartlett's test of sphericity were used to assess the independence of the eight dependent variables. The hypothesis of independence was rejected (*F* maximum criterion = 1.28071 with [8,245] df, $p = 0.000$). Next, MANOVA tests were run to find out if there were any significance differences among the three nations on the eight dependent variables taken together (these comprise the Multidimensional Ethics Measure). The results from MANOVA based on Pillai's criterion reveal significant difference among the three nations (approximate $F = 4.06776$, hypothetical df = 16, error df = 478, $p = 0.000$).[23] As discussed earlier, to investigate differences between each of the three pairs of countries, follow-up results from Stepdown Analysis provide the most useful approach.

Roy–Bargman's Stepdown *F* tests showed that there were significant differences among the three nations on three of the four dependent variables comprising the Moral Equity Dimension, on both items comprising the Relativism Dimension, and on one item comprising the Contractualism Dimension.[24]

The details of Roy–Bargman's Stepdown *F* tests are as follows:

- *Moral Equity Dimension.* Fair/unfair ($p = 0.000$), just/unjust ($p = 0.004$) and morally right/not morally right ($p = 0.000$).
- *Relativism Dimension.* Culturally acceptable/culturally unacceptable ($p = 0.000$) and traditionally acceptable/traditionally unacceptable ($p = 0.019$).
- *Contractualism Dimension.* Does not violate an unwritten social contract/ violates an unwritten social contract ($p = 0.000$).

The next section discusses the results of follow-up tests to find any differences between the three pairs of countries on each of the dependent variables that showed significant results in Stepdown Analysis.

FOLLOW-UP TESTS

Table 6.10 shows results of the follow-up tests after finding significant differences from Roy–Bargman's Stepdown *F* tests. Both parametric and nonparametric tests are reported where the assumption of homogeneity of variance was violated (Levene's test). "Yes" in the table indicates that the results were significant ($p < 0.05$), and "No" indicates that the results were not significant with respect to the follow-up tests shown on the left-hand column of the table.

Case Three: Hypothesis H2a: Likelihood of Engaging in Whistle-blowing

Again, data to test H2a were obtained by asking two single-item questions which measured the likelihood that respondents in each of the three nations would make the same decision ("you" question), and respondent's perception of whether their colleagues would make the same decision ("your colleagues" question), as the actor in Case Three who decided against whistle-blowing. Note that Table 6.1B, presented earlier, shows that on each of the 11 dependent variables, the mean scores of Australian professional accountants are higher than those of Chinese Malaysian and Indian professional accountants, with a higher score indicating a greater likelihood of engaging in whistle-blowing. These scores are in the direction predicted in the hypotheses.

Responses on both questions (you, and colleagues) violated the assumption of homogeneity of variances (Levene's test, 2-tailed $p = 0.0440$ for the "you" question and 0.0060 for the "colleague" question). Therefore, results of both parametric and nonparametric tests are presented.

Table 6.10. Follow-Up Tests.

	Australia/Malaysia	Australia/India	India/Malaysia
Moral Equity Dimension			
Fair/unfair			
Parametric			
Tukey's HSD	Yes	No	No
Scheffe's	Yes	No	No
Nonparametric			
Mann–Whitney U	Yes ($z = -3.66$)	No	No
Just/unjust			
Parametric			
Tukey's HSD	Yes	Yes	No
Scheffe's	Yes	Yes	No
Nonparametric			
Mann–Whitney U	Yes ($z = -4.27$)	Yes ($z = -2.94$)	no
Morally right/not			
Parametric			
Tukey's HSD	Yes	No	No
Scheffe's	Yes	No	No
Nonparametric			
Mann–Whitney U	Yes ($z = -4.91$)	No	No
Relativism Dimension			
Culturally acceptable/not			
Parametric			
Tukey's HSD	Yes	Yes	No
Scheffe's	Yes	Yes	No
Nonparametric			
Mann–Whitney U	Yes ($z = -5.08$)	Yes ($z = -2.92$)	No
Traditionally acceptable/not			
Parametric			
Tukey's HSD	Yes	Yes	No
Scheffe's	Yes	Yes	No
Nonparametric			
Mann–Whitney U	Yes ($z = 5.52$)	Yes ($z = -3.71$)	No
Contractualism Dimension			
Unwritten contract			
Parametric			
Tukey's HSD	Yes	No	Yes
Scheffe's	Yes	No	Yes

One-way ANOVA tests were run to establish if any significant differences existed among respondents from the three countries on each of the two single-item questions. The results are shown in Table 6.11, Panels A and B.

Table 6.11 shows that there are significant differences among respondents from Australia, India and Malaysia on their responses to each of the two questions. Tukey's HSD and Scheffe's tests to follow-up significant results from Table 6.11, Panel A (scores of respondents' own judgement) showed that there was a significant difference between Australians and Chinese Malaysians, and between Australians and Indians. In addition, results from follow-up Mann–Whitney U tests provided support for the hypothesis, and also showed differences between Indians and Chinese Malaysians (Australia and India, $z = -1.9642$, 2-tailed $p = 0.0495$; Australia and Malaysia, $z = -4.6969$, 2-tailed $p = 0.0000$; India and Malaysia, $z = -2.5853$, 2-tailed $p = 0.0097$). The results from Table 6.1B indicate that the direction of difference was also as hypothesised (i.e., Australian professional accountants are more likely to engage in whistle-blowing as an internal control mechanism than Indian and Chinese Malaysian professional accountants).

With respect to the dependent variable that measured respondents' perception of their colleagues' judgement (colleague question), follow-up Tukey's HSD and Scheffe's tests, and Mann–Whitney U tests (Australia and India, $z = -2.5749$, 2-tailed $p = 0.0100$; Australia and Malaysia, $z = -4.5538$, 2-tailed $p = 0.0000$), showed support for the hypothesis (i.e., significant difference was found between Australians on the one hand, and Indian and Chinese Malaysians, on the other, with the results from Table 6.1B indicating that the direction of difference was also as hypothesised).

Table 6.11

Source	DF	Sum of Squares	Mean Squares	F Ratio	F Probability
Panel A: ANOVA, Respondents' judgements ("You" Question) by Country					
Between groups	2	75.32	37.66	11.79	0.0000
Within groups	245	782.03	3.19		
Total	247	857.35			
Panel B: ANOVA, Respondents' judgements of their Colleagues ("Colleague") Question by Country					
Between groups	2	76.52	38.26	12.20	0.0000
Within groups	245	768.37	3.13		
Total	247	844.89			

Hypothesis H2b: Acceptance of Engaging in Whistle-Blowing

Data to examine differences in judgements related to acceptance of engaging in whistle-blowing as an internal control mechanism, was measured on the single-item ethical/unethical question and on the Multidimensional Ethics Measure. Results with respect to each of these are discussed in turn.

Single-item Ethical/Unethical Question. Since the assumption of homogeneity of variance was violated on this question (Levene's test, 2-tailed $p = 0.000$), results from both, parametric and nonparametric tests are discussed. Table 6.12 shows the results from ANOVA.

Table 6.12 shows that there are significant differences among professional accountants from Australia, India and Malaysia on their judgements relating to how ethical was the behaviour of the actor described in Case Three who decided against whistle-blowing. Follow-up Tukey's HSD and Scheffe's tests, and Mann–Whitney U tests (Australia and Malaysia, $z = -3.3152$, 2-tailed $p = 0.0009$; Malaysia and India, $z = -2.8269$, 2-tailed $p = 0.0047$), indicate that there was a significant difference between Australians and Chinese Malaysians, and between and Indians and Chinese Malaysians. However, no difference was found between Australians and Indians. Thus, the results suggest that on the single-item ethical/unethical question, hypothesis H2b is partially supported.

Multidimensional Ethics Measure. Results from Bartlett's test of sphericity were used to reject the hypothesis that the eight dependent variables are independent (F maximum criterion = 1.19101 with [8,245] df, $p = 0.0000$). Next, MANOVA tests were run to find out if there was any significance difference among the three nations on the eight dependent variables taken together (these comprise the Multidimensional Ethics Measure). The results from MANOVA based on Pillai's criterion reveal significant difference among the three nations (approximate $F = 4.21492$, hypothetical df = 16,

Table 6.12. ANOVA: Respondents judgements on Single-Item Ethical Question by Country.

Source	DF Squares	Sum of Squares	Mean	*F* Ratio	*F* Probability
Between groups	2	64.55	32.27	10.70	0.0000
Within groups	245	738.51	3.01		
Total	247	803.06			

error df = 478, $p = 0.000$).[25] This was followed by Stepdown Analysis to establish differences between each of the three pairs of countries under examination.

Roy–Bargman's Stepdown *F* tests showed that there was significant difference among the three nations on three of the four dependent variables comprising the Moral Equity Dimension, and on one each of the two dependent variables that comprise the Relativism and Contractualism Dimensions.[26]

The details of Roy–Bargman's Stepdown *F* tests are as follows:

- *Moral Equity Dimension.* Fair/unfair ($p = 0.000$), just/unjust ($p = 0.011$), morally right/not morally right ($p = 0.000$).
- *Relativism Dimension.* Culturally acceptable/culturally unacceptable ($p = 0.000$).
- *Contractualism Dimension.* Does not violate an unwritten social contract/violates an unwritten social contract ($p = 0.000$).

The next section discusses the results of follow-up tests on each of the dependent variables that showed significant results in Stepdown Analysis.

FOLLOW-UP TESTS

Table 6.13 shows the results of the follow-up tests, which were performed after finding significant differences from Roy–Bargman's Stepdown *F* tests. Both parametric and nonparametric tests are reported where the assumption of homogeneity of variance was violated (Levene's test). "Yes" in the table indicates that the results were significant ($p < 0.05$), and "No" indicates that the results were not significant with respect to the follow-up tests shown on the left-hand column of the table.

Summary of Results on Whistle-Blowing as an Internal Control Mechanism

Table 6.14 provides a summary of the results from the two cases related to whistle-blowing as an internal control mechanism. "Support" indicates that, with respect to the relevant dependent variables shown in the left-hand column, the results supported the two hypotheses H2a and H2b. "Partial" indicates partial support for the hypotheses (that is, these results suggest that there was a significant difference between Australian and Chinese Malaysians professional accountants, but no difference was found between Australians and Indians).

Table 6.13. Follow-Up Tests.

	Australia/Malaysia	Australia/India	India/Malaysia
Moral Equity Dimension			
Fair/unfair			
Parametric			
Tukey's HSD	Yes	Yes	No
Scheffe's	Yes	Yes	No
Nonparametric			
Mann-Whitney *U*	Yes ($z = -3.59$)	Yes ($z = -2.91$)	No
Just/unjust			
Parametric			
Tukey's HSD	Yes	Yes	No
Scheffe's	Yes	Yes	No
Nonparametric			
Mann-Whitney *U*	Yes ($z = -4.20$)	Yes ($z = -3.88$)	No
Morally right not			
Parametric			
Tukey's HSD	Yes	No	Yes
Scheffe's	Yes	No	Yes
Nonparametric			
Mann-Whitney *U*	Yes ($z = -3.99$)	No	Yes ($z = -3.51$)
Relativism Dimension			
Culturally acceptable/not			
Parametric			
Tukey's HSD	Yes	Yes	No
Scheffe's	Yes	Yes	No
Contractualism Dimension			
Unwritten contract			
Parametric			
Tukey's HSD	Yes	Yes	Yes
Scheffe's	Yes	Yes	Yes
Nonparametric			
Mann-Whitney *U*	Yes ($z = -4.40$)	Yes ($z = -2.57$)	Yes ($z = -2.10$)

The word "no" indicates that the results did not support the hypotheses. Table 6.14 shows that, with respect to Case Two, results from four of the 11 dependent variables support the hypotheses (H2a and H2b). In contrast, with respect to Case Three, results from six dependent variables provide support for these hypotheses.

The additional support for the hypotheses from Case Three may be attributable to the greater seriousness of the wrongdoing in Case Three compared to

Table 6.14. Summary of Results: Whistle-Blowing Hypotheses.

Dependent Variables	Findings	
	Case Two	Case Three
Single-item questions		
Ethical/unethical	Partial	Partial
You would make the same decision	Partial	Support
Your colleagues would make the same decision	Support	Support
Multidimensional Ethics Measures		
Moral Equity Dimension		
Fair	Partial	Support
Just	Support	Support
Morally right	Partial	Partial
Acceptable to my family	No	No
Relativism Dimension		
Culturally acceptable	Support	Support
Traditionally acceptable	Support	No
Contractualism Dimension		
Unwritten contract	Partial	Support
Unspoken contract	No	No

Case Two. The wrongdoing in Case Three involved an organisation that is a primary contractor for the government and the actor (internal auditor) discovered a series of inflated or falsified invoices to customers that had already been paid. In contrast, the wrongdoing in Case Two was an internal matter where the marketing manager claimed reimbursement for items such as a moderately expensive necklace, and a bill related to his wife's personal secretary. Additionally, compared to Case Two, the threatened retaliation for the potential whistle blower is greater in Case Three. The potential whistle blower in Case Three is told that he would be "fired" and the case further describes that the potential whistle blower is aware that, with his qualifications, he is not likely to find another such well-paid position in the current economic climate. In contrast, the threatened retaliation for the potential whistle blower is less serious in Case Two (his promotion chances could be greatly reduced if he reported the wrongdoing). Thus, these findings may suggest that both greater seriousness of the wrongdoing and/or the threat of retaliation for the potential whistle blower, highlight the culturally expected differences. It is suggested that future studies consider both these factors in designing research instruments for examining cross-cultural differences on whistle-blowing between Eastern and Western countries or between countries generally.

The results for both cases, shown in Table 6.14, provide support for hypothesis H2a with respect to the item asking respondents for judgements on their colleagues' likelihood of engaging in whistle-blowing. That is, results from this question provided support for the hypothesis that Australian professional accountants are more likely to engage in whistle-blowing as an internal control mechanism than Indian and Chinese Malaysian professional accountants. However, with regard to the item asking respondents to evaluate their own judgement on their likelihood of engaging in whistle-blowing, results for Case Three supported this hypothesis, but only partial support was found from the results in Case Two (that is, a significant difference was found between Australians and Chinese Malaysians, but no difference was found between Australians and Indians).

In relation to the single-item ethical question, both Cases Two and Three provided partial support for hypothesis H2b. There was a significant difference between Australians and Chinese Malaysians, but no difference was found between Australians and Indians.

With regard to the Multidimensional Ethics Measure, there was some support for hypothesis H2b. Results from both cases supported hypothesis H2b only on one of the four items, which comprise the Moral Equity Dimension (just/unjust), and on one of the two items included in the Relativism Dimension (culturally acceptable/culturally unacceptable). Furthermore, as discussed earlier, compared to Case Two, results from Case Three provided greater support for the hypothesis. Specifically, statistical tests from Case Three provided support for hypothesis H2b on one additional item included in the Moral Equity Dimension (fair/unfair), and also on one of the two items comprising the Contractualism Dimension (does not violate an unwritten social contract/violates an unwritten social contract).

Another item comprising the Multidimensional Ethics Measure (morally right/not morally right) provided partial support for hypothesis H2b with regard to results from both Cases Two and Three. There was a significant difference between Australians and Chinese Malaysians, but no difference was found between Australians and Indians.

In conclusion, the results from the study are generally supportive of the hypotheses related to whistle-blowing as an internal control mechanism. Furthermore, results from both issues examined in this study (auditor–client conflict resolution and whistle-blowing as an internal control mechanism) reveal the usefulness of the Multidimensional Ethics Measure in comparing judgements of professional accountants from Australia, India and Malaysia. This issue is discussed later in the chapter.

The results presented in this chapter also support the usefulness of considering SDRB in cross-cultural studies. The next section provides a discussion of such bias found in the study.

SOCIAL DESIRABILITY RESPONSE BIAS

Chapter 4 provided some insight into SDRB in cross-cultural studies. Cohen et al. (1995, 1996a) demonstrated the seriousness of SDRB in accounting contexts. This study provides additional insight into SDRB found among senior professional accountants from Australia, India and Malaysia.

Consistent with the approach used by Cohen et al. (1995, 1996a), this study measured SDRB through asking the two questions of respondents in each of the three cases, the "you question" and the "colleague question". Responses were captured on a 7-point Likert scale ranging from 1 (highly probable) to 7 (highly improbable). The difference in responses between these two questions is a measure of SDRB (Tyson, 1992; Cohen et al., 1995, 1996a).

Table 6.15, Panels A–C, reveal that in relation to each of the three cases in the three nations, compared to the "you" questions, the mean scores were

Table 6.15. Social Desirability Response Bias.

Dependent Variables	Mean Scores		
	Australia	India	Malaysia
Panel A: Case One			
You would make the same decision	5.18	4.51	3.79
Your colleagues would make the same decision	4.53	3.80	3.22
SDRB	0.65	0.71	0.57
Panel B: Case Two			
You would make the same decision	5.65	5.17	4.37
Your colleagues would make the same decision	5.11	4.29	3.50
SDRB	0.54	0.88	0.87
Panel C: Case Three			
You would make the same decision	5.44	4.81	4.09
Your colleagues would make the same decision	4.78	4.05	3.40
SDRB	0.66	0.76	0.69

Response scale 1–7, where 1 = highly probable and 7 = highly improbable. Note that standard deviations are provided in Tables 6.1A–C.

lower on the "colleague" questions. These results show that respondents from all three nations present themselves as acting more ethically than their colleagues. That is, compared to their own judgements, respondents attributed greater probability to the likelihood of their colleagues resolving audit conflicts by acceding to clients, and respondents also believed that their colleagues were less likely to engage in whistle-blowing.

Furthermore, the tables show that, in all cases, SDRB was highest among Indian professional accountants. In contrast, Australians had the lowest scores on this bias in Cases Two and Three. Additionally, there was a significant difference between Australian and Chinese Malaysian professional accountants on SDRB with respect to Case Two (assumption of homogeneity of variance was violated, Levene's test, 2-tailed $p = 0.0007$; nonparametric Mann–Whitney U Wilcoxon Rank Sum W test provided 2-tailed $p = 0.0293$). No other difference was found between respondents from the three countries on SDRB.

To find out whether SDRB existed among professional accountants within each of the three nations, T tests for paired samples and the nonparametric Wilcoxon Matched-Pairs Signed-Ranks tests were used. T tests for paired samples demonstrated that there were significant differences between the scores on "you" and "colleague" questions in each of the three cases within Australia, India and Malaysia (2-tailed $p = 0.000$ in all nine cases, three tests for each country).[27] These results reveal the existence of SDRB among senior professional accountants in each of the three nations under examination. However, as discussed earlier, the only between country difference was found between Australian and Chinese Malaysian professional accountants with respect to Case Two.

The importance of measuring SDRB in this study is reflected in the results with respect to Case Two on whistle-blowing. Table 6.14 presented earlier shows that there was only partial support for the hypothesis in relation to Case Two on the question which measured respondents' own judgement. This result suggested that Australian professional accountants were more likely to engage in whistle-blowing as an internal control mechanism than Chinese Malaysian professional accountants. However, no difference was found between Australians and Indians. In contrast, the hypothesis was fully supported in relation to the question that measured respondents' judgements of their colleagues.

In conclusion, if this study had only used Case Two and not taken into account the effect of SDRB, the results from the study would have been inconclusive. The findings in this study support that SDRB cannot be ignored in any research in accounting where respondents are asked to provide their evaluation on controversial accounting constructs. It is suggested that future studies use research instruments that capture both respondents' judgements of their colleagues as well as their own judgements. This would provide some control over, and insight into, the results from this study, which suggest that professional accountants from Australia, India and Malaysia tend to perceive their colleagues as less ethical than themselves.

USEFULNESS OF THE MULTIDIMENSIONAL ETHICS MEASURE

Differences in Explanatory Power

The use of both the univariate and the multidimensional measures enables this study to provide empirical evidence on the proposition that the explanatory power of the Multidimensional Ethics Measure is greater than that of the univariate (ethical/unethical) measure.

Consistent with the approach used by Flory et al. (1992), measures of behavioural intention are the criterion or dependent variable for testing the above proposition. Evidence suggests that a person's willingness to behave in a certain way is related to his or her behavioural intention (Hunt & Vitell, 1986). The theoretical basis for using behavioural intention as a surrogate measure of behaviour is based on the previous studies that have "demonstrated empirically that intention can be used as an immediate precursor to behavior. Intention represents the individual subjective probability of engaging in the behavior" (Flory et al., 1992, p. 295).

Flory et al. (1992) used only one item to measure behavioural intention (respondents' own judgement of their behavioural intention). However, this study also included the additional question (respondents' judgement of their colleagues' behavioural intention) to provide additional insight into measures of behavioural intention among respondents in the three nations.

The usefulness of the Multidimensional Ethics Measure is corroborated by comparing its results with the univariate ethics measure (ethical/unethical) in terms of their ability to "explain behavioral intention" (Flory et al., 1992, p. 296). The results based on Multiple Linear Regression Analysis for all respondents in the three nations, with respect to this comparison, are provided in Table 6.16, Panel A (respondents' judgements of their own behavioural intention) and Panel B (respondents' judgements of their colleagues behavioural intention).

Table 6.16. Differences in Explanatory Power of Multidimensional Ethics Measure Over the Univariate (Ethical/Unethical) Measure.

Case Number	Behavioural Intention (Adjusted R^2)		
	Univariate	Multidimensional	Difference
Panel A: Respondents' Own Behavioural Iintention			
One	0.36	0.47	0.11*
Two	0.42	0.53	0.11*
Three	0.31	0.51	0.20*
Panel B: Respondents' judgements of their Colleagues Intention			
One	0.34	0.43	0.09
Two	0.36	0.47	0.11*
Three	0.28	0.47	0.19*

*Significant at $p<0.05$

Table 6.16 shows that in all cases the Multidimensional Ethics Measure accounted for more "explained" variance than the univariate measure by 9 to 20 percentage points. If a one-tailed Z test is used to determine statistically significant differences between correlations, all except Case One in Table 6.16, Panel B, are significant at the 95% level.[28] These results provide empirical evidence that the explanatory power of the Multidimensional Ethics Measure is greater than that of the univariate (ethical/unethical) measure, thus providing additional insight into the judgements of professional accountants from Australia, India and Malaysia.[29]

Furthermore, adjusted R^2 ranged from 0.43 to 0.53, indicating that the Multidimensional Ethics Measure "explained" almost one half of the variance in the behavioural intention of respondents own judgements as well as respondents' judgements of their colleagues' behavioural intention.

The usefulness of the Multidimensional Ethics Measure in this study is reflected in the findings with respect to the hypotheses on whistle-blowing. The results from the univariate question (ethical/unethical) provided only partial support for the hypothesis (there was a significant difference between Australians and Chinese Malaysians, but no difference was found between Australians and Indians) (see Table 6.14). However, the results for a number of the items comprising the Multidimensional Ethics Measure showed significant differences between both Australians and Chinese Malaysians, and Australians and Indians; thus providing support for the hypothesis that Australian professional accountants are more accepting of engaging in whistle-blowing as an internal control mechanism than Indian and Chinese Malaysian professional accountants.

More importantly, the results from the Multidimensional Ethics Measure allow this research to go beyond a simplistic understanding of "what" professional accountants in Australia, India and Malaysia believe, and begins the process of understanding "why" they believe it. The findings from the various items comprising the three dimensions included in the Multidimensional Ethics Measure suggest that professional accountants in the three countries use more than one rationale in arriving at their judgements. These rationales are a function of the situation faced by the individual and "each rationale used represents a necessary dimension in any measure that expects to capture a true sense of that ethical judgement" (Reidenbach & Robin, 1990, p. 640).

The relative strength and consistency of results on the Multidimensional Ethics Measure in this study are consistent with prior research (such as Tsalikis & Nwachukwu, 1989; Reidenbach & Robin, 1988, 1990; Flory et al., 1992 and Cohen et al., 1993a, 1996b) in that a broad based Moral Equity Dimension is a fundamental decision rule for evaluating judgements.

The finding of consistent results across all three cases for one of the two questions on the Relativism Dimension (culturally acceptable/culturally unacceptable) suggest that this may be an important dimension in understanding differences in judgements among professional accountants from different nations. Recall that the essence of Relativism is that all values are a function of culture, and as a result, there are no universal ethical rules.

Furthermore, one of the two questions on the Contractualism Dimension (does not violate an unwritten social contract/violates an unwritten social contract) also provided some useful insight into comparative judgements of professional accountants in the three nations under examination. Recall that the Contractualism Dimension is important in examining differences in judgements among people from various cultures because most business exchanges incorporate either implicit or explicit promises or contracts. Individuals from various cultures tend to take the idea of contracts to include "an ethics of exchange" (Reidenbach & Robin, 1990, p. 647).

The relative importance (adjusted R^2) of the Moral Equity, Relativism and Contractualism dimensions for all respondents in the three nations are shown in Table 6.17, Panel A (respondents' judgements of their own behavioural intention) and Panel B (respondents' judgements of their colleagues behavioural intention). The table reveals that with respect to explaining differences in judgements among professional accountants from Australia, India and Malaysia, the explanatory power of the Moral Equity Dimension is superior to the Relativism and Contractualism dimensions, respectively.

Table 6.17. Differences in Explanatory Power of Three Dimensions Comprising Multidimensional Ethics Measure.

Case Number	Behavioural Intention (Adjusted R^2)		
	Moral Equity	Relativism	Contractualism
Panel A: Respondents' Own Behavioural Intention			
One	0.45	0.28	0.25
Two	0.52	0.35	0.34
Three	0.47	0.40	0.33
Panel B: Colleagues' Behavioural Intention			
One	0.41	0.28	0.20
Two	0.45	0.34	0.29
Three	0.42	0.41	0.33

The adjusted R^2 range from 0.41 to 0.52, 0.28 to 0.41 and 0.20 to 0.34 for the Moral Equity, Relativism and Contractualism dimensions, respectively.

These findings support the proposition that the three dimensions of the Multidimensional Ethics Measure capture a substantial amount of the decision dynamics used by professional accountants in the three countries to make ethical judgements.

SUMMARY

The results of the hypotheses tests presented in this chapter are generally supportive of the two hypotheses formulated in the study. With respect to the first hypothesis related to resolution of auditor–client conflicts, the results suggest that Australian professional accountants are both less likely and less accepting of resolving audit conflicts by acceding to clients than Indian and Chinese Malaysian professional accountants. The results are also supportive of the second hypothesis, showing that Australian professional accountants are more likely and more accepting of engaging in whistle-blowing as an internal control mechanism than Indian and Chinese Malaysian professional accountants.

However, the results of the hypotheses tests also revealed that there were significant differences between Indian and Chinese Malaysian professional accountants in relation to two items, which comprise the Multidimensional Ethics Measure.[30] These results suggest that in relation to these two items, Indians were less likely and less accepting of resolving audit conflicts by acceding to clients than Chinese Malaysians. Additionally, with respect to these items, Indians were more likely and more accepting of engaging in whistle-blowing as an internal control mechanism than Chinese Malaysians. Also note that with respect to all 11 dependent variables shown in Tables 6.1A–C, the mean scores of Indians are higher than those of Chinese Malaysians. A possible reason for this difference may be traced to the various historical influences of Confucianism and Hinduism. Specifically, the literature suggests that compared to Hinduism, Confucianism may be more enduring, resistant to change and stronger in its influence on cultural values.[31] Therefore, the difference in judgements between Indians and Chinese Malaysian found in this study may be attributed to the comparatively more enduring and stronger influence of Confucianism on the Chinese people, and hence on the dependent variables examined in the study. However, it is suggested that these results be regard as exploratory to enable further cross-cultural studies between Indian and Chinese Malaysian professional accountants.

The implications of the findings from the study are discussed in the next chapter.

CHAPTER 7
CONCLUSIONS

This study has examined the influence of Australian, Indian and Chinese Malaysian cultures on judgements of senior professional accountants from 'big-five' accounting firms with respect to two accounting issues, namely, resolution of auditor–client conflicts and whistle-blowing as an internal control mechanism. The importance of cultural values in influencing accountants' professional judgements has been examined by a number of researchers in this area, but prior to this study, no research has systematically examined that influence with respect to these issues. Such an examination was conducted in this study through the formulation and testing of two hypotheses relating to the resolution of auditor–client conflicts and whistle-blowing as an internal control mechanism.

The remainder of the chapter is organised as follows. The following sections summarise the theory development and hypotheses formulation, research method, results from Hofstede's Values Survey Module (1994) and the results from interviews with university academics with an interest in culture, the results of the hypotheses tests, the usefulness of the Multidimensional Ethics Measure and the SDRB found in the study. This is followed by the implications and contributions of the findings. Finally, the study concludes with the limitations and suggestions for further research.

THEORY DEVELOPMENT AND HYPOTHESES FORMULATION

It was shown in Chapter 2 that most cross-cultural studies in accounting have relied extensively on the five-dimensional model of culture, identified by Hofstede (1980) and Hofstede and Bond (1988), to examine various accounting issues such as management control systems design, ethical judgements, standard setting practices and organisational culture in accounting firms. While these studies demonstrated the importance of culture, their insights may be limited because most of the studies neglected findings from other disciplines, such as the sociological, psychological and historical literatures, specifically that the form and nature of cultural dimensions may be different among various countries. As a result, most cross-cultural studies in accounting have provided only a limited insight into the depth, richness and complexity of cultural differences.

While it is useful to classify culture into distinct dimensions, such as those identified by Hofstede (1980) and Hofstede and Bond (1988), a more holistic approach is needed to provide insight into the specific nature of the cultural values applicable to Indians, Chinese Malaysians and Australians. Therefore, rather than solely relying on Hofstede's cultural dimensions in theory development and hypotheses formulation, the approach adopted in this study provided insight into the specific nature of cultural values that are applicable to Chinese Malaysians and Indians by drawing on the relevant features of Confucianism and Hinduism, respectively. Additionally, relevant historical and sociological literatures were analysed to provide insight into those aspects of Australian culture that are particularly applicable to the issues examined in this study. Based on these insights, the study drew out the various features of cultural differences between Indians and Chinese Malaysians in one cluster and Australians in another cluster, to formulate hypotheses on auditor–client conflict resolution and whistle-blowing as an internal control mechanism. Specifically, the following hypotheses were formulated and tested in the study:

H1a: Australian professional accountants are *less likely* to resolve audit conflicts by acceding to clients than Indian and Chinese Malaysian professional accountants.

H1b: Australian professional accountants are *less accepting* of resolving audit conflicts by acceding to clients than Indian and Chinese Malaysian professional accountants.

H2a: Australian professional accountants are *more likely* to engage in whistle-blowing as an internal control mechanism than Chinese Malaysian and Indian professional accountants.

H2b: Australian professional accountants are *more accepting* of engaging in whistle-blowing as an internal control mechanism than Chinese Malaysian and Indian professional accountants.

RESEARCH METHOD

Four important features were employed to enhance the reliability and validity of the results of the study. Firstly, the use of realistic accounting scenarios, in contrast to questions about a code of professional conduct, was included in the survey questionnaire. The use of scenarios was motivated by the empirical evidence, which shows that they lead to a richer explanation of differences in ethical judgements among professional accountants.

Secondly, the use of both the univariate and multidimensional measures enabled the study to show the usefulness of using the multidimensional ethics measure to examine complex comparative judgements of professional accountants in the three countries.

Thirdly, an extensive pilot testing provided confidence about the reliability and validity of the survey questionnaire. In addition, the choice of the three countries further reduced the threats to internal validity. Specifically, Australia, India and Malaysia belong to the British Commonwealth model of accounting development and this lends some confidence about content equivalence of the accounting concepts that were examined. Additionally, the selection of senior staff from the big-five accounting firms in the three countries provided assurance that respondents had similar rank and were broadly influenced by similar organisational culture. Moreover, various steps were taken to gain insight into the potential for SDRB in the survey questionnaire.

Finally, to overcome some of the limitations of survey research, interviews were conducted in each of the three countries with university academics, with an interest in culture, to provide a more holistic understanding of the cultural values.

RESULTS FROM HOFSTEDE'S SURVEY

The results based on Hofstede's Values Survey Module (1994) supported that there were significant differences in Power Distance and Individualism indices between Australian professional accountants on one hand, and Chinese Malaysians and Indians, on the other. Specifically, the results suggest that the Chinese Malaysian and Indian respondents were drawn from the cluster comprising large Power Distance and low Individualism societies, and the Australians from a cluster comprising small Power Distance and high Individualism societies.

However, the results failed to distinguish the three countries on the Long-term Orientation dimension. Since the Long-term Orientation dimension is important in differentiating between Western- and Chinese-based (including Indian) societies, it is suggested that additional validation is required with respect to the items included in Hofstede's Values Survey Module (1994), which measure this dimension.

SUMMARY OF INTERVIEW RESULTS

The major findings based on the interviews with university academics in each of the three countries are broadly consistent with the cultural differences between Australians in one cluster, and Indians and Chinese Malaysians in another cluster, invoked in theory development and hypotheses formulation. Additionally, the findings from the interviews are also consistent with the theory invoked that, compared with Indian and Chinese cultures, Australians place less emphasis on the influence "other people", such as their family and their superior officers, when making judgements about what is considered ethical or unethical.

RESULTS OF HYPOTHESES TESTS

Table 7.1 provides a summary of the results related to auditor–client conflict resolution (Case One), and whistle-blowing as an internal control mechanism (Cases Two and Three). 'Support' indicates that with respect to the relevant dependent variables shown in the left-hand column, the results supported the hypotheses. 'Partial' indicates partial support for the hypotheses (these results suggest that there was significant difference between Australian and Chinese Malaysians professional accountants, but no difference was found between Australians and Indians). The word 'no' indicates that the results did not support the hypotheses.

Summary of the Results with Respect to Auditor–Client Conflict Resolution

Table 7.1 shows that the results from the study were supportive of hypothesis H1a that Australian professional accountants are less likely to resolve audit conflicts by acceding to clients than Indian and Chinese Malaysian professional accountants. Furthermore, these results were consistent for both respondents' own judgements, as well as their perception of their colleagues' judgements.

With respect to the single-item ethical question, the results supported hypothesis H1b that Australian professional accountants are less accepting of resolving audit conflicts by acceding to clients than Indian and Chinese

Table 7.1. Summary of Results.

Dependent Variables	Auditor–Client Conflict	Whistle-Blowing	
	Case One	Case Two	Case Three
Single Item Questions			
Ethical/unethical	Support	Partial	Partial
You would make the same decision	Support	Partial	Support
Your colleagues would make the same decision	Support	Support	Support
Multidimensional Ethics Measures			
Moral Equity Dimension			
Fair	Support	Partial	Support
Just	Support	Support	Support
Morally right	Partial	Partial	Partial
Acceptable to my family	Support	No	No
Relativism Dimension			
Culturally acceptable	Support	Support	Support
Traditionally acceptable	No	Support	No
Contractualism Dimension			
Unwritten contract	Partial	Partial	Support
Unspoken contract	No	No	No

Malaysian professional accountants. The results from judgements measured on the Multidimensional Ethics Measure are also generally supportive of hypothesis H1b.

Results from three dependent variables, which comprise the Moral Equity Dimension (fair/unfair, just/unjust, acceptable to my family/unacceptable to family), and from one of the two dependent variables, which comprise the Relativism Dimension (culturally acceptable/culturally unacceptable), also provided support for hypothesis H1b that Australian professional accountants are less accepting of resolving audit conflicts by acceding to clients than Indian and Chinese Malaysian professional accountants.

However, the results only partially supported hypothesis H1b with respect to one item for each of the Moral Equity Dimension (morally right/not morally right) and the Contractualism Dimension (does not violate an unwritten social contract/violates an unwritten social contract). Results from these two items suggest that Australian professional accountants are less accepting of resolving audit conflicts by acceding to clients than Chinese Malaysians. However, there was no difference between judgements of Australians and Indians.

Summary of Results on Whistle-Blowing as an Internal Control Mechanism

With respect to Case Two, results from four of the 11 dependent variables supported hypotheses H2a and H2b. In contrast, with respect to Case Three, results from six dependent variables provided support for the above hypotheses. The additional support for the hypotheses from Case Three may be attributable to the greater seriousness of the wrongdoing, and of the threatened retaliation for the potential whistle blower, in Case Three compared to Case Two.

The results from both cases provided support for hypothesis H2a with respect to the item asking respondents for judgements on their colleagues' likelihood of engaging in whistle-blowing. That is, results from this question provided support for the hypothesis that Australian professional accountants are more likely to engage in whistle-blowing as an internal control mechanism than Indian and Chinese Malaysian professional accountants. However, with regard to the item asking respondents to evaluate their own judgement on their likelihood of engaging in whistle-blowing, results from Case Three supported this hypothesis, but only partial support was found from the results in Case Two (i.e., a significant difference was found between Australians and Chinese Malaysians, but no difference was found between Australians and Indians).

In relation to the single-item ethical question, both Cases Two and Three provided partial support for hypothesis H2b. There was a significant difference between Australians and Chinese Malaysians, but no difference was found between Australians and Indians.

With regard to the Multidimensional Ethics Measure, there was some support for hypothesis H2b. Results from both cases provided support for hypothesis H2b only from one of the four items, which comprise the Moral Equity Dimension (just/unjust), and on one of the two items included in the Relativism Dimension (culturally acceptable/culturally unacceptable). Furthermore, as discussed earlier, compared to Case Two, results from Case Three provided greater support for this hypothesis.

Another item comprising the Multidimensional Ethics Measure (morally right/not morally right) provided partial support for hypothesis H2b with regard to the results from both Cases Two and Three. There was significant difference between Australians and Chinese Malaysians, but no difference was found between Australians and Indians.

The results of all four hypotheses tests also revealed that there were significant differences between Indian and Chinese Malaysian professional accountants in relation to the two items, which comprise the Multidimensional

Ethics Measure (morally right/not morally right and does not violate an unwritten social contract/violates an unwritten social contract). These results suggest that in relation to these two items, Indians were less likely and less accepting of resolving audit conflicts by acceding to clients than Chinese Malaysians. Additionally, with respect to these items, Indians were more likely and more accepting of engaging in whistle-blowing as an internal control mechanism than Chinese Malaysians. A possible reason for this difference may be traced to the literature which suggests that, compared to Hinduism, Confucianism may be more enduring, more resistant to change and stronger in its influence on cultural values.

In conclusion, the results presented in this study are generally supportive of the hypotheses formulated in the study.

USEFULNESS OF MULTIDIMENSIONAL ETHICS MEASURE

The use of both the univariate and the multidimensional measures enabled this study to show the usefulness of using Multidimensional Ethics Measure to examine complex comparative judgements of professional accountants in the three countries. The results reveal that the explanatory power of the Multidimensional Ethics Measure is significantly greater than that of the univariate (ethical/unethical) measure. Moreover, the findings support the proposition that the Moral Equity, Relativism and Contractualism dimensions, which comprise the Multidimensional Ethics Measure, capture a substantial amount of the decision dynamics used by professional accountants in the three countries to make ethical judgements.

SOCIAL DESIRABILITY RESPONSE BIAS

The results showed that in relation to each of the three cases, respondents from the three countries presented themselves as acting more ethically than their colleagues. That is, compared to their own judgements, respondents who attributed greater probability that their colleagues were more likely to resolve audit conflicts by acceding to clients, and respondents also believed that their colleagues were also less likely to engage in whistle-blowing.

Furthermore, the results showed that in all cases, SDRB was highest among Indian professional accountants. In contrast, Australians had the lowest overall scores on this bias. Moreover, there was a significant difference between Australian and Chinese Malaysian professional accountants on SDRB with respect to one of the cases. In conclusion, these results reveal the importance of taking into account SDRB in cross-cultural research.

IMPLICATIONS AND CONTRIBUTIONS

Accounting as the 'language' of business is a socio-technical activity in which the values and judgements of preparers and users of financial information are important. An enhanced awareness of the impact of culture on accounting information has resulted from a multiplicity of factors, particularly the recent increase in economic activities related to globalisation. An understanding of the similarities and differences in judgements of professional accountants across countries should improve the quality and comparability of international accounting information, systems and procedures. Specifically, the findings from this study have implications for the following three important areas in accounting: effective management of multinational enterprises, the international convergence and harmonisation of accounting and auditing standards and cross-cultural accounting research including accounting education. Each of these is discussed in turn.

MANAGEMENT OF MULTINATIONAL ENTERPRISES

Auditor–Client Conflict Resolution

The movement towards globalisation is reflected in the mergers, demise and further concentration of services provided by the big multinational accounting firms. For example, on 1 July 1998, 140,000 employees in 70 countries of Price Waterhouse and Coopers & Lybrand merged to formed PricewaterhouseCoopers (PwC), pooling 8,500 partners and revenues of $A21.37 billion (The Australian, 24 June 1998, p. 36), and reducing the "big-six" to 'big-five'. The collapse of Arthur Andersen in 2002 resulted in only four firms that are potentially capable of serving the largest global public companies. At one time, there was serious concern whether the big-four would be reduced to big-three as Ernst & Young was facing a damages claim of approximately US$3.5 billion from Equitable Life, a failed insurance company (http://in.rediff.com/money/2005/nov/01guest.htm). This globalisation and concentration of services provided by big accounting firms have created some serious problems. For example, big-four audit 78% of all US public companies and 97% of those with sales of more than $250 million. The big-four also dominate the international audit market (The Future of the Accounting Profession: Auditor Concentration, 2005, p. 6).

The problems facing the big-four accounting firms include the export and refinement of largely Anglo-American accounting and auditing techniques, the worldwide management of the standardisation of activities such as the audit process, hiring and promotion criteria and implementation of the firm's code of professional conduct in diverse cultures. The big-four firms have to further ensure that they comply with IFAC Code of Ethics.

Developing a uniform approach to ethical behaviour is a major problem for the big-four. Specifically, developing guidelines for a global set of code of professional conduct on issues related to independence remains one of the most serious problems. Indeed, on many occasions auditors in the largest and most respected accounting firms have yielded to management pressure, permitting management to file incomplete or misleading financial statements. Evidence also suggests that many of our recent accounting scandals can be traced to auditors' failure to resist pressure to accept misleading financial statements (The Future of the Accounting Profession, 2003, p. 9); that is, the problem relates to ethical resolution of auditor–client conflicts.

Each of the big-five accounting firms has compiled a comprehensive manual, which provides guidance to their professional accountants, auditors and tax experts on how to deal with technical issues in various countries. The single most important element in applying the firm's audit approach is the exercise of informed judgement at the various stages of the audit. However, an examination of the manuals reveals that almost no guidance is provided about the influence culture may have on professional judgements of employees in big-four accounting firms. The results from this study have implications with respect to this issue.

Specifically, the results from the study may be of interest to those involved in developing manuals and the training programmes of the big-four accounting firms. The globalisation of large accounting firms has created a need for those firms to integrate diverse cultural norms and audit engagement procedures into a single global practice. Professional accountants of big-four may find it useful to have guidance on how various cultures may influence resolution of auditor–client conflicts.

The results from this study show that the attainment of 'single global' audit procedures and a single global code of professional conduct is likely to be problematic because cultural values have an influence on judgements of professional accountants. However, research related to establishing consistent patterns of differences in judgements of professional accountants on various controversial ethical issues serves as a starting point. Additional discussion and training programmes in Indian- and Chinese-based societies with respect to resolution of auditor–client conflicts may be useful in providing an optimum solution to this problem.

Whistle-Blowing as an Internal Control System

The US Sarbanes-Oxley Act of 2002 and the Securities and Exchange Commission (SEC) have clearly established the importance of improving corporate internal control systems. Largely based on this American initiative, the policy makers and the accounting profession in many countries have also emphasised high-quality internal controls because it is considered to be an important factor in achieving good quality financial reporting.

Designing effective internal control systems is an integral component of managing complex operations of both domestic and multinational enterprises. However, Choi and Meek (2005, p. 382) conclude that, "Studies have revealed that the systems employed by a number of multinational enterprises to control their foreign operations are identical in many respects to those used domestically".[1] Since cultural values influence the effectiveness of control systems, enforcing uniformity in control systems in various countries may lead to dysfunctional behavioural consequences and unnecessary costs. Managers of multinational enterprises may find it useful to understand that domestic standardised internal audit procedures may not be simply transferred to other cultures. Compatibility between cultural values and organisational systems is important when designing effective control procedures.

It was shown in Chapter 1 that whistle-blowing is an important factor that contributes to improvements in both internal control and in evaluations of the control environment by management and external auditors. The results from the study also have implications with regard to this issue. Specifically, it is suggested that compared with Indian and Chinese cultures, whistle-blowing as an internal control mechanism is likely to be more effective in Australian culture.

Social Desirability Response Bias

The findings from the hypotheses tests showed that SDRB existed among professional accountants from the three countries. This evidence is consistent with results from business ethics research which consistently reveals that individuals believe that they are more ethical than comparable others. A possible implication of the results is that individuals may not feel any pressure to improve their own ethical conduct. A more serious problem is that employees "might rationalize unethical behavior as being necessary to compete evenly with others who are far less principled" (Tyson, 1990, p. 715). The findings from the study with respect to SDRB may be useful to managers of multinational enterprises in general, and big-four accounting firms in particular.

INTERNATIONAL CONVERGENCE AND HARMONISATION OF ACCOUNTING AND AUDITING STANDARDS

The globalisation of business and investment markets has highlighted a need for internationally converged and harmonised accounting and auditing standards. Accounting convergence and harmonisation is expected to improve international comparability of financial statements, enhance international capital flows and reduce financial reporting costs for multinational enterprises (Radebaugh & Gray, 2002; Choi & Meek, 2005).

International convergence and harmonisation of auditing standards is important in ensuring the global capital market participants that high-quality audit process is consistently applied across countries. This would enhance the creditability of corporate financial reports and would lead to more effective and efficient allocation of resources in global capital markets (Doupnik & Perera, 2005). Moreover, convergence and harmonisation of auditing standards would increase global efficiency and effectiveness of the audit process (Doupnik & Perera, 2005). In recent years, comparability with the International Standards on Auditing, issued respectively by the IFAC through its International Auditing and Assurance Board, has become a major objective of global auditing and assurance systems and procedures.[2] All three countries in this study, namely, Australia, India and Malaysia, are strongly supportive of international convergence and harmonisation of accounting and auditing standards.

Professional accounting bodies in Australia, India and Malaysia, together with 70 other countries, are members of the IFAC. A requirement of IFAC membership is that professional accounting bodies should support the objectives of IFAC and specifically to incorporate IFAC's pronouncements into their national standards (www.ifac.org/MediaCenter/files/IAASB_Fact_Sheet.pdf).[3] Recall that in Chapter 1 it was concluded that professional judgements pervade virtually all aspects of contemporary financial statement audits. Moreover, audit manuals of most multinational accounting firm reinforces that the single most important element in applying the firm's audit approach is the exercise of informed judgement at the various stages of the audit. Also, recognising the importance of professional judgements in auditing, the International Auditing and Assurance Board is currently working on a number of projects to examine various issues related to professional judgements. However, both the IFAC and its International Auditing and Assurance Board provide no discussion of cultural influences on interpreting auditing standards in various countries. On the contrary, the IFAC has implicitly adopted the assumption that accounting and auditing information is 'neutral' and 'value-free'; that is, the influence of culture on judgements of professional accountants can be ignored.

Such a simplistic assumption with regards to accounting and auditing has long been rejected. For example, Gray (1988, p. 4) concluded that, "the influence of culture on accounting would seem to have been largely neglected in the development of ideas about international classification". Moreover, to show the importance of culture in accounting development, Gray (1988) proposed a comprehensive theoretical model that linked accounting values to Hofstede's (1980) cultural dimensions (Gray's model and the cultural dimensions were discussed in Chapter 1). Salter and Niswander (1995) operationalised Gray's (1988) model and showed a significant relationship between accounting values and cultural dimensions. Additionally, with respect to international harmonisation of accounting and auditing standards, Salter and Niswander (1995, p. 393) aptly concluded that, "Even if the IASC[4] were successful de jure, culture may frustrate the results by making the quality of financial reporting unclear. Persons seeking information on companies globally may believe they are receiving the same information but may well be missing certain subtleties and, as a result, make, poor decisions...even companies that voluntarily disclose information above required national levels still retain a national flavor to those disclosures and are limited by those national predilections".

The findings of this study provide empirical evidence to complement Gray's (1988), Salter and Niswander's (1995) and other cross-cultural studies (these were discussed in Chapter 2), which show the importance of incorporating culture as a significant variable in the convergence and harmonisation accounting and auditing standards. Specifically, greater comparability in accounting information should result from identifying consistent differences in judgements among professional accountants from various countries when they are presented with similar accounting information. It is therefore suggested that while international convergence and harmonisation of accounting and auditing standards may be a laudable objective, greater attention should be paid to incorporate culture as an important variable in this process.

CROSS-CULTURAL ACCOUNTING RESEARCH

Chapter 2 identified the theoretical and methodological weaknesses in prior accounting research with particular reference to cross-cultural studies on professional accountant and auditor values, perceptions and judgements. The findings from this study have the following implications for improving cross-cultural accounting research.

Firstly, it was discussed in Chapter 2 that the simplistic treatment of culture, which relies on one or a limited number of Hofstede's cultural dimensions have tended to limit theoretical advances in cross-cultural accounting research. It was suggested that if any of the five dimensions are not applied in theory development, then the study needs to explain the reason(s) for the omission, and needs also to discuss the theoretical implications of the omitted cultural dimension(s). The 'pick and choose' approach to the selection of relevant cultural dimensions used in a number of studies may limit our understanding of the influence of culture on various accounting constructs selected for the study. Consequently, studies need to pay attention to developing a more comprehensive and holistic perspective on cultural differences and similarities.

To overcome this limitation in cross-cultural research, it is suggested that Hofstede's cultural dimensions be complemented by historical, sociological, psychological and other relevant literatures. The combination of the five-dimensional cultural model and the supporting literatures from other disciplines would identify and provide an understanding of the core and the peripheral values in a given society. To further enrich understanding of cultural values in a country, it may be useful to conduct interviews with selected subjects with an interest in culture, to obtain additional evidence on attributes of culture that are of importance to the accounting profession, and the particular dependent variables that are examined in the particular study. Conducting such interviews provides additional insight into core cultural norms and values that may impact on the dependent variables. Theory development and hypotheses formulation can then proceed driven largely by the differences in core cultural values. Consistent results obtained in this study may be attributable to this approach.

Additionally, two methodological considerations emerge from the current study. Firstly, the findings show that the Multidimensional Ethics Measure is useful in capturing the various complexities of differences in cross-cultural judgements of professional accountants. Secondly, the findings suggest that SDRB cannot be ignored in any research in accounting where respondents are asked to provide their evaluations on controversial accounting constructs.

In conclusion, the implications discussed above are related to accounting education because it is through education, broadly defined, that research can have the most significant long-term impacts. Indeed, it is generally recognised that research, education and practice in accounting are closely interrelated. The findings from the study contribute to accounting education in general, and international accounting in particular.

LIMITATIONS AND SUGGESTIONS FOR FURTHER RESEARCH

A significant discussion of culture in this study is based on the structural functionalist perspective, which conceptualises 'cultural reality' in terms of norms and values in a given society. As such, the conception of culture based on shared norms and values may limit our understanding of cross-cultural similarities and differences because it is argued that any conception of culture needs to address the following questions: "How do strategies of representation of empowerment come to be formulated in the competing claims of communities where, despite shared histories of deprivation and discrimination, the exchange of values, meanings and priorities may not always be collaborative and dialogical, but may be profoundly antagonistic, conflictual and even incommensurable?" (Bhabha, 1994, p. 2).

Future studies may examine cultural influences on professional accountants' judgements with respect to auditor–client conflict resolution and whistle-blowing as an internal control mechanism, by conceptualising culture as being embedded and entangled in the exercise of power, resistance and conflict.

However, while the post-modernism, post-colonialism and post-feminism perspectives largely reject the contributions to the literature made by conceptualising culture in terms of norms and values, it is suggested that there is a need to devise ways of integrating different disciplinary perspectives, which will achieve greater forms of completeness from the point of view of understanding the cultural process as a whole. In this regard, Bennett (1998,

p. 59) aptly proposes that, "a more definite and limited set of disciplinary attributes for itself (cultural studies), viewing these, more modestly, as existing alongside other disciplinary norms and paradigms rather than auguring their dissolution into its own totalising ambition".

Two additional recommendations for future studies emerge from the results of this study. Firstly, with respect to the findings for whistle-blowing as an internal control mechanism, it is suggested that both greater seriousness of the wrongdoing and/or the threat of retaliation for the potential whistle-blower, affect judgements of professional accountants from Australia, India and Malaysia. Therefore, it is recommended that future studies consider both these factors in designing research instruments for examining cross-cultural differences in whistle-blowing.

Secondly, based on the findings from Lee (1997) and this study, it is suggested that additional research needs to be done to validate Hofstede's Values Survey Module (1994) with respect to calculation of the Long-term Orientation index. Although the Value Survey Module (1994) did not show differences between Australia on one hand, and India and Malaysia on the other on the Long-term Orientation index, the psychological, sociological and historical literatures suggest that differences do exist. As suggested earlier, this problem may be overcome by developing a more comprehensive and holistic perspective when examining cultural differences and similarities across countries.

With respect to the overall findings, it is suggested that caution needs to be exercised when generalising to other countries and accounting constructs. Finally, it is critical to recognise that differing cultural values across societies do not imply or justify individual ethnic or cultural stereotypes. It is inappropriate to apply collective attributes of a cultural group to a particular individual from that group.

NOTES

Chapter 1: Introduction

1. Professional accountants are defined as members of either the Australian Society of Certified Practising Accountants, the Institute of Chartered Accountants in Australia, the Institute of Chartered Accountants in India, the Malaysian Institute of Accountants (Institut Akauntan Malaysia) or the Malaysian Association of Certified Public Accountants (Institut Akauntan Umum Malaysia). The big-five accounting firms include KPMG Peat Marwick, Ernst & Young, PricewaterhouseCoopers, Arthur Anderson and Deloitte Ross Tohmatsu. On 31 August, 2002, Arthur Anderson after conviction on Enron's audit surrendered its licenses and its right to practice to the Securities and Exchange Commission of the USA.

2. This dimension relates to the teachings of Confucius, a Chinese philosopher around 500 BC. Confucianism is not a religion but a set of pragmatic rules derived from Chinese history. Since this dimension also applied to countries such as India and Brazil which do not have Confucian heritages, Hofstede (1994b) suggested that "Long versus Short-term Orientation" is a better description of this fifth cultural dimension.

3. This study focuses on the consequences (of culture) side of the framework, and is not directed towards the antecedents of culture.

4. Salter and Niswander (1995) and Eddie (1996) operationalised the model of Gray (1988) and showed a significant relationship between accounting values and cultural dimensions.

Chapter 2: Literature Review

1. Papers reviewed by Harrison and McKinnon (1999) include: Lincon, Hanada, and Olson (1981), Birnberg and Wong (1985), Lincoln et al. (1986), Snodgrass and Grant (1986), Birnberg and Snodgrass (1988), Chow, Shields, and Chan (1991), Frucot and Shearon (1991), Vance, McClaine, Boje, and Stage (1992), Harrison (1992, 1993), Ueno and Sekaran (1992), Ueno and Wu (1993), Harrison et al. (1994), Chow et al. (1994), O'Connor (1995), Lau et al. (1995), Chow, Kato, and Merchant (1996).

2. Core cultural values are those that are the most important, enduring and stable. In contrast, peripheral values are not as important and may not be shared by most members of the society (Lachman, Nedd, & Hinings, 1994). Indeed, cross-cultural researchers need to draw on the core cultural values in their theory development and hypothesis formulation. In the next chapter, examples of how to draw on the core cultural values are presented.

3. Reviews and edited collections of studies in international accounting are available in the literature. See for example, Gernon and Wallace (1995) in relation to reviews and the five volumes Library of International Accounting (1996) for edited collections.

4. Studies from cross-cultural research in management control systems design that treated culture as an unspecified independent variable include studies by Chiu and Chang (1979) and Daley, Jiambalvo, Sundem, and Kondo (1985). After finding differences in the adoption of certain management accounting techniques between companies in the USA and Taiwan, Chiu and Chang (1979) attributed these differences to culture with no further elaboration. Similarly, Daley et al. (1985) treated culture as a "black-box" in their examination of perceptual differences in financial control systems including autonomy in purchases, budget development and participation and motivation between controllers and managers in the US and Japan.

5. The Uncertainty Avoidance scores (scores and rankings are from low to high Uncertainty Avoidance) identified by Hofstede (1980) for these three countries are: Canada with a score 48 is ranked 12th of the 53 countries that were studied, USA with a score of 46 is ranked 11th and Great Britain scored 35 and is ranked 6th.

6. The countries examined were: Argentina, Australia, Belgium, Brazil, Canada, Chile, Colombia, Denmark, Finland, France, Germany, Hong Kong, Italy, Korea, Malaysia, Mexico, the Netherlands, New Zealand, Norway, Philippines, Portugal, Singapore, South Africa, Spain, Sweden, Taiwan, United Kingdom and United States.

7. Based on Hofstede's original instrument, Harrison et al. (1994) scored 63 for Hong Kong and 61 for Australia, compared with Hofstede's (1980) scores of 29 and 51, respectively.

8. Yamamura et al. (1996, p. 361) noted that rank consciousness was equivalent to Hofstede's cultural dimension of Power Distance.

9. Yamamura et al. (1996, p. 361) also stated that group orientation was equivalent to Hofstede's cultural dimension of Individualism.

10. A detailed discussion of this study and the Defining Issues Test (DIT) is provided because scores from the DIT are extensively used in ethics research in accounting (Ponemon, 1992; Louwers, Ponemon, & Radtke, 1997; Bailey et al., 2005).

11. Confucian Dynamism is unlikely to have been invoked in Karnes et al.'s (1990) theory development because this dimension was introduced in the literature by Hofstede and Bond (1988) and gained prominence in cross-cultural accounting literature only in the early 1990s.

12. For example, multinational accounting firms operate an "up or out" policy (Soeters & Schreuder, 1988, p. 77). It is very unlikely, given the importance placed on Confucian Dynamism in Taiwan (The Chinese Culture Connection, 1987, p. 153), and the Confucian tradition of respect for one's social network and the tradition of "patriarchal authority" (Kao, 1993, p .25), that local accounting firms would have adopted such a policy.

13. This bias refers to the desire, at either a conscious or an unconscious level, to give a particular picture of oneself in the way one responds to questionnaire items (Watkins & Cheung, 1995, p. 490). SDRB is a pervasive problem in behavioral ethics research (Rossi et al., 1983; Tyson, 1992). How this study attempts to deal with the potential for SDRB in the survey questionnaire is discussed in Chapter 4.

14. Additional details regarding the background of managers and professional staff are not provided.

15. *Ren Qin* is described as social favours that are exchanged in the form of money, goods, information, status, service and affection according to an implicit set of rules (Hwang, 1987, pp. 949–951).

Chapter 3: Theory Development and Hypotheses Formulation

1. Similar ideas have been expressed by a number of researchers such as Hu (1944), Lu (1983), Bharati (1985), Brindley (1989) and Sinha & Sinha (1990). These are discussed later in the chapter.

2. Recall that the focus of this study is on Chinese Malaysians.

3. Recall that Hofstede's taxonomy is based on comparative differences, and therefore the comparisons provided between Australians on one hand and Indians and Chinese Malaysians on the other, are relative to each other in degree and intensity.

4. For example, the Federal Constitution of Malaysia defines a Malay as, "...a person who professes the Muslim religion, habitually speaks the Malay language, conforms to Malay "adapt" (customs) and is a Malaysian citizen" [The Federal Constitution, Article 160 (2)].

5. Also see Hu (1993) and Alamgir (1994) for additional details.

6. For example, since the race riots of 13 May, 1969, it is unacceptable for the Chinese to question sensitive issues such as the special privileges of the Malays (Federal Territory MCA Liaison Committee, 1982).

7. Although Confucius was the founder and thus the most prominent member of the Confucianism school, his ideas are sometimes different from those of other philosophers such as Mencius and Xun Zi, and are different also from other schools of the later Confucianism. All these different ideas must be included as part of Confucianism. In its broad sense, Confucianism comprises the ideas and doctrines of all Confucianists in the history of Chinese philosophy (Lu, 1983).

8. It is under this historic interpretation that Confucius has been criticized in mainland China as "stubbornly supporting the aristocratic slavery system..., and condemned to symbolize all that is backward, conservative, reactionary, anti-reform and anti-revolutionary" (Guo, 1972, pp. 1–2). However, Stover (1974) rejected this interpretation and argued that Confucianism was espoused because its ideology was congruent with the cultural values of the agrarian state.

9. The current concept of a Chinese family (chia or chia-ting; this concept was also used in imperial times) refers to a "unit consisting of members related to each other by blood, marriage, or adoption and having a common budget and common property" (Lang, 1968, p. 13). A joint Chinese family may consist of parents, their unmarried children, their married sons and sons' wives and children; and sometimes a fourth or fifth generation (Lang, 1968).

10. In studying Confucius' humanism, the most crucial concept is "ren", which has been variously translated in English as love, benevolence, human-heartedness, perfect virtue, or humanity (Lu, 1983, p. 5).

11. Taoism and Buddhism continued in the Chinese empire as an undercurrent of Chinese religious and philosophical thought. Consequently, religious tolerance

became one of the outstanding features of Chinese society. This tolerance was facilitated partly by the fact that Taoism and Buddhism allowed themselves to be influenced considerably by Confucianism, influencing it in turn (Lang, 1968, p. 8).

12. The closest Chinese approximation for the English "to save face" is a person who continually strives to show himself or herself better situated, more capable, possessing better social connections or a better character than actually is the case (Hu, 1944, p. 58).

13. Hu (1944) and Ho (1976) are classic references in this area. The use of these references in this study is relevant, given the longevity and permanence of the influence of the cultural phenomena being drawn on, and their combination with more recent citations (such as Bond & Hwang, 1986 and Cheung et al., 1996) providing corroborating evidence.

14. This concept has some similarities with Confucius' criteria for a "chun-tze" (the perfect gentleman) that were described earlier in the chapter.

15. The Chinese preoccupation with "social order is the same way as the Oedipal drama underscores the Western preoccupation with individual freedom" (Bond & Hwang, 1986, p. 213).

16. Even the concept of beauty (t'i-mien) is associated with that of social approval (Hu, 1944, p. 55).

17. Social stratification is a "hierarchical ranking of status positions in a society. It is the outcome of social inequalities within the social structure which are transmitted by society's major institutions" (Edgar et al., 1993, p. 172).

18. Aryans were white skinned and were called "Svityano". They dominated and colonized the original inhabitants, "Krsnatvac", who were of darker complexion (Sinha, 1995, p. 29).

19. The reputation of female members in Indian families is largely derived from that of the male members. For example, the key term in a matrimonial transaction "rasa" (literal meaning is juice) means that a woman merges and loses her entire personality into her "husband's substance at the wedding" (Marriott, 1976, p. 111).

20. Literally the cognate vocation, "sahajam karma" (Bharati, 1985, p. xviii).

21. "Outcastes" have also been called the "untouchables" or the "Harijans". They prefer to call themselves "Dalits", Hindi for the oppressed. There are approximately 160 million Dalits in India (http://www.dalits.org/default.htm).

22. Running organisations as if they were their "personal fiefdoms" is a value that is also shared by the Chinese.

23. Triandis (1994, p. 4) noted that: "We in the west think that if X is true, non-X cannot be true". This view makes relatively little sense in cultures such as India, where "philosophical monism is widely used i.e., 'everything is one', and the 'opposite of a great truth is also a great truth'".

24. In a collectivist society, one says what the other wants to hear, and one does not contradict the other (Triandis, 1994, p. 185). The importance of harmony in collectivist cultures is illustrated in the following Indonesian missionary's parable: A man had two sons. He went to the first and said: 'Son, go and work in the vineyard today.' The son replied, 'I will go, sir,' but he did not go. The man went to his second son and said the same thing, and the son replied 'I will not go,' but later changed his mind and did go. Which of the two sons did the bidding of the father? The collectivist missionary argued that it was the first, because he did not contradict his father (Hofstede, 1991, p. 58).

25. The influence of the Australian landscape on its societal values was aptly described: "If we ask what the bush has meant for Australians, it has stood for anti-romantic attitudes towards an unfruitful nature. The continent and the landscape...have been the setting in which a man or a woman shows they are not 'soft' Europeans, that they do not give in to nature or to corrupt authority. Their errand...has been to do without Europe and to see life without the 'illusions' of European culture...withoutromantic agony" (in Goodnow et al., 1989, p. 40).

26. For example, it was only in 1967 that the Australian people voted overwhelmingly in support of a referendum to remove the constitutional restriction on the federal government from making laws affecting the welfare of the Aboriginal people in any state and to repeal Section 127 of the Constitution so that the census could count Aboriginal people among the Australian citizenry (Jones, 1989, p. 104). The final leap to the abolition of racial discrimination came when the Whitlam Labor government decreed in 1973 that future immigration policy would be based on the "avoidance of discrimination on any ground of race or colour of skin or nationality" (Borrie, 1989, p. 129).

27. Withers (1989, p. 9) noted the relatively advantaged position of migrants in Australia compared to the experience with guest worker migrants in post-war Europe: "we find a broad equity of treatment. Record of equal access to social facilities and amenities".

28. Amongst the convicts, the male–female ratio was 5:1; by 1985 the ratio has been reduced to 1.4:1 (Borrie, 1989, p. 120) and in 2005 the ratio was 0.99:1 (http://www.cia.gov/cia/publications/factbook/geos/as.html).

29. A literature review of nineteenth-century Australia shows that today's children are not unique in the frequency with which they are not cared for by two parents. For example, nineteenth-century Australia "saw families disrupted by a series of events-migration, the gold rushes, the demands of the pastoral and mining industries and the great depression of the 1890s – that left many children to be reared by single parents and some children without either parent. In the year 1870, for example, family separations were so common that 2,498 children passed through the charitable institutions of New South Wales: 0.5 percent of all persons of all ages in the colony" (Goodnow et al., 1989, p. 28).

30. In contrast, in low individualistic cultures, "family members are connected; younger relatives are an integral part of their elders' lives. Because social support tends to be derived almost exclusively from the family, it is culturally normative for relatives to assume responsibility for family members" (Hart & Poole, 1995, p. 97).

31. Another point of view states that "Australian families are marked by patriarchy (power in the hands of men) and by matriduxy (leadership in the hands of mothers)" (Withers, 1989, p. 33). However, the important issue for this study is that there are differences between Indian/Chinese and Australians in terms of exercise of power within families.

32. The difference between America and Australia on equalitarianism and egalitarianism was aptly described by Withers (1989, p. 18): "Americans favour equality of opportunity and Australians favour equality of outcome".

33. Withers (1989, p. 16) cited another story that reveals the importance of egalitarian values in Australia: "Lord Bertrand Russell left our shores with more hope for mankind than when he arrived: oral tradition has it that among his formative

experiences in Australia in arriving at that conclusion was that of asking for his suitcase to be carried up to his hotel room. The clerk responded, What's wrong with you mate? You look healthy enough to me".

34. Tall poppy syndrome is defined as "a desire to diminish in stature those people who have attained excellence" (The Macquarie Dictionary, 1991, p. 1784).

35. Self-actualisation was identified by Maslow (1954) as the highest level in his five-order hierarchy of needs theory. The self-actualisation need deals with fulfilling one's self to grow, and use one's abilities to the fullest and most creative extent. Maslow (1954, p. 81) defined self-actualisation as the "desire to become more and more what one is, to become everything one is capable of becoming". In contrast, the researcher's reading of the literature suggests that among Indians and Chinese Malaysians, "social needs" are regarded more highly. In Maslow's hierarchy of needs theory which comprised of five categories, social need was categorised in group three. Social needs are related to the social nature of people and their need for companionship.

36. Interviews with partners of selected big-five firms in each of the three nations further confirmed the highly competitive nature of the audit markets in India, Australia and Malaysia.

37. Daft (1988, p. 458) in describing Western approaches to managing conflict argues that, "If an organization achieves the ideal of no conflict, the organization is probably in trouble. Conflict is a sign of an active, ongoing, forceful organization".

Chapter 4: Research Method

1. The big-five accounting firms include KPMG Peat Marwick, Ernst & Young, PricewaterhouseCoopers, Arthur Anderson, and Deloitte Ross Tohmatsu. On 31 August 2002, Arthur Anderson after conviction on Enron's audit surrendered its licenses and its right to practice to the Securities and Exchange Commission of the USA.The big-five accounting firms include KPMG Peat Marwick, Ernst & Young, Coopers & Lybrand, PricewaterhouseCoopers, Arthur Anderson, and Deloitte Ross Tohmatsu. On 31 August 2002, Arthur Anderson after conviction on Enron's audit surrendered its licenses and right to practice to the Securities and Exchange Commission of the USA.

2. Tables 1 and 2 in chapter 2 provide details of these studies.

3. See Radebaugh and Gray (2002) and Nobes and Parker (2004) for the different patterns of accounting development in these countries.

4. Note that the European Union, as part of its move towards convergence of accounting standards, in 2005 adopted International Financial Reporting Standards (IFRS). IFRS requires substantial exercise of accountants' professional judgements.

5. The AAA (1977) provides the following classification of five zones of influence: British, Franco–Spanish–Portuguese, German/Dutch, United States and Communistic (now mixed economy). Recent studies have broadly continued to use this method of classification.

6. Professional accountants in the three countries selected for examination are defined as members of either the Australian Society of Certified Practising Accountants, the Institute of Chartered Accountants in Australia, the Institute of Chartered Accountants in India, the Malaysian Institute of Accountants (Institut Akauntan

Malaysia), or the Malaysian Association of Certified Public Accountants (Institut Akauntan Umum Malaysia).

7. Interviews with partners in Kuala Lumpur revealed that a vast majority of senior professional accountants in the big-five accounting firms in Malaysia are Chinese Malaysian. The purpose of this study was to draw respondents of Chinese Malaysian origin. Since ethnicity is a highly sensitive issue in Malaysia, this issue could not be openly discussed with partners of all four firms that had agreed to participate in this study. However, since the topic of ethnicity in Malaysia was raised by two of the four partners and they were comfortable in discussing this, the researcher was able to request these two partners to select only Chinese Malaysian respondents in their firms. The results which showed that there were no significant differences in responses between the two firms where the respondents were Chinese Malaysian, and the two firms where the ethnic background of respondents were not known, are discussed in Chapter 5.

8. These hypotheses and their formulation were discussed in Chapter 3.

9. The three scenarios used in this study satisfy these criteria.

10. The importance of applying Multidimensional Ethics Measure to examine ethical judgements is shown by Tsalikis and Nwachukwu (1989), Reidenbach and Robin (1988; 1990), Flory et al. (1992), and Cohen et al. (1993b; 1996a).

11. It was necessary to do this to check that there were no significant differences in judgements among the respondents from each of the three firms in Australia. Similar tests were also conducted among the three firms that participated in the study in India, and also among the four firms in Malaysia. No such differences were found. Furthermore, statistical tests showed that there was no significant difference between the two methods of collecting responses in Australia. That is, there was no significant difference between completed responses that were collected personally and those that were sent in pre-paid, self-addressed envelopes. The details are elaborated on in Chapter 5.

12. Defined as rank of supervisor or higher in a professional accounting firm.

13. For example, Spitzer (1979, p. 69) noted that he was "...disturbed by the subcontinent's entrenched colonial legacy of class distinction between European and Indian. Since the authoritarian days of the British Raj, Westerners have been defined as 'high caste' and many Indians still expect Caucasians to treat them as inferiors. Unfortunately, to act with courtesy and consideration only confuses that pattern of behavior so rigorously instilled by the British".

14. Interviews were conducted with 11 academics in India, 9 in Malaysia and 10 in Australia.

15. It was suggested in Chapter 3 that in comparison with Australian subjects, subjects from India and Malaysia are more likely to be influenced by other people, such as their family and their superior officers, in their judgements. The purpose of this question was to gain further insight into this proposition.

Chapter 5: Results: Cultural Values

1. The differences between the three countries with respect to the indices calculated in this study and those calculated by Hofstede (1980) (shown in brackets) are as follows: Australia and India 47 (41); Australia and Malaysia 75 (68) and India and Malaysia 28 (27).

2. The decrease in differences between Australia and Malaysia and between India and Malaysia with respect to their Individualism indices calculated in this study and those by Hofstede (1983a) may be attributed to Malaysia's higher economic growth compared to India and Australia. Hofstede (1983b, p. 80) postulated that the degree of individualism in a country is statistically related to that country's wealth.

3. The results from this study show Australia to be higher than India and Malaysia on the Individualism indices. Taking these scores and their differences in conjunction with Hofstede's (1980) cluster matrices, there is support for these countries being seen to lie in the high and low Individualism clusters of countries generally.

4. Note that the Long-term Orientation was not included in Hofstede's Value Survey (1980). However, with respect to Long-term Orientation indices, Hofstede and Bond's (1988) findings show Australia at 31 (out of an observed range of 0 to 96) and ranked 11 (out of 20 countries), and India at 61, rank 6. Hofstede and Bond (1988) did not include Malaysia in the study.

5. Recall that the literature suggests that compared to the Chinese-based societies, Australians are likely to be lower on the Long-term Orientation index. That is, Australians are likely to be Short-term Oriented, while Chinese societies are more Long-term Oriented. Indeed, Long-term Orientation is also referred to as "Confucian Dynamism".

6. Also note that Lee's (1997) results for the Power Distance and Individualism indices were in the direction predicted by Hofstede (1980), and consistent with the directional results obtained in this study.

7. This study has adopted one aspect of "content analysis" in the use of frequency counts as a method of analysing interview responses. A complete application of content analysis was not considered appropriate in the context of the study. It is acknowledged that the potential for researcher bias in interpretation and classification of responses may be present.

8. The meaning of the terms positive and negative with respect to interviewees' perceptions of their organisational and national cultures was explained to them to ensure that they were clear on each of the structured interview questions.

9. One academic rather aptly described this as "management by affectionate domination".

10. To facilitate discussion on sensitive issues such as racial discrimination, when interviewing Chinese and Indians in Malaysia, this researcher when introducing himself also explained that he was forced to migrate from his country (Fiji) because of legal and social discrimination practised in the country after the military coups in 1987. This strategy seemed to work because a number of non-Malays felt comfortable in describing examples of racial discrimination they had faced in their organisations and the country.

11. Malays are called "Bumiputra" (literal meaning is "son of the soil") (Chien, 1987, p. 8).

12. Since "Bahasa Malaysia" was adopted as the national language in 1957, "the government has made great efforts to attain this language goal through various programs, particularly through formal education. It has vigorously promoted Bahasa Malaysia among its people of different ethnic groups with a wide range of activities" (Hu, 1993, p. 53).

13. Some of these statements by Australian academics relate to the attributes of high Power Distance as manifest in organisational settings. However, compared to the Indian and Malaysian responses, the frequency of appearance of these attributes is lower among the Australian interviewees.

14. Consistent with the suggestion, this study asked interviewees questions about both their national culture and organisational culture, to gain insight into their core cultural values.

15. High regard for senior citizens and elders is based on their greater "wisdom", which they are expected to pass on to the younger generation.

16. For example, unlike the West, separate residential facilities for senior citizens are almost non-existent in India and Malaysia. The virtues of "filial piety" demand that children look after their aged parents in their own homes.

17. An example of mutual support may include the extended family contributing money to send a family member to study abroad (USA, UK, Canada and Australia are highly regarded). Eventually on return and when financially secure, he or she is supposed to provide necessary financial support to other family members. Better still, an individual would be highly regarded if he or she migrated and then in turn sponsored other family members for migration.

18. One academic appropriately described this as a "flexible culture".

19. In Chapter 3 it was suggested that the reputation of female members in Indian families is largely derived from that of male members.

20. Tall poppy syndrome is defined as "a desire to diminish in stature those people who have attained excellence" (The Macquarie Dictionary, 1991, p. 1784).

21. Since discrimination against the Chinese in Malaysia has been identified as a pervasive issue, both at the national as well as organisational levels, this study needs to provide a further explanation of this within the Confucian model. A brief explanation of this follows. Historically, the Chinese in Malaysia have more or less accepted the legal and social discrimination against them (Alamgir, 1994). With respect to the Chinese in Malaysia, Hu (1993, p. 45) further explains that "most of them never thought of Malaya as their home until the 20th century. Perhaps that is why the seizure of political power was not the ambition of the Chinese in Malaysia. All they wanted was to make enough money to keep the family comfortable in a peaceful haven, and to have a good education for their children". This acceptance of discrimination may be traced to the doctrines of Confucianism in which "Authority [political power], supersedes the law" (Shengqing, 1992, p. 6). That is, in Chinese culture, "the laws, in the minds of the people, reflect the authority of the state, not the rights of the people. The concept of human rights, has not been given importance" (Shengqing, 1992, p. 6). Again, this "cultural concern for harmony-within-hierarchy" may explain the current political status of the Chinese in Malaysia.

22. Recall that the reason for asking respondents about their colleagues' judgements, rather than their own judgements, was to minimise any SDRB.

23. With respect to the question on "their distant relatives", the assumption of homogeneity of variance was violated. Therefore results from one-way ANOVA as well as nonparametric Kruskal–Wallis one-way ANOVA and follow-up Mann–Whitney U-tests were performed.

24. Again, the reason for asking respondents about their colleagues' judgements rather than their own judgements, was to minimise any SDRB.

Chapter 6: Results: Hypotheses Tests

1. A total of 98 responses was received, but six were eliminated because of incomplete data.

2. A total of 95 responses was received, but 11 were eliminated because of incomplete data.

3. A total of 81 responses was received, but two incomplete responses, and seven responses from those whose nationality and/or country of birth were other than Australia were eliminated.

4. Recall that the Multidimensional Ethics Measure consists of eight bipolar scales divided into three dimensions. These are the Moral Equity dimension, which comprises four items, and Relativism and Contractualism dimensions, each comprising two items.

5. Interviews with partners of the big-five accounting firms in each of the three countries revealed that their employees were required to pass examinations set by the respective professional accounting bodies and meet other requirements for professional membership before promotion to a senior position, However, in India partners generally encouraged their employees to also study for a master's degree while preparing for professional examinations.

6. This variable has been included in the study because it has been suggested that provision of management advisory services or consulting services may influence how audit–client conflicts are resolved (Gul, 1991; Lindsay, 1992; The Future of Accounting Profession, 2005). Results of statistical tests discussed later in this chapter in the section entitled, Aggregation of Data, suggested that there was no difference among respondents within each of the three countries with respect to the percentage of working time spent in provision of management advisory services.

7. It is important to note that the mean differences cannot be tested by univariate statistics. This assures protection against the effects of positive correlations among the dependent variables as well as the tendency for individual differences to be significant merely by chance as more responses are included in the variate vectors (Morrison, 1967, p. 127; Tabachnick & Fidell, 1989, p. 399).

8. Tabachnick and Fidell (1989, p. 405) further explain that "Bartlett's test of sphericity tests the null hypothesis that correlations among dependent variables are zero; if they are, univariate F is used instead of stepdown F to test the importance of dependent variables".

9. Bray and Maxwell (1985, p. 35) further state that Box's M is "generally not useful because the test itself is extremely sensitive to departures from normality".

10. Nonparametric Kruskal–Wallis one-way ANOVA is used in this study if the homogeneity of variance assumption is violated because it is "the most efficient of the nonparametric tests for k independent samples. It has power-efficiency of 95.5%, when compared with the F-test, the most powerful parametric test" (Siegel, 1956, p. 194).

11. These are the single item "ethical/unethical" question, and two additional questions which measure the likelihood that respondents would make the same decision, and whether their colleagues would make the same decision as the actors in the three cases.

12. Specific p-values and other details from the statistical tests are not shown in this section because of the large number of tests conducted before the aggregation of the data (132 statistical tests in total, 44 for each of the three nations.

13. Note that Table 1A, presented earlier, shows that for each of the 11 dependent variables, the mean scores of Australian professional accountants are higher than those of Chinese Malaysian and Indian professional accountants. These mean scores are in the direction predicted in the hypotheses.

14. It is recommended that Tukey's HSD and Scheffe's follow-up tests are used because these tests are more conservative than Fisher's LSD, Duncan's New Multiple Range and Newman-Keuls (Huck et al., 1974, p. 69; Cooksey, 1995, p. 13).

15. A possible theoretical explanation for the significant difference between Indian and Chinese Malaysian professional accountants with respect to their judgements is discussed later in the conclusion section of this chapter.

16. It is suggested that ANOVA could still be used despite any violation of homogeneity of variance because of its additional power (Huck et al., 1974, p. 197). This study reports both ANOVA and relevant nonparametric statistic, to overcome the criticism directed at nonparametric statistical tests that they "do not use all of the information in the sample" or that they "throw away information" (Siegel, 1956, p. 32).

17. Huck et al. (1974, p. 216) and Conover (1980, p. 236) recommend that the Mann–Whitney *U*-test is the appropriate follow-up test after finding significant results from Kruskal–Wallis one-way ANOVA.

18. Results from Wilks' Lambda and Hotelling's trace criterion also provided a *p*-value of 0.000.

19. Univariate *F*-tests (2,245 df) showed significant difference ($p = 0.000$) among the three nations on all four items comprising the Moral Equity Dimension, and on each of the two items comprising the Relativism and Contractualism Dimensions. However, as discussed earlier, results from only the Stepdown Analysis are used for hypotheses testing because of its theoretical relevance to the study.

20. In each case follow-up Mann–Whitney *U*-tests were run only after finding significant results on the Kruskal–Wallis one-way ANOVA tests for the three nations.

21. Responses on both questions (you and your colleague) violated the assumption of homogeneity of variances (Levene's test showed 2-tailed $p = 0.001$ for the "you" question and 0.001 for the "colleague" question). Consequently, results of both parametric and nonparametric tests are presented.

22. A possible theoretical explanation for the significant difference between Indian and Chinese Malaysian professional accountants with respect to their judgements is discussed later in the conclusion section of this chapter.

23. Results from Wilks' Lambda and Hotelling's trace criterion also provided *p*-values of 0.000.

24. Univariate *F*-tests (2,245 df) showed significant difference ($p = 0.000$) among the three nations on all four items comprising the Moral Equity Dimension, and on each of the two items comprising the Relativism and Contractualism Dimensions.

25. Results from Wilks' Lambda and Hotelling's trace criterion also provided *p*-values of 0.000.

26. Univariate *F*-tests (2,245 df) showed significant difference ($p = 0.000$) among the three nations on all four items comprising the Moral Equity Dimension, and on each of the two items comprising the Relativism and Contractualism Dimensions.

27. Nonparametric Wilcoxon Matched-Pairs Signed-Ranks tests also showed *p*-values of 0.000 in all cases.

28. The use of a one-tailed Z-test is consistent with the approach used by Flory et al. (1992).

29. Additional insight refers to both the greater R and in terms of the specific components comprising the Multidimensional Ethics Measure. These issues are discussed later in this chapter.

30. With respect to Case One (auditor–client conflict resolution) and Case Three (whistle blowing), significant differences were found in relation to two items comprising the Multidimensional Ethics Measure ("morally right/not morally right", and "does not violate an unwritten social contract/violates an unwritten social contract"). With regards to Case Two, a difference was found only on the latter item.

31. The influence of Confucianism on the Chinese people is unique in the world because of China's "unbroken and almost unbreakable longevity of a highly centralized political system (which) finds no precedence anywhere in the world" (Chang, 1992, p. 179). The Chinese communists came to power in 1949 determined "to break the hold of Chinese familism on Chinese society" (Fukuyama, 1995, p. 83). However, the basic Chinese values were never replaced largely because "the Celestial Empire functioned on the basis of Confucian humanism which is an intellectually structured belief system" (Chang, 1992, p. 182). On the contrary, Mao Zedong's revolution of 1949 may have further strengthened the influence of Confucianism on the Chinese society (Fukuyama, 1995, p. 84). In contrast, the subcontinent of India has "never even achieved a nation-wide political unification" (Chang, 1992, p. 179). India is "very much akin to a deep net into which various races and peoples of Asia have drifted and been caught" (Kangayappan, 1992, p. 42). As such, despite various external invasions, Hinduism was never seriously threatened. The Hindu value system has been described as "encompassing", in which the various external influences are "tolerated, balanced, accommodated or just allowed to coexist (Sinha & Sinha, 1990, p. 706).

Chapter 7: Conclusions

1. It is agued that former domestic managers working overseas and their corporate superiors may be more comfortable if they continued to use domestic systems largely because they were promoted to the highest levels of management by mastering their domestic systems (Choi & Meek, 2005, p. 383).

2. Other pronouncements issues by the International Auditing and Assurance Board include: International Standards on Assurance Engagements, International Standards on Related Services, International Standards on Quality Control and International Auditing Practice Statements.

3. The objective of IFAC and its International Auditing and Assurance Standards Board is to, "...serve the public interest by setting high-quality auditing, assurance, quality control and related services standards by facilitating the convergence of international and national standards, thereby enhancing the quality of practice throughout the world and strengthening public confidence in the global auditing and assurance profession" (http://www.ifac.org/IAASB/) (http://www.ifac.org/MediaCenter/files/IAASB).

4. IASC stands for International Accounting Standards Committee, now known as International Accounting Standards Board.

REFERENCES

Agacer, G. M., & Doupnik, T. M. (1991). Perceptions of auditor independence: A cross-cultural study. *The International Journal of Accounting, 26*(2), 220–237.

Ahmed, F., Ganguly, M., Belaur, M. R., & Bhagwan, S. (1997). Asia. *Time* (October), 33–39.

Alamgir, J. (1994). Formula and fortune: Economic development in Malaysia. *Journal of Contemporary Asia, 24*(1), 67–80.

Alexander, C. S., & Becker, H. J. (1978). The use of vignettes in survey research. *Public Opinion Quarterly, 42*(1), 93–104.

Americ, J. H., Kanungo, R., & Aranya, N. (1983). Professional and work values of accountants: A cross-cultural study. *Journal of Accounting Education and Research, 18*(2), 177–192.

American Accounting Association (AAA). (1977). Report of the committee on international accounting operations and education 1975–76. *The Accounting Review*, (Suppl.), 65–101.

American Accounting Association (AAA) (1983). *A Special Issue Ethics in Accounting, 18* (March).

Andersen, W. K. (1995). India in 1994 economics to the fore. *Asian Survey, XXXV*(2), 127–139.

Arnold, D. F., Sr., & Ponemon, L. A. (1991). Internal auditors perceptions of whistle-blowing and the influence of moral reasoning: An experiment. *Auditing: A Journal of Practice & Theory, 10*(2), 1–15.

Australian Society of Certified Practising Accountants and the Institute of Chartered Accountants in Australia (Middleton Report). (1994). *A research study on financial reporting and auditing-bridging the gap*. Sydney: Prentice-Hall.

Bagranoff, N. A., Houghton, K. A., & Hronsky, J. (1994). The structure of meaning in accounting: A cross-cultural experiment. *Behavioral Research in Accounting, 6*(Suppl.), 36–61.

Bailey, C. D., Philips, T. J., Jr., & Scofield, S. B. (2005). Does political bias in the DIT or DIT-2 threaten validity in studies of CPAs. *Behavioral Research in Accounting, 17*, 23–42.

Baumhart, R. C. (1961). How ethical are businessmen? *Harvard Business Review*, (August), 10–11.

Bayles, M. D., & Henley, K. (1983). *Right conduct: Theory and applications*. New York: Random House.

Bazley, M., Hancock, P., Berry, A., & Jarvis, R. (2003). *Contemporary accounting* (5th ed.). Sydney: Thomson Learning.

Beauchamp, T. (1982). *Philosophical ethics*. New York: McGraw-Hill.

Beauchamp, T., & Bowie, N. E. (1983). *Ethical theory and business*. Englewood Cliffs, NJ: Prentice-Hall.

Belkaoui, A. R., & Picur, R. D. (1991). Cultural determinism and perception of accounting concepts. *International Journal of Accounting, 26*(3), 118–130.

Bennett, T. (1998). *Culture a reformer's science*. Sydney: Allen & Unwin.

Berry, J. W., Poortinga, Y. H., Segall, M. H., & Dasen, P. R. (1992). *Cross-cultural psychology: Research and applications*. Cambridge: Cambridge University Press.

Bhabha, H. K. (1994). *The location of culture*. London: Routledge.

Bhagat, R. S., & McQuaid, S. J. (1983). Role of subjective culture in organizations: A review and directions for future research. *Journal of Applied Psychology*, *68*, 653–695.

Bharati, A. (1985). The self in Hindu thought and action. In: A. J. Marsella, G. DeVos & F. L. K. Hsu (Eds), *Culture and self Asian and Western perspectives*. New York: Tavistock Publishers.

Birnberg, J. G., & Snodgrass, C. (1988). Culture and control: A field study. *Accounting Organization and Society*, *13*(5), 447–464.

Birnberg, P. H., & Wong, G. Y. Y. (1985). Organisational structure of multinational banks in Hong Kong from culture free prospective. *Administrative Science Quarterly*, *30*, 262–277.

Bloom, R., & Naciri, M. A. (1989). Accounting standard setting and culture: A comparative analysis of the United States, Canada, England, West Germany, Australia, New Zealand. *The International Journal of Accounting*, *24*(1), 70–97.

Bloom, R., & Schirm, C. (2005). Consolidation and Competition in Public Accounting: An Analysis of the GAO Report. *The CPA Journal* (pp. 21–23). New York State Society of CPAs.

Bolton, G. (1984). The image of Australia in Europe. *Journal of the Royal Society of Arts*, (February), p. 176.

Bond, M. H. (1991). *Beyond the Chinese face: Insights from psychology*. Oxford: Oxford University Press.

Bond, M. H., & Hwang, K. (1986). The social psychology of Chinese people. In: M. H. Bond (Ed.), *The psychology of the Chinese people* (pp. 213–264). Hong Kong: Oxford University Press.

Borrie, W. D. (1989). The population. In: K. Hancock (Ed.), *Australian society* (pp. 119–142). Sydney: Cambridge University Press.

Bowie, N. E. (Ed.) (2002). *The Blackwell guide to business ethics*. Oxford: Blackwell.

Brabeck, M. (1984). Ethical characteristics of whistle blowing. *Journal of Personality*, *18*, 41–53.

Bray, J. H., & Maxwell, W. E. (1985). *Multivariate analysis of variance*. Beverly Hills, CA: Sage.

Bredemeier, H. (1978). Exchange theory. In: T. Bottomore & R. Nishet (Eds), *A history of sociological analysis*. New York: Basic Books.

Brenner, S. N., & Molander, E. A. (1977). Is the ethics of business changing? *Harvard Business Review*, *55*(January–February), 57–71.

Brewster-Smith, M. (1968). Socialization and competence. In: J. Clausen (Ed.), *Socialization and society* (pp. 161–171). Boston: Little Brown.

Brief, A. P., & Motowidlo, S. (1986). Prosocial organizational behaviors. *Academy of Management Review*, *11*(4), 710–725.

Brindley, T. A. (1989). Socio-psychological values in the Republic of China I. *Asian Thought and Society*, *XIV*(41–42), 98–115.

Brindley, T. A. (1990). Socio-psychological values in the Republic of China II. *Asian Thought and Society*, *XV*(43), 1–15.

Briston, R. J. (1978). The evolution of accounting in developing countries. *The International Journal of Accounting Education and Research*, (Fall), 105–120.

Brownell, P. (1995). *Research methods in management accounting*. Australia: Coopers & Lybrand.

Bryce, J. (1921). *Modern democracies*. London: Macmillan.

Cable, D., & Patel, C. (2000). Cultural influences on aggressive financial reporting practices. *Asian Review of Accounting*, *8*(2), 60–80.

Carpenter, B. W., Dirsmith, M. W., & Gupta, P. P. (1994). Materiality judgements and audit firm culture: Social-behavioral and political perspectives. *Accounting, Organizations and Society, 19*(4/5), 355–380.

Cavanagh, S. J., & Fritzsche, F. D. J. (1985). Using vignettes in business ethics research. In: L. Preston (Ed.), *Research in corporate social performance and policy* (pp. 279–293). Greenwich, CT: JAI Press.

Chan, W. (1963). *A source book in Chinese philosophy*. Princeton: Princeton University Press.

Chand, P., Patel, C., & Patel, A. (2005). judgements of professional accountants in Fiji: Implications for convergence of accounting standards. *Emerging issues in accounting, business and technologies conference*. Niagara Falls, USA.

Chang, D. W. (1992). Confucianism, democracy and socialism: The communist search for a new political typology with Chinese characteristics. *Asian Thought and Society, XVII*(51), 179–193.

Chang, M. H. (1995). Greater China and the Chinese global tribe. *Asian Survey, XXXV*(10), 955–967.

Cheung, F. M. (1986). Psychopathology among Chinese people. In: M. H. Bond (Ed.), *The psychology of the Chinese people* (pp. 171–211). Hong Kong: Oxford University Press.

Cheung, F. M., Leung, K., Fan, R. M., Song, W. Z., Zhang, J. X., & Zhang, J. P. (1996). Development of the Chinese personality assessment inventory. *Journal of Cross-Cultural Psychology, 27*(2), 181–199.

Chien, D. J. (1987). *Public bank*. Malaysia: Public Bank.

Child, J. (1981). Culture, contingency and capitalism in the cross-national study of organizations. In: L. L. Cummings & B. M. Staw (Eds), *Research in organizational behavior* (pp. 303–356). Greenwich, CT: JAI Press.

Chiu, J. S., & Chang, D. L. (1979). Management accounting in Taiwan. *Management Accounting*, (June), 50–55.

Choi, F. D. S., & Meek, G. (2005). *International accounting*. Englewood Cliffs, NJ: Pearson Education Inc.

Choi, F. D. S., & Mueller, G. G. (1992). *International accounting*. Englewood Cliffs, NJ: Prentice-Hall.

Chow, C. W., Kato, Y., & Merchant, K. A. (1996). The use of organisational controls and their effects on the data manipulations and management myopia: A Japan vs. U.S. comparison. *Accounting, Organizations and Society, 21*, 175–192.

Chow, C. W., Kato, Y., & Shields, M. D. (1994). National culture and the performance for management controls: An exploratory study of the firm–labor market interface. *Accounting, Organizations and Society, 19*(4/5), 381–400.

Chow, C. W., Shields, M. D., & Chan, Y. K. (1991). The effects of management controls and national culture on manufacturing performance: An experimental investigation. *Accounting, Organizations and Society, 16*(3), 209–226.

Chua, W. F. (1986). Radical developments in accounting thought. *The Accounting Review, LXI*(4), 601–632.

Chui, A. C. W., Lloyd, A. E., & Kwok, C. C. (2002). The determination of capital structure: Is national culture a missing piece to the puzzle. *Journal of International Business Studies, 33*, 99–127.

Clarke, F. L., Dean, G. W., & Oliver, K. G. (1997). *Corporate collapse*. Cambridge: Cambridge University Press.

Cohen, J. R., Pant, L. W., & Sharp, D. J. (1992). Cultural and socioeconomic constraints on international codes of ethics: Lessons from accounting. *Journal of Business Ethics*, *11*, 687–700.

Cohen, J. R., Pant, L. W., & Sharp, D. J. (1993a). Culture based ethical conflicts confronting multinational accounting firms. *Accounting Horizons*, (September), 1–13.

Cohen, J. R., Pant, L. W., & Sharp, D. J. (1993b). A validation and extension of a multi-dimensional ethics scale. *Journal of Business Ethics*, *12*, 13–26.

Cohen, J. R., Pant, L. W., & Sharp, D. J. (1995). An exploratory examination of international differences in auditors ethical perceptions. *Behavioral Research in Accounting*, *7*, 37–64.

Cohen, J. R., Pant, L. W., & Sharp, D. J. (1996a). Measuring ethical awareness and ethical orientation of Canadian auditors. *Behavioral Research in Accounting*, *8*(Suppl.), 98–119.

Cohen, J. R., Pant, L. W., & Sharp, D. J. (1996b). A methodological note on cross-cultural accounting research. *The International Journal of Accounting*, *31*(1), 55–66.

Committee of Sponsoring Organizations of the Treadway Commission (COSO). (1992). *Internal control: Integrated framework*. Harborside, NJ: AICPA.

Conover, W. J. (1980). *Practical nonparametric statistics*. New York: Wiley.

Cooksey, R. (1995). *Multivariate methods for behavioral research*. Armidale, Australia: University of New England.

Cornberg, D. (1994). Cross-cultural moral experience: A view from Taiwan. *Asian Thought and Society*, *XIX*(56), 136–147.

Cronbach, L. J. (1951). Coefficient alpha and the internal structure of tests. *Psychometrika*, *16*(3), 297–334.

Daft, R. L. (1988). *Organizational theory and design*. St. Paul, USA: West Publishing Co.

Daley, L., Jiambalvo, J., Sundem, G. L., & Kondo, Y. (1985). Attitudes towards financial control systems in the United States and Japan. *Journal of International Business Studies*, (Fall), 91–110.

Dane, F. C. (1990). *Research method*. CA: Brooks Cole Publishing Co.

De Vaus, D. A. (1991). *Surveys in social research*. London: Allen & Unwin.

Doupnik, T., & Perera, H. (2005). *International accounting*. New York: McGraw-Hill.

Doupnik, T. S., & Richer, M. (2004). The impact of culture on the interpretation of in context verbal probability expressions. *Journal of International Accounting Research*, *3*(1), 1–21.

Doupnik, T. S., & Tsakumis, G. T. (2004). A critical review of tests of Gray's theory of cultural relevance and suggestions for future research. *Journal of Accounting Literature*, *23*, 1–29.

Dozier, J., & Miceli, M. (1985). Potential predictors of whistle blowing: A prosocial behavior perspective. *Academy of Management Review*, *10*, 823–836.

Dumont, L. (1970). *Homohierarchus: The caste system and its implications*. Chicago: Chicago University Press.

Eddie, I. A. (1996). Consolidation accounting disclosures in corporate annual reports: An empirical study of Asian-Pacific corporations. Paper presented at 8th Asian-Pacific conference on international accounting issues, October, Vancouver.

Edgar, D., Earle, L., & Fopp, R. (1993). *Introduction to Australian society*. Australia: Prentice-Hall.

Elliot, J. (1997). India's challenge: The next 50 years. *Fortune* (September), 40–55.

Epstein, M. J., & Geiger, M. A. (1994). Investor views of audit assurance: Recent evidence of the expectation gap. *Journal of Accountancy*, (January), 60–66.

Ettredge, M. (1988). Audit firm size and the association between reported earnings and security. *Auditing: A Journal of Practice & Theory*, (Spring), 29–42.

Farmer, T. A., Rittenberg, L. E., & Trompeter, G. M. (1987). An investigation of the impact of economic and organizational factors on auditor independence. *Auditing: A Journal of Practice & Theory, 7*(1), 1–14.

Federal Territory MCA Liaison Committee. (1982). *The Malaysian Chinese towards national unity*. Kuala Lumpur: Eastern Universities Press.

Ferrel, O. C., & Weaver, K. M. (1978). Ethical beliefs of marketing managers. *Journal of Marketing, 42*(July), 69–73.

Ferris, K. R., Dillard, J. F., & Nethercott, L. (1980). A comparison of V-I-E model predictions: A cross-national study in professional accounting firms. *Accounting, Organizations and Society, 5*(4), 361–368.

Flory, S. M., Phillips, T. J., Jr., Reidenbach, R. E., & Robin, D. P. (1992). A multidimensional analysis of selected ethical issues in accounting. *The Accounting Review, 67*(2), 284–302.

Frank, R. H., Hofstede, G., & Bond, M. H. (1991). Cultural roots of economic performance: A research note. *Strategic Management Journal, 12*, 165–173.

Fried, D., & Schiff, A. (1981). CPA switches and associated market reactions. *The Accounting Review, LVI*(2), 326–341.

Frucot, V., & Shearon, W. T. (1991). Budgetary participation, locus of control, and Mexican managerial performance and job satisfaction. *The Accounting Review, 66*(1), 80–99.

Fukuyama, F. (1995). *Trust the social virtues and the creation of prosperity*. London: Penguin Books Ltd.

Gernon, H. (1993). Discussion of an investigation of the reporting of questionable acts in an international setting. *Journal of Accounting Research, 31*(Suppl.), 104–110.

Gernon, H., & Wallace, R. S. O. (1995). International accounting research: A review of its ecology, contending theories and methodologies. *Journal of Accounting Literature, 14*, 54–106.

Ghurye, G. S. (1969). *Caste and race in India*. Bombay: Popular Prakashan.

Gibbs, J. (1977). Kohlberg's stages of moral judgement: A constructive critique. *Harvard Educational Review*, 110–125.

Gillin, J. (1944). Cultural adjustment. *American Anthropologist, 46*(4), 429–447.

Glazer, M. (1983). Ten whistle-blowers and how they fared. *Hastings Center Report*, (December), 33–41.

Goodnow, J., Burns, A., & Russell, G. (1989). Australian families. In: K. Hancock (Ed.), *Australian society* (pp. 23–43). Sydney: Cambridge University Press.

Gray, S. J. (1988). Towards a theory of cultural influence on the development of accounting systems internationally. *Abacus, 24*(1), 1–15.

Greenberger, D., Miceli, M., & Cohen, D. (1987). Oppositionists and group norms: The reciprocal influence of whistle blowers and co-workers. *Journal of Business Ethics, 6*, 527–542.

Gul, F. A. (1991). Size of audit fees and perceptions of auditors' ability to resist management pressure in audit conflict situations. *Abacus*, (September), 162–172.

Gul, F. A., & Tsui, J. (1993). A comparative study of auditors' attitudes to uncertainty qualifications: An empirical test of strong versus weak uncertainty avoidance hypothesis. *International Journal of Accounting, 28*(4), 356–364.

Gunn, M. (1997). The loneliness epidemic. *The Australian*, 12 November, p. 17.

Guo, M. (1972). *Slavery period*. Peking: People's Publishing Agency.

Harrison, G. L. (1990). *Reliance on accounting performance measures in superior evaluative style–the influence of national culture*. Unpublished Ph.D. thesis, Macquarie University, Sydney.

Harrison, G. L. (1992). The cross-cultural generalisability of the relation between participation, budget emphasis and job related attitudes. *Accounting, Organizations and Society*, *17*(1), 1–15.

Harrison, G. L. (1993). Reliance on accounting performance measures in superior evaluative style–the influence of national culture and personality. *Accounting, Organizations and Society*, *18*(4), 319–339.

Harrison, G. L., & McKinnon, J. L. (1998). Cross-cultural research in management control systems design: A review of the current state. Revisions to the paper presented at the AOS conference on comparative management accounting, University of Siena, 7–9 November 1996.

Harrison, G. L., & McKinnon, J. L. (1999). Cross-cultural research in management control systems design: A review of the current state. *Accounting, Organizations and Society*, *24*, 483–506.

Harrison, G. L., McKinnon, J. L., Panchapakesan, S., & Leung, M. (1994). The influence of culture on organizational design and planning and control in Australia and the United States compared with Singapore and Hong Kong. *Journal of International Financial Management and Auditing*, *5*(3), 242–262.

Hart, I., & Poole, G. D. (1995). Individualism and collectivism as considerations in cross-cultural health research. *The Journal of Social Psychology*, *135*, 97–99.

Ho, D. Y. (1976). On the concept of face. *American Journal of Sociology*, *81*(4), 867–884.

Hofstede, G. (1980). *Culture's consequences: International differences of work related values.* Beverly Hills, CA: Sage.

Hofstede, G. (1983a). *Culture and management development*. Geneva: International Labour Office.

Hofstede, G. (1983b). The cultural relativity of organizational practices and theories. *Journal of International Business Studies*, (Fall), 75–89.

Hofstede, G. (1984a). Cultural dimensions in management and planning. *Asia Pacific Journal of Management*, (January), 83–84.

Hofstede, G. (1989). Organizing for cultural diversity. *European Management Journal*, *7*, 390–397.

Hofstede, G. (1991). *Cultures and organizations software of the mind.* Berkshire, UK: McGraw-Hill.

Hofstede, G. (1994a). Cultural constraints in management theories. *Academy of Management Executive*, *7*(1), 81–94.

Hofstede, G. (1994b). *Cultures and organizations software of the mind.* Glasgow: HarperCollins.

Hofstede, G., & Bond, M. H. (1984). Hofstede's cultural dimensions: An independent validation using Rokeach's value survey. *Journal of Cross-Cultural Psychology*, (December), 417–433.

Hofstede, G., & Bond, M. H. (1988). The Confucius connection: From cultural roots to economic growth. *Organizational Dynamics*, 5–21.

Hofstede, G., & Hofstede, G. J. (2005). *Cultures and organizations: Software of the mind.* New York: McGraw-Hill.

Hofstede, G., Neuijen, B., Ohayv, D., & Sanders, G. (1990). Measuring organizational cultures: A qualitative and quantitative study across twenty cases. *Administrative Science Quarterly*, *35*, 286–316.

Hong, T. T. (1982). Educational and manpower training for the Chinese – an appraisal. In: *The Malaysian Chinese – towards national unity*. Kuala Lumpur: MCA Federal Territory Research & Service Centre.

Hooks, K. L., Kaplan, S. E., & Schultz, J. J., Jr. (1994). Enhancing communication to assist in Fraud prevention and detection. *Auditing: A Journal of Practice & Theory, 13*(2), 86–117.

Hope, O. K. (2003). Firm-level disclosures and the relative roles of culture and legal origin. *Journal of International Financial Management and Accounting, 14*, 218–248.

Hopwood, A. G. (1996). Introduction. *Accounting, Organizations and Society, 21*(2/3), 217–218.

Hu, H. C. (1944). The Chinese concepts of 'face'. *American Anthropologist, 46*(4), 45–64.

Hu, S. M. (1993). Education in Malaysia: Multilingual, bilingual, or monolingual. *Asian Thought and Society, XVIII*(52), 44–56.

Huck, S. W., Cormier, W. H., & Bounds, W. G., Jr. (1974). *Reading statistics and research*. New York: Harper & Row.

Humphrey, C., Moizer, P., & Turley, S. (1993). The audit expectation gap in Britain: An empirical investigation. *Accounting and Business Research, 23*(91A), 395–411.

Hunt, S. D., & Vitell, S. (1986). A general theory of marketing ethics. *Journal of Macromarketing, 6*(Spring), 5–16.

Hwang, K. K. (1987). Face and favor: The Chinese power game. *American Journal of Sociology, 92*, 944–974.

Indian Financial Markets. (2005). http://www.rediff.com/money/2005/apr/12guest1.htm

International Accounting Standards Board (IASB). (2005). *International financial reporting standards*. London: IASC.

International Federation of Accountants. (2005a). *Code of ethics for professional accountants*. New York: International Federation of Accountants.

International Federation of Accountants. (2005b). *Projects and project histories*. http://www.ifac.org/IAASB/Projects.php

Jaggi, B. L. (1979). The impact of the cultural environment on financial disclosures. In: *Notable contribution to the periodical international accounting literature–1975–78*. CA: American Accounting Association.

Jaggi, B. L., & Low, P. Y. (2000). Impact of culture, market forces, and legal systems on financial disclosures. *The International Journal of Accounting, 35*, 495–519.

Jahoda, G. (1984). Do we need a concept of culture? *Journal of Cross Cultural Psychology, 15*(2), 139–151.

Jeffrey, C. (1993). Ethical development of accounting students, non-accounting business students, and liberal arts students. *Issues in Accounting Education, 8*(1), 86–96.

Jha, R. J. (2005). Blowing the whistle on corruption in construction: One man's fatal struggle. *Global Corruption Report*. http://www.globalcorruptionreport.org/download.html

Johns, S. K., Smith, L. M., & Strand, C. A. (1999). Impact of cultural environment on information technology. Paper presented at Emerging Issues in International Accounting Conference, Niagara Falls, New York, August.

Johnson, R. A. (2002). *Whistle-blowing: When it works–and why*. London: Lynne Rienner Publishers.

Jones, F. L. (1989). Changing attitudes and values in post-war Australia. In: K. Hancock (Ed.), *Australian society* (pp. 94–118). Cambridge: Cambridge University Press.

Kachelemeier, S. J., & Shehata, M. (1997). Internal auditing and voluntary co-operation in firms: A cross-cultural experiment. *The Accounting Review, 72*(3), 407–431.

Kahn, H. (1979). *World economic development: 1979 and beyond*. London: Croom Helm.

Kangayappan, K. (1992). The caste system: Social stratification in India. *Asian Thought and Society*, (January–April), 42–50.

Kant, I. (1964). *Foundations of the metaphysics of morals.* (H.J. Paton, trans.). New York: Harper & Row Publishers.

Kao, J. (1993). The worldwide web of Chinese business. *Harvard Business Review*, (March–April), 24–36.

Kapadia, K. M. (1966). *Marriage and family in India.* London: Oxford University Press.

Karnes, A., Sterner, J., Welker, R., & Wu, F. (1989). A bicultural study of independent auditors' perceptions of unethical business practices. *International Journal of Accounting, 24*(1), 29–41.

Karnes, A., Sterner, J., Welker, R., & Wu, F. (1990). A bi-cultural comparison of accountants' perceptions of unethical business practices. *Accounting, Auditing & Accountability Journal, 3*(3), 45–64.

Kerlinger, F. N. (1986). *Foundations of behavioral research* (3rd ed.). New York: Holt, Rinehart & Winston.

King, A. Y. C., & Bond, M. H. (1985). The Confucian paradigm of man: A sociological view. In: W. S. Tseng & D. Y. H. Wu (Eds), *Chinese culture and mental health* (pp. 29–46). New York: Academic Press.

Kinney, W. (1986). Audit technology and preferences for auditing standards. *Journal of Accounting and Economics*, (March), 73–89.

Knapp, M. C. (1985). Audit conflict: An empirical study of the perceived ability of auditors to resist management pressure. *The Accounting Review, LX*(2), 202–211.

Knapp, M. C. (1993). *Contemporary Auditing: Issues and Cases.* Los Angeles: West Publishing Co.

Kohlberg, L. (1969). Stages and sequences: The cognitive developmental approach to socialization. In: D. Goslin (Ed.), *Handbook of socialization theory and research.* Chicago: Rand McNally.

Kohlberg, L. (1984). *Essays in moral development, Vol. 2: Psychology of moral development.* San Francisco: Harper & Row.

Kroeber, A. L., & Kluckhohn, C. (1952). *Culture: A critical review of concepts and definitions.* Cambridge, MA: Peabody Museum of American Archaeology and Ethnology, Harvard University.

Lachman, R., Nedd, A., & Hinings, B. (1994). Analyzing cross-national management and organizations: A theoretical framework. *Management Science*, (January), 40–55.

Lachman, R., Nedd, A., & Hinings, B. (1995). Analyzing cross-national management and organizations: A theoretical framework. In: T. Jackson (Ed.), *Cross-cultural management.* New York: Butterworth-Heinemann.

Lachowicz, R. (1997). *Culture and conflict resolution in Australia: Teaching guide.* Australia: Griffith University.

Lampe, J. C., & Finn, D. W. (1992). A model of auditors' ethical decision processes. *Auditing: A Journal of Practice & Theory*, (Suppl.), 33–59.

Lang, O. (1968). *Chinese family and society.* New Haven, CT: Yale University Press.

Lapierre, D. (1986). *The city of joy.* London: Arrow Books.

Lau, C. M., Low, L. C., & Eggleton, I. R. C. (1995). The impact of reliance on accounting performance on job-related tension and managerial performance: Additional evidence. *Accounting, Organizations and Society, 20*(5), 359–381.

Laurent, A. (1983). The cultural diversity of Western conceptions of management. *International Studies of Management and Organizations, 13*, 75–79.

Lee, A. (1997). The appropriateness of reliance on accounting performance measures: Is it a case of culture or task uncertainty. Paper presented at the Department of Accounting & Finance. Macquarie University, Australia.

Lehman, C. R. (1992). *Accounting's changing roles in social conflict*. New York: Markus Wiener Publishing Inc.

Leung, K., & Bond, M. H. (1984). The impact of cultural collectivism on reward allocation. *Journal of Personality and Social Psychology*, *47*(4), 793–804.

Leung, K., & Iwawaki, S. (1988). Cultural collectivism and distributive behavior. *Journal of Cross-Cultural Psychology*, *19*(1), 35–49.

Library of International Accounting (1996). In: C. A. Adams, G. K. Meek, G. K. Roberts, C. W. Nobes & P. J. Walton (Eds), *Library of international accounting*. UK: An Elgar Reference Collection.

Lincon, J. R., Hanada, M., & Olson, J. (1981). Cultural orientations in individual reactions to organizations: A study of employees of Japanese owned firms. *Administrative Science Quarterly*, *6*, 93–115.

Lindsay, D. (1992). Auditor-client conflict resolution: An investigation of the perceptions of the financial community in Australia and Canada. *The International Journal of Accounting*, *27*, 342–365.

Liu, I. (1986). Chinese cognition. In: M. H. Bond (Ed.), *The psychology of the Chinese people* (pp. 73–102). Hong Kong: Oxford University Press.

Louwers, T. J., Ponemon, L. A., & Radtke, R. R. (1997). Examining accountants' ethical behavior: A review and implication for future research. In: V. Arnold & S. G. Sutton (Eds), *Behavioral Accounting, Research Foundations and Frontiers*. Sarasota, Florida: American Accounting Association.

Low, A. M. (1989). The auditor's detection responsibility: Is there an 'expectation gap'. *Journal of Accounting Singapore*, (October), 65–70.

Lu, M. (1983). *Confucianism: Its relevance to modern society*. Singapore: Federal Publishers Ltd.

Lyons, L. H. L., & Tong, M. (1992). The effects of management advisory services involvement by audit firms on Hong Kong bankers perceptions on auditor and financial statement credibility. *Proceedings of the 4th Asian-Pacific conference on international accounting issues*, Dunedin, November, pp. 95–99.

Ma, H. K., & Cheung, C. (1996). A cross-cultural study of moral stage structure in Hong Kong Chinese, English, and Americans. *Journal of Cross-Cultural Psychology*, *27*(6), 700–713.

Mahimalia, A. K. (1997). Fudging the figures. *The Chartered Accountant in India*, (June), 36–40.

Marriott, M. (1976). Hindu transactions: Diversity without dualism. In: B. Kapferer (Ed.), *Transactions and meaning directions in the anthropology of exchange and symbolic behavior*. Philadelphia: Institute of the Study of Human Issues.

Maslow, A. H. (1954). *Motivation and personality*. New York: Harper & Row.

Mautz, R. K., & Sharaf, H. A. (1961). *The philosophy of auditing*. Sarasota, FL: American Accounting Association.

McDonald, G. M., & Zepp, R. A. (1988). Ethical perceptions of Hong Kong Chinese business managers. *Journal of Business Ethics*, *7*, 835–845.

McKinnon, J. (1984). Cultural constraints on audit independence in Japan. *The International Journal of Accounting*, *20*(1), 17–44.

Meier, M., & Rittenberg, L. (1986). Dealing with known corporate wrongdoing. *The Internal Auditor*, (April), 37–39.

Miceli, M. P., & Near, J. P. (1984). The relationship among beliefs, organizational position and whistle blowing status: A discriminant analysis. *Academy of Management Journal*, *27*, 687–705.

Miceli, M. P., & Near, J. P. (1992). *Blowing the whistle: The organizational and legal implications for companies and employers*. New York: Lexington Books.

Miceli, M. P., Near, J. P., & Schwenk, C. R. (1991). Who blows the whistle and why? *Industrial and Labor Relations Review*, *45*(1), 113–130.

Mitchell, I. (1995). Correspondents whistle blowing. *Chartered Accountants Journal*, (March), 79.

Monroe, G. S., & Woodliff, D. R. (1994). Great expectations: Public perceptions of the auditor's role. *Australian Accounting Review*, (November), 42–53.

Morrison, D. F. (1967). *Multivariate statistical methods*. New York: McGraw-Hills.

Mueller, G.G. (1968). Accounting principles generally accepted in the United States versus those generally accepted elsewhere. *International Journal of Accounting Education & Research*, (Spring), 91–103.

Mueller, G. G., Gernon, H., & Meek, G. (1991). *Accounting an international perspective*. IL: Richard D. Irwin.

Mueller, G. G., Gernon, H., & Meek, G. (1994). *Accounting an international perspective* (3rd ed.). IL: Richard D. Irwin.

Murphy, J., & Gilligan, C. (1980). Moral development in late adolescence and adulthood: A critique and reconstruction. *Human Development*, 77–104.

Near, J., & Miceli, M. (1985). Organizational dissidence: The case of whistle blowing. *Journal of Business Ethics*, *4*, 1–16.

Near, J., & Miceli, M. (1986). Retaliation against whistle blowers: Predictors and effects. *Journal of Applied Psychology*, *71*, 137–145.

Nikhilananda, S. (1968). *Hinduism: Its meaning for the liberation of the spirit*. Madras: Sri Ramakrishna Nath.

Nobes, C., & Parker, R. H. (1981). *Comparative international accounting*. Oxford: Philip Allan.

Nobes, C., & Parker, R. H. (1995). *Comparative international accounting* (4th ed.). UK: Prentice-Hall.

Nobes, C., & Parker, R. H. (2004). *Comparative international accounting*. Essex: Pearson Education Ltd.

Nunnally, J. C. (1967). *Psychometric methods*. New York: McGraw-Hill.

Nunnally, J. C. (1978). *Psychometric theory* (2nd ed.). New York: McGraw-Hill.

O'Connor, N. G. (1995). The influence of organizational culture on the usefulness of budget participation by Singaporean-Chinese managers. *Accounting, Organizations and Society*, *20*(5), 383–403.

O'Malley, S. F. (1993). Commentary legal liability is having a chilling effect on the auditor's role. *Accounting Horizons*, *7*(2), 82–87.

Palkhivala, N. (1997). Squandered legacy. *The Hindustan Times*, 15 August, p. 13.

Patel, C. (1992). External auditors' independence and culture: Perceptions in Fiji and New Zealand. *Journal of Accounting & Finance*, (Fall), 391–422.

Patel, C. (2004). Some theoretical and methodological suggestions for cross-cultural accounting studies. *International Journal of Accounting, Auditing and Performance Evaluation*, *1*(1), 61–84.

Patel, C., & Psaros, J. (2000). Perceptions of external auditors' independence: Some cross-cultural evidence. *The British Accounting Review*, *32*, 311–338.

Patel, C., Psaros, J., & Roberts, C. (1996). A comparative study of the influence of culture and acculturation on perceptions of external auditors' independence. Paper presented at the 8th Asian-Pacific conference on international accounting issues, October, Vancouver.

Phegade, G. D. (1997). All this business about ethics. *Indian Management*, (July), 75–78.

Pitt, L. F., & Abratt, R. (1986). Corruption in business: Are management attitudes right? *Journal of Business Ethics*, *5*, 39–44.

Ponemon, L. A. (1990). Ethical judgements in accounting: A cognitive-developmental perspective. *Critical Perspectives on Accounting, 1*(2), 191–215.
Ponemon, L. A. (1992). Ethical reasoning and selection-socialization in accounting. *Accounting, Organizations and Society, 17*(3 4), 239–258.
Ponemon, L. A. (1993). Commentary on ethical reasoning research in accounting. Newsletter of the public interest section of American accounting association. *A Special Issue, Ethics in Accounting*, (March), 5–7.
Ponemon, L. A. (1994). Comment whistle-blowing as an internal control mechanism: Individual and organizational considerations. *Auditing: A Journal of Practice & Theory, 13*(2), 118–130.
Ponemon, L. A., & Gabhart, D. (1990). Auditor independence judgements: A cognitive-developmental model and experimental evidence. *Contemporary Accounting Research, 7*(1), 227–251.
Ponemon, L. A., & Glazer, A. (1990). Accounting education and ethical development: The influence of liberal learning on students and alumni in accounting practice. *Issues in Accounting Education, 5*(2), 195–208.
Power, C. (1999). *The audit society: Rituals of verification.* Oxford: Oxford University Press.
Prather-Kinsey, J., & Rueschhoff, N. G. (2004). An analysis of international accounting research in US and non-US based academic accounting journals. *Journal of International Accounting Research, 3*(1), 63–81.
Pratt, J., & Beaulieu, P. (1992). Organizational culture in public accounting: Size, technology, rank, and functional area. *Accounting, Organization and Society, 17*(7), 667–684.
Pratt, J., Mohrweis, L. C., & Beaulieu, P. (1993). The interaction between national and organizational culture in accounting firms: An extension. *Accounting, Organizations and Society, 8*(7 8), 621–628.
Psaros, J., & Patel, C. (2003). A study of uncertainty expressions in Australian accounting and auditing standards. *Pacific Accounting Review, 15*(2), 1–28.
Radebaugh, L. H., & Gray, S. J. (1993). *International accounting and multinational enterprises* (3rd ed.). Canada: Wiley.
Radebaugh, L. H., & Gray, S. J. (2002). *International accounting and multinational enterprises* (5th ed.). New York: Wiley.
Redding, G., & Wong, G. Y. Y. (1986). The psychology of Chinese organizational behavior. In: M. H. Bond (Ed.), *The psychology of the Chinese people* (pp. 267–293). Hong Kong: Oxford University Press.
Reidenbach, R. E., & Robin, D. P. (1988). Some initial steps towards improving the measurement of ethical evaluations of marketing activities. *Journal of Business Ethics, 7*, 871–879.
Reidenbach, R. E., & Robin, D. P. (1990). Toward the development of a multidimentional scale for improving evaluations of business ethics. *Journal of Business Ethics, 9*, 639–653.
Rest, J. R. (1979). *Development in judging moral issues.* Minneapolis: University of Minnesota Press.
Rieger, F., & Wong-Rieger, D. (1988). Model building in organizational cross-cultural research: The need for multiple methods, indices, and cultures. *International Studies of Management and Organizations, 18*, 19–30.
Roberts, C., Weetman, P., & Gordon, P. (2005). *International financial reporting: A comparative study.* Essex: Pearson Education Inc.
Rohner, R. P. (1984). Towards a conception of culture for cross-cultural psychology. *Journal of Cross-Cultural Psychology*, (June), 111–138.

Roland, A. (1984). The self in India and America. In: V. Kavolis (Ed.), *Designs of selfhood*. NJ: Associated University Press.

Ronen, S., & Shenkar, O. (1985). Clustering countries on attitudinal dimensions: A review and synthesis. *Academy of Management Review*, 435–454.

Ross, A. D. (1961). *The Hindu family in its urban setting*. Toronto: University of Toronto Press.

Rossi, P. H., Wright, J. D., & Anderson, A. B. (1983). *Handbook of survey research*. Orlando, FL: Academic Press.

Salter, S. B., & Niswander, F. (1995). Cultural influence on the development of accounting systems internationally: A test of Gray's [1988] theory. *Journal of International Business Studies*, *26*(2), 379–397.

Saudagaran, S. M., & Diga, J. G. (1999). Evaluation of contingency based approach in comparative international accounting: A case for alternative research paradigms. *Journal of Accounting Literature*, *18*, 1–30.

Schulberg, L. (1968). *Historic India great ages of man: A history of the world culture series*. Amsterdam: Time-life International.

Schulte, A. (1965). Compatibility of management consulting and auditing. *The Accounting Review*, *XL*(3), 587–593.

Schultz, J. J., Johnson, D. A., Morris, D., & Dyrnes, S. (1993). An investigation of the reporting of questionable acts in an international setting. *Journal of Accounting Research*, *31*(Suppl.), 75–103.

Schwartz, S. H. (1990). Individualism–collectivism critique and proposed refinements. *Journal of Cross-Cultural Psychology*, *21*(2), 139–157.

Schwartz, S. H. (1994). Cultural dimensions of values: Towards an understanding of national differences. In: V. Kim, H. C. Triandis, C. Kagitcibasi, S. C. Choi & G. Yoon (Eds), *Individualism and collectivism: Theoretical and methodological issues* (pp. 85–119). Thousand Oaks, CA: Sage.

Securities and Exchange Commission of the USA. (2004). *Initial decision release 249*, 16 April.

Selvadurai, S. (1997). Leadership in the co-operatives. *Indian Management*, (July), 40–45.

Shaub, M. K., Finn, D. W., & Munter, P. (1993). The effects of auditors' ethical orientation on commitment and ethical sensitivity. *Behavioral Research in Accounting*, *5*, 145–169.

Shengqing, C. (1992). Chinese legal culture: The traditional and contemporary. *Asian Thought and Society*, *XVII*(49), 3–8.

Shils, E. (1961). *The intellectual between tradition and modernity: The Indian situation*. The Hague: Mouton Press.

Shockley, R. A. (1981). Perceptions of auditors' independence: An empirical analysis. *The Accounting Review*, *LVI*(4), 785–800.

Siegel, S. (1956). *Nonparametric statistics for behavioral sciences*. Tokyo: McGraw-Hill.

Sinha, D. (1995). Caste as an economic institution in India: An interdisciplinary study. *Asian Economics*, (March), 27–45.

Sinha, J. B. P., & Sinha, D. (1990). Role of social values in Indian organizations. *International Journal of Psychology*, *25*(5/6), 705–714.

Smith, P. B., & Bond, M. H. (1993). *Social psychology across cultures analysis and perspectives*. Hertfordshire: Harvester Wheatsheaf.

Smith, P. B., Dugan, S., & Trompenaars, F. (1996). National culture and the values of organizational employees. *Journal of Cross-Cultural Psychology*, *27*(2), 231–264.

Snodgrass, C., & Grant, J. H. (1986). Cultural influences on strategic planning and control system. *Advances in Strategic Management*, *4*, 205–228.

Soeters, J., & Schreuder, H. (1988). The interaction between national and organizational cultures in accounting firms. *Accounting Organizations and Society*, *13*(1), 75–85.

Spitzer, D. (1979). *Wanderlust*. New York: Richard Marek Publishers.

Stover, L. E. (1974). *The cultural ecology of Chinese civilization*. NewYork: New American Library.

Strauch, J. (1981). *Chinese village politics in the Malaysian state*. Cambridge, MA: Harvard University Press.

Tabachnick, B. G., & Fidell, L. S. (1989). *Using multivariate statistics*. New York: Harper Collins Publishers.

Tay, J. S. W. (1993). Malaysia. In: T. E. Cooke & R. H. Parker (Eds), *Financial reporting in West Pacific rim*. London: Routledge.

The Chinese Culture Connection. (1987). Chinese values and the search for culture-free dimensions of culture. *Journal of Cross-Cultural Psychology*, *18*(2), 143–164.

The Future of the Accounting Profession. (2003). 103rd The American Assembly, Columbia University.

The Future of the Accounting Profession: Auditor Concentration. (2005). The American Assembly, Columbia University.

The Macquarie Dictionary. (1991). *The Macquarie dictionary*. Macquarie University, Sydney: Macquarie Library Pty. Ltd.

Tourish, D., & Hargie, O. (Eds) (2005). *Key issues in organizational communications*. London: Routledge.

Triandis, H. C. (1994). *Culture and social behavior*. New York: McGraw-Hill.

Triandis, H. C. (1995). *Individualism and collectivism*. Boulder, CO: Westview Press Inc.

Triandis, H. C., Betancourt, H., Iwao, S., Leung, K., Salazar, J. M., Setiadi, B., Sinha, J. B. P., Touzard, H., & Zaleski, Z. (1993). An etic-emic analysis of individualism and collectivism. *Journal of Cross-Cultural Psychology*, *24*(3), 366–383.

Tripathi, R. C. (1990). Interplay of values in the functioning of Indian organizations. *International Journal of Psychology*, *25*(5/6), 715–734.

Trompenaars, F. (1993). *Riding the waves of culture understanding cultural diversity in business*. London: Nicholas Brealey Publishing Ltd.

Truell, P., & Gurwin, L. (1992). *False profits the inside story of BCCI, the world's most corrupt financial empire*. New York: Houghton Mifflin.

Tsalikis, J., & Nwachukwu, O. (1989). Cross-cultural business ethics: Ethical beliefs differences between black and white. *Journal of Business Ethics*, *7*, 45–63.

Tsalikis, J., & Nwachukwu, O. (1991). A comparison of Nigerian to American views of bribery and extortion in international commerce. *Journal of Business Ethics*, *10*, 85–99.

Tsui, J. (1996). Commentary on measuring the ethical awareness and ethical orientation of Canadian auditors. *Behavioral Research in Accounting*, *8*(Suppl.), 120–123.

Tsui, J., & Gul, F. A. (1994). Auditors' behavior in an audit conflict situation: An empirical analysis of the role of locus of control and ethical reasoning. Paper presented at faculty of economics & administration, University of Malaya, Malaysia.

Tyson, T. (1990). Believing that everyone else is less ethical: Implications for work behavior and ethics instruction. *Journal of Business Ethics*, (9), 715–721.

Tyson, T. (1992). Does believing that everyone else is less ethical have an impact on work behavior? *Journal of Business Ethics*, *11*, 707–717.

Ueno, S., & Wu, F. H. (1993). The comparative influence of culture on budget control practices in the United States and Japan. *The International Journal of Accounting*, *28*, 17–39.

Values Survey Module Manual. (1994). *Values survey module manual.* Netherlands: Institute for Research on Intercultural Cooperation.

Vance, C. M., McClaine, S. R., Boje, D. M., & Stage, H. D. (1992). An examination of the transferability of traditional performance appraisal principals across cultural boundaries. *Management International Review, 32,* 313–326.

Venkataraman, N. S. (2002). Where will corruption rake India? *PUCL Bulletin,* (November), 1–2.

Waters, M. (1990). *Sociology one: Principles of sociological analysis for Australians.* Melbourne: Longman Cheshire.

Watkins, D., & Cheung, S. (1995). Culture, gender, and response bias. *Journal of Cross-Cultural Psychology, 26*(5), 490–504.

Weber, D. (1992). Scenarios in business ethics research: Review, critical assessment and recommendations. *Business Ethics Quarterly, 2*(2), 137–160.

Welton, R. E., & Davis, J. R. (1990). Accounting implications of the perceptions of professional ethics: A comparative analysis of American and New Zealand students. *The International Journal of Accounting, 25,* 268–283.

Werhane, P. H., Bowie, N., & Radin, T. (2003). *Employment and employee rights.* Oxford: Blackwell.

Wheeler, R., Felsig, M., & Reilly, T. (1987). Large or small CPA firms: A practioner's perspective. *CPA Journal,* (April), 29–33.

Whiting, B. B. (1976). The problem of the packaged variable. In: K. F. Reigel & J. A. Meacham (Eds), *The developing individual in a changing world.* The Hague: Moulton.

Withers, G. (1989). Living and working in Australia. In: K. Hancock (Ed.), *Australian society* (pp. 1–22). Sydney: Cambridge University Press.

Wu, C. C. (1927). The Chinese family: Organizations, names and kinship terms. *American Anthropologist, XXIX*(July–September), 316–324.

Wyatt, A. R. (1997). Review the accounting profession major issues: Progress and concerns. *Accounting Horizons, 11*(2), 127–131.

Yamamura, J. H., Frakes, A. H., Sanders, D. L., & Ahn, S. K. (1996). A comparison of Japanese and US auditor decision-making behavior. *The International Journal of Accounting, 31*(3), 347–364.

Yamamura, J. H., Stedham, Y. E., & Satoh, M. (2004). Accountants in Japan: Culture, organisational factors and job satisfaction. *International Journal of Accounting, Auditing and Performance Evaluation, 1*(1), 85–102.

Yang, K. (1981). Social orientation and individual modernity among Chinese students in Taiwan. *Journal of Social Psychology, 113,* 159–170.

Zimmer, H. (1951). *Philosophies of India.* New York: Bollingen Foundation.

Zimmerman, C. C., & Unnithan, T. K. N. (1975). *Family and civilisation in the East and the West.* Bombay: Thacker & Co. Ltd.

www.ingramcontent.com/pod-product-compliance
Ingram Content Group UK Ltd.
Pitfield, Milton Keynes, MK11 3LW, UK
UKHW020844290926
15470UKWH00004B/1533